A Culture of Conspiracy

COMPARATIVE STUDIES IN RELIGION AND SOCIETY

Mark Juergensmeyer, editor

A Culture of Conspiracy

Apocalyptic Visions
in Contemporary America

Michael Barkun

UNIVERSITY OF CALIFORNIA PRESS

Berkeley / Los Angeles / London

Portions of chapter 7 first appeared as Michael Barkun, "Myths of the
Underworld in Contemporary American Millennialism," in *Experiences of
Place,* edited by Mary N. MacDonald. Cambridge, Mass.: Center for the
Study of World Religions, Harvard Divinity School, 2003.

University of California Press
Berkeley and Los Angeles, California

University of California Press, Ltd.
London, England

Library of Congress Cataloging-in-Publication Data

Barkun, Michael.
  A culture of conspiracy : apocalyptic visions in contemporary America /
Michael Barkun.
      p.   cm. — (Comparative studies in religion and society ; 15)
  Includes bibliographical references and index.
  ISBN 0-520-23805-2 (alk. paper)
    1. Millennialism—United States.   2. Conspiracies—United States.
3. Human-alien encounters—United States.   I. Title.   II. Series.
BL503.2 .B37   2003
306'.1—dc21   2002155793

Manufactured in the United States of America

11 10 09 08 07 06 05 04 03
10 9 8 7 6 5 4 3 2 1

The paper used in this publication is both acid-free and totally chlorine-
free (TCF). It meets the minimum requirements of ANSI/NISO Z39.48–
1992 (R 1997) ⊗ .

For Natalie Rose

Contents

Preface

In the summer of 1994, less than a year before he blew up the Oklahoma City federal building, Timothy McVeigh visited Area 51, the secret installation north of Las Vegas, Nevada, where legend has it that the U.S. government keeps captured UFOs. McVeigh apparently made the visit to protest restrictions on public access to the base, but he also had had a long-standing fascination with flying saucers and tales of alien life forms. On death row he watched the film *Contact,* a story of a scientist contacted by aliens, six times in two days. McVeigh was also said to have been a regular listener to the shortwave-radio broadcasts of Milton William Cooper, an Arizona-based conspiracy theorist who first emerged in UFO circles in the 1980s and later acquired a large audience among antigovernment activists. A friend of Cooper's claims that McVeigh visited Cooper shortly before the Oklahoma City bombing. The substance of their conversation is unknown.[1]

While McVeigh's interests may seem merely the peculiarities of an individual whose true motives remain difficult to fathom, the connection he made between antigovernment politics and UFOs was not unique. Throughout the 1990s, right-wing conspiracy theories increasingly came together with beliefs about visiting creatures from outer space. We do not know whether McVeigh himself was affected by these speculations, but it is clear that his interests were shared by others.

Similar hybrids emerged after the terrorist attacks on New York and Arlington, Virginia, in September 2001. They mingled the prophecies of Nostradamus, UFOs, and theories about the Illuminati in strange and unpredictable ways. These were not combinations I would have expected to find. Like most people, I had assumed that those with a right-wing, antigovernment agenda were altogether different from believers in UFOs. But the first inkling I had that such boundaries might be crossed had come some years before the 2001 attacks, as I was reading through the extremist literature that served as a basis for my book *Religion and the Racist Right*. While much of this literature was predictable, with its diatribes against Jews and blacks, there were unexpected intrusions of material that, though certainly not considered mainstream, was neither racist nor antigovernment. It dealt with such matters as processed foods (which the writers condemned), garlic (whose medicinal attributes they touted), and environmental pollution (which they wished to eliminate). Indeed, this was material that would not have been out of place in leftist publications or those for New Age readers. Consequently, when I found right-wing conspiracism emerging in UFO circles, it suggested that the odd juxtapositions I had found earlier might be part of a larger pattern in which seemingly discrete beliefs cohabited.

Despite the many references to UFOs, this is not a book about flying saucers. I do not know whether they exist or, if they do, where they come from; and I do not address either of those questions. What this work does concern is the fusion of right-wing conspiracy theories with UFO motifs. This is a study of how certain dissimilar ideas have migrated from one underground subculture to another.

Many readers may regard both sets of ideas as bizarre and may question whether this is terrain worth exploring. I have addressed such skepticism in earlier books on millennialism—belief in the imminent perfection of human existence—and my response here is the same: it makes little sense to exclude ideas from examination merely because they are not considered respectable. Failing to analyze them will not keep some people from believing them, and history is littered with academically disreputable ideas that have had devastating effects—for example, the scientific acceptance of racial differences in the nineteenth century. Failure to examine them did not cause them to disappear. My examination of certain odd beliefs does not signify my acceptance of them.[2]

The convergence of conspiracy theories with UFO beliefs is worth examining for two reasons. First, it has brought conspiracism to a large new audience. UFO writers have long been suspicious of the U.S. government, which they believe has suppressed crucial evidence of an alien presence on earth, but in the early years they did not, by and large, embrace strong political positions. That began to change in the late 1980s and early 1990s, with the first appearance in UFO circles of references to right-wing conspiracism. Over the next decade, such borrowing accelerated and, as a result, brought right-wing conspiracism to people who otherwise would not have been aware of it.

Second, this combination provides a striking example of a new and growing form of millennialism, which I call *improvisational millennialism*. Unlike earlier forms, which elaborated themes from individual religious or secular traditions, improvisational millennialism is wildly eclectic. Its undisciplined borrowings from unrelated sources allow its proponents to build novel systems of belief.

Mapping fringe ideas is a difficult undertaking. Familiar intellectual landmarks are unavailable, and the inhabitants of these territories tend to speak languages difficult for outsiders to penetrate. Some of these ideas have begun to filter into mainstream popular culture, a process I describe in chapter 11. But their origins lie in obscure and barely visible subcultures—millenarian religion, occultism, and radical politics among them.

As to the subculture of UFO speculation itself, I occasionally refer to it as *ufology*, borrowing a term from UFO writers, though I employ it in a narrower sense. The ufology literature ranges widely, from conventional scientific investigation to fringe conspiracism. Because my concern is with the latter, the reader should be aware that I use *ufology* to apply only to the ideas of this minority within the larger community of UFO believers.

In citing sources, I have limited citations to the ends of paragraphs. In each note, sources are listed in the order they are utilized in the accompanying paragraph. When Internet sources are cited, the dates in parentheses at the end of the citation refer to the dates I viewed the pages.

In the course of this research, I have incurred many institutional and intellectual debts. If they cannot be fully repaid, they can at least be gratefully acknowledged. My own institution, the Maxwell School at Syracuse University, provided a timely research leave, as well as support through the Appleby-Mosher Fund. A number of libraries and repositories generously provided access to their materials. I am particularly appreciative of the courtesies extended to me by the George Arents Research Library at Syracuse University; the Alternative Press collection at the Wisconsin State Historical Society; the American Religions collection at the University of California, Santa Barbara, Library; the Millennium Archive at the Van Pelt Library of the University of Pennsylvania; the Anti-Defamation League; and the Library of Congress.

I had the opportunity of presenting preliminary versions of some of the ideas in this book before audiences of colleagues, which gave me the chance both to shape inchoate ideas and to modify them in light of the listeners' comments. Much of the material on the Illuminati in chapter 3 was first presented at a conference titled "Millenarianism and Revolution," organized by Richard H. Popkin at the William Andrews Clark Memorial Library at UCLA in 1998. The examination of "inner earth" ideas in chapter 7 was facilitated by an invitation from Mary N. MacDonald to participate in a 2000 lecture series called "Experiences of Place and the History of Religions," at the Center for the Study of World Religions at Harvard University. An opportunity to discuss the role of nativism in conspiracy theory was afforded when Richard Landes asked me to deliver the keynote address at the 1999 International Conference on Millennialism at Boston University. In similar fashion, I was able to develop ideas about the movement of fringe ideas into the mainstream at a conference, "American Apocalypse: Beyond the Fringe and back to the Center," held in 1999 at the University of Pennsylvania to mark the opening of the Millennium Archive collected by Ted Daniels.

Many individuals have graciously given their time to read manuscripts, provide materials, answer queries, and otherwise be of assistance. They have also saved me from numerous errors of omission and commission, and I am responsible for any that remain. Joscelyn Godwin, at neighboring Colgate University, shared his knowledge of esotericism, as Chip Berlet did his equally formidable command of American conspiracism. Vance Pollock responded patiently to numerous queries about William Dudley Pelley. Brad Whitsel, of Pennsylvania State University–Fayette, was an important source of "inner earth" material. Sue Lewis and Candy Brooks provided valuable assistance in manuscript preparation. I am also grateful to Matthew Kalman, Philip Lamy, Mark Pitcavage, Jeffrey Kaplan, and Charles Strozier. And, of course, my debt to Janet, my wife, for her unfailing love and support is beyond measure.

CHAPTER I

The Nature of Conspiracy Belief

On January 20, 2002, Richard McCaslin, thirty-seven, of Carson City, Nevada, was arrested sneaking into the Bohemian Grove in Northern California. The Grove is the site of an exclusive annual men's retreat attended by powerful business and political leaders. When McCaslin was discovered, he was carrying a combination shotgun–assault rifle, a .45-caliber pistol, a crossbow, a knife, a sword, and a bomb-launching device. He said he was acting alone.

McCaslin told police he had entered the Bohemian Grove in order to expose the satanic human sacrifices he believed occurred there. He fully expected to meet resistance and to kill people in the process. He had developed his belief in the Grove's human sacrifices based on the claims of a radio personality, Alex Jones, whose broadcasts and Web site present alleged evidence of ritual killings there. Similar charges against the Bohemian Grove—along with allegations of blood drinking and sexual perversions—have been spread for several years on the Web and in fringe publications, some of which also suggest that the Grove's guests include nonhuman species masquerading as human beings. These and similar tales would be cause for little more than amusement were it not for individuals like McCaslin, who take them seriously enough to risk killing and being killed.[1]

They also form part of a conspiracist subculture that has become more visible since September 11, 2001. Immediately after the terrorist attacks, strange reports burgeoned on the Internet; many never migrated to mainstream news outlets. Among them were that Nostradamus had foretold the attacks; that a UFO had appeared near one of the World

I

Trade Center towers just as a plane crashed into it; that the attacks had been planned by a secret society called the Illuminati; that U.S. president George W. Bush and British prime minister Tony Blair had advance knowledge of the attacks; and that the attacks signaled the coming of the millennial end-times prophesied in the Bible.

On one level, such ideas might be attributed simply to the anxieties of a deeply shaken people, desperate to make sense of the shocking events. On another level, however, these and similar beliefs alert us to the existence of significant subcultures far outside the mainstream. Surfacing in times of crisis and bound up with heterodox religion, occult and esoteric beliefs, radical politics, and fringe science, they have had a long-standing and sometimes potent influence in American life. It is with these beliefs—which in chapter 2 I refer to as *stigmatized knowledge*—that I am concerned. Binding these disparate subjects together is the common thread of conspiracism—the belief that powerful, hidden, evil forces control human destinies.

"Trust no one" was one of the mantras repeated on *The X-Files*, and it neatly encapsulates the conspiracist's limitless suspicions. Its association with a popular end-of-the-millennium television program is a measure of how prevalent conspiracy thinking has become. Indeed, the period since the assassination of President John F. Kennedy in 1963 has seen the rise of a veritable cottage industry of conspiracism, with ever more complex plots and devious forces behind it.

Although much of this mushrooming can be traced to the traumatic effect of specific events, that seems an insufficient explanation on its own. Conspiracist preoccupations have grown too luxuriantly to be fully explained even by events as shocking as the Kennedy assassination or the rapid spread of AIDS. Rather, they suggest an obsessive concern with the magnitude of hidden evil powers, and it is perhaps no surprise that such a concern should manifest as a millennium was coming to a close and the culture was rife with apocalyptic anxiety.

Belief in conspiracies is central to millennialism in the late twentieth and early twenty-first centuries. That is scarcely surprising—millennialist worldviews have always predisposed their adherents to conspiracy beliefs. Such worldviews may be characterized as Manichaean, in the sense that they cast the world in terms of a struggle between light and darkness, good and evil, and hold that this polarization will persist until the end of history, when evil is finally, definitively defeated.

To be sure, one can believe in a struggle between good and evil without believing in conspiracies. In such a scenario, evil would operate openly—a picture often drawn by millenarian preachers when they point to widespread manifestations of greed, unbridled sexuality, or hostility to religion. But millennialists tend to gravitate toward conspiracism for two specific reasons. First, a millenarian movement without a mass following finds hidden evil an attractive way to explain its lack of popularity. Surely the masses would believe if only they knew what the concealed malefactors were up to. Second, the more elusive the end-times are, the more tempting it is to blame their delay on secret evil powers, whether in the form of a capitalist conspiracy or of the minions of Satan. Conspiracism explains failure, both for organizations and for the larger world. Yet significant though conspiracy is for millenarians, it is a slippery concept.

Defining Conspiracy

Despite the frequency with which conspiracy beliefs have been discussed at the end of the second millennium, the term *conspiracy* itself has often been left undefined, as though its meaning were self-evident. Courts and legislatures have devoted considerable attention to defining a crime of conspiracy, but the meaning of the broader concept has rarely been addressed.

The essence of conspiracy beliefs lies in attempts to delineate and explain evil. At their broadest, conspiracy theories "view history as controlled by massive, demonic forces." The locus of this evil lies outside the true community, in some "Other, defined as foreign or barbarian, though often . . . disguised as innocent and upright." The result is a worldview characterized by a sharp division between the realms of good and evil.[2]

For our purposes, a *conspiracy belief* is the belief that an organization made up of individuals or groups was or is acting covertly to achieve some malevolent end. As I indicate later in this chapter, such a definition has implications both for the role of secrecy and for the activities a conspiracy is believed to undertake.

A conspiracist worldview implies a universe governed by design rather than by randomness. The emphasis on design manifests itself in three principles found in virtually every conspiracy theory:

· *Nothing happens by accident.* Conspiracy implies a world based on intentionality, from which accident and coincidence have been removed. Anything that happens occurs because it has been willed. At its most extreme, the result is a "fantasy [world] . . . far more coherent than the real world."[3]

· *Nothing is as it seems.* Appearances are deceptive, because conspirators wish to deceive in order to disguise their identities or their activities. Thus the appearance of innocence is deemed to be no guarantee that an individual or group is benign.

· *Everything is connected.* Because the conspiracists' world has no room for accident, pattern is believed to be everywhere, albeit hidden from plain view. Hence the conspiracy theorist must engage in a constant process of linkage and correlation in order to map the hidden connections.

In an odd way, the conspiracy theorist's view is both frightening and reassuring. It is frightening because it magnifies the power of evil, leading in some cases to an outright dualism in which light and darkness struggle for cosmic supremacy. At the same time, however, it is reassuring, for it promises a world that is meaningful rather than arbitrary. Not only are events nonrandom, but the clear identification of evil gives the conspiracist a definable enemy against which to struggle, endowing life with purpose.

CONSPIRACY AND SECRECY

Conspiracy and *secrecy* seem indissolubly linked. Yet conspiracy beliefs involve two distinguishable forms of secrecy. One concerns the group itself; the second concerns the group's activities. A group may be secret or known, and its activities may be open or hidden. Table 1 identifies four types of groups based on combinations of secrecy and openness.

Type I, a secret group acting secretly, is a staple of conspiracy theories. Indeed, such groups are often believed to hold virtually unlimited power, even though people who claim to expose them assert that these groups are entirely invisible to the unenlightened observer. For example, the famous anti-Semitic forgery *The Protocols of the Elders of Zion* (discussed in chapter 3) purports to reveal the existence of a Jewish conspiracy to rule the world. Concocted by Czar Nicholas II's secret police at the end of the nineteenth century, it was published in Russian in 1905 and in English in 1920. Despite its early unmasking as a forgery, it has continued to be disseminated. In 2002, despite international pro-

TABLE 1. Secrecy versus Openness

		ACTIVITIES	
		Secret	Not Secret
GROUP	Secret	I Illuminati	II Anonymous philanthropists
	Not Secret	III Masons	IV Democratic political parties

tests, television stations throughout the Arab world broadcast a forty-one-part Egyptian series in which *The Protocols* were prominently featured. A comparably tenacious mythology revolves around the Bavarian Illuminati, a Masonic organization founded in 1776 that was supposedly the catalyst for the French Revolution and subsequent upheavals worldwide. The Illuminati was quickly dissolved by suspicious governments, but it lives on in countless conspiracist tracts discussed in chapter 3.[4]

By contrast, Type II lies outside conspiracy theory, for it concerns a group that, while concealing its existence from the public, nonetheless acts openly. An example might be a group of philanthropists who desire to keep their benefactions anonymous. Thus they conceal their identities, though the beneficiaries are free to reveal the nature of the gifts as long as they do not expose the identities of the givers.

Type III returns us to the conspiracist world, for it combines known groups with secret activities. A stock feature of conspiracy theories is the known group or institution that engages in some activities so sinister it must conceal them from public view. The implication is that such an organization exists on two levels, one at least relatively open and benign, but serving to mask the true, hidden function. Among the groups that have been described in this fashion are the Masons (discussed in chapter 8), the Trilateral Commission (see chapter 4), and the CIA.

Finally, the residual Type IV includes all those known and open associations that proliferate in democracies, including political parties and interest groups, whose identities and activities are reported and made parts of the public record.

TYPES OF CONSPIRACY THEORIES

Although all conspiracy theories share the generic characteristics described earlier in this chapter, they may be distinguished, principally by their scope. They range from those directed at explaining some single, limited occurrence to those so broad that they constitute the worldviews of those who hold them. They may be categorized, in ascending order of breadth, as follows:

- *Event conspiracies.* Here the conspiracy is held to be responsible for a limited, discrete event or set of events. The best-known example in the recent past is the Kennedy assassination conspiracy literature, though similar material exists concerning the crash of TWA flight 800, the spread of AIDS in the black community, and the burning of black churches in the 1990s. In all of these cases, the conspiratorial forces are alleged to have focused their energies on a limited, well-defined objective.

- *Systemic conspiracies.* At this level, the conspiracy is believed to have broad goals, usually conceived as securing control over a country, a region, or even the entire world. While the goals are sweeping, the conspiratorial machinery is generally simple: a single, evil organization implements a plan to infiltrate and subvert existing institutions. This is a common scenario in conspiracy theories that focus on the alleged machinations of Jews, Masons, and the Catholic Church, as well as theories centered on communism or international capitalists.

- *Superconspiracies.* This term refers to conspiratorial constructs in which multiple conspiracies are believed to be linked together hierarchically. Event and systemic conspiracies are joined in complex ways, so that conspiracies come to be nested within one another. At the summit of the conspiratorial hierarchy is a distant but all-powerful evil force manipulating lesser conspiratorial actors. These master conspirators are almost always of the Type I variety—groups both invisible and operating in secrecy. Superconspiracies have enjoyed particular growth since the 1980s, in the work of authors such as David Icke, Valdamar Valerian, and Milton William Cooper (discussed in chapters 5 and 6).

THE EMPIRICAL SOUNDNESS OF CONSPIRACY THEORIES

Conspiracy theories purport to be empirically relevant; that is, they claim to be testable by the accumulation of evidence about the observable world. Those who subscribe to such constructs do not ask that the constructs be taken on faith. Instead, they often engage in elaborate presentations of evidence in order to substantiate their claims. Indeed, as Richard Hofstadter has pointed out, conspiracist literature often mimics the apparatus of source citation and evidence presentation found in conventional scholarship: "The very fantastic character of [conspiracy theories'] conclusions leads to heroic strivings for 'evidence' to prove that the unbelievable is the only thing that can be believed."[5]

But the obsessive quest for proof masks a deeper problem: the more sweeping a conspiracy theory's claims, the less relevant evidence becomes, notwithstanding the insistence that the theory is empirically sound. This paradox occurs because conspiracy theories are at their heart nonfalsifiable. No matter how much evidence their adherents accumulate, belief in a conspiracy theory ultimately becomes a matter of faith rather than proof.

Conspiracy theories resist traditional canons of proof because they reduce highly complex phenomena to simple causes. This is ordinarily a characteristic much admired in scientific theories, where it is referred to as "parsimony." Conspiracy theories—particularly the systemic theories and the superconspiracy theories discussed above—are nothing if not parsimonious, for they attribute all of the world's evil to the activities of a single plot, or set of plots.

Precisely because the claims are so sweeping, however, they ultimately defeat any attempt at testing. Conspiracists' reasoning runs in the following way. Because the conspiracy is so powerful, it controls virtually all of the channels through which information is disseminated—universities, media, and so forth. Further, the conspiracy desires at all costs to conceal its activities, so it will use its control over knowledge production and dissemination to mislead those who seek to expose it. Hence information that appears to put a conspiracy theory in doubt must have been planted by the conspirators themselves in order to mislead.

The result is a closed system of ideas about a plot that is believed not only to be responsible for creating a wide range of evils but also to be so clever at covering its tracks that it can manufacture the evidence adduced by skeptics. In the end, the theory becomes nonfalsifiable, because every attempt at falsification is dismissed as a ruse.

The problem that remains for believers is to explain why they themselves have not succumbed to the deceptions, why they have detected a truth invisible to others. This they do through several stratagems. They may claim to have access to authentic pieces of evidence that have somehow slipped from the conspirators' control and thus provide an inside view. Such documents have ranged from *The Protocols* to UFO documents that purport to be drawn from highly classified government files. Another stratagem is to distance themselves ostentatiously from mainstream institutions. By claiming to disbelieve mass media and other sources, believers can argue that they have avoided the mind control and brainwashing used to deceive the majority. This also accounts in part for their fondness for what in chapter 2 I call stigmatized knowledge—that is, knowledge claims that run counter to generally accepted beliefs.

Conspiracy Theory and Paranoia

The connection made between conspiracy and paranoia has two interrelated origins. The first, and more general, source is the similarity between the delusional systems of paranoids and the plots imagined by conspiracy theorists. The second source is Richard Hofstadter's widely cited essay "The Paranoid Style in American Politics," first presented the month of John F. Kennedy's assassination and published in its final form in 1965. Hofstadter sought to make clear that his use of *paranoid* was metaphorical rather than literal and clinical. Indeed, he argued that, unlike the clinical paranoid, the political paranoid believes that the plot is directed not against himself or herself personally, but "against a nation, a culture, a way of life whose fate affects not himself alone but millions of others." Despite this caveat, Hofstadter, partly by the force of his writing and argument, introduced clinical terminology into the stream of discourse, where it could be employed more broadly by others.[6]

Unlike Hofstadter, some have argued that the clinical and the political may overlap. Robert Robins and Jerrold Post assert that the domain of political paranoia encompasses a range of exemplars, including such clinical paranoids as James Forrestal and Joseph Stalin; borderline paranoids whose "delusion is likely to involve exaggeration and distortion of genuine events and rational beliefs rather than pure psychotic invention"; and cultures in which, at least temporarily, conspiracy beliefs become a culturally defined norm. In this view, conspiracy beliefs become neither determinative of paranoia nor divorced from it. Instead, conspiracism straddles a blurred and shifting boundary between pathology and normalcy.[7]

The precise nature of the relation between conspiracism and paranoia is unlikely to be definitively determined, if only because the two concepts are subject to varying definitions, depending on theoretical orientation. The effect of introducing such terms as *paranoid* into the discussion of conspiracism is double-edged. On the one hand, the connection—whether metaphorical or literal—captures the belief that devotees of conspiracy theory have severed important ties with a realistic and accurate view of the world. They inhabit a world of the mind more orderly than the world that "is." On the other, *paranoid* has an unmistakably pejorative connotation. Indeed, it seems clear that Hofstadter utilized it precisely because of its judgmental quality. Its overtones are such that its use, even in careful hands, runs the risk of merely labeling people whose ideas we disapprove of.

Conspiracy Theory and Millennialism

In addition to his ruminations about the suspicious tendency of political paranoids, Hofstadter also linked the paranoid style to millennialism. He noted that the millenarian figures described in such works as Norman Cohn's *The Pursuit of the Millennium* manifested precisely the complex of plots and fears that Hofstadter called the "paranoid style." Yet it turns out that while a relation exists between conspiracism and millennialism, it is not a simple one.[8]

Conspiracism is neither a necessary nor a sufficient condition for millennialism. It is not a necessary condition because some millenarian movements lack significant conspiracist components. For instance, Millerite Second Adventism in the 1840s, perhaps the most significant American millenarian movement of the nineteenth century, never constructed a major conspiracist structure. Millerism—named after its founder, Baptist preacher William Miller—coalesced around Miller's interpretation of biblical prophecy. According to him, Christ would return to earth sometime between March 21, 1843, and March 21, 1844. When the latter date passed without an end-time event, his followers persuaded Miller to accept a revised deadline of October 22, 1844. On that date, the "Great Disappointment" destroyed the movement, but not before it had attracted tens of thousands of supporters throughout the Northeast, including prominent abolitionists and evangelicals. The movement attempted to maintain a harmonious relationship with existing Protestant churches, and only in a late phase did adherents heed the call to "come out of Babylon" by withdrawing from their congregations.[9]

Likewise, conspiracism is not a sufficient condition for millennialism, for all conspiracism does is to impose a strongly dualistic vision on the world. It does not necessarily guarantee that good will triumph or predict that such a triumph will mean the perfection of the world. Indeed, conspiracism can sometimes lead to an antimillenarian conclusion, in which the evil cabal is depicted as virtually invincible. Fixation on a conspiracy whose indestructible tentacles are believed to extend everywhere can give rise to the belief that the forces of good are perilously close to defeat. Some conspiracy-minded survivalists have retreated into the wilderness at least in part because they fear that if they do not, they risk being destroyed.[10]

Despite the absence of a systematic connection between conspiracy and millennialism, the two are in fact often linked. Many millenarian movements are strongly dualistic and often ascribe to evil a power believed to operate conspiratorially. As Stephen O'Leary notes, "The discourses of conspiracy and apocalypse . . . are linked by a common function: each develops symbolic resources that enable societies to address and define the problem of evil." Conspiracy theories locate and describe evil, while millennialism explains the mechanism for its ultimate defeat. Hence the two can exist in a symbiotic relationship, in which conspiracism predisposes believers to be millennialists and vice versa, though each can exist independently. They are thus best viewed as mutually reinforcing.[11]

There is reason to believe that conspiracy theories are now more common elements of millennialism than they were in the past. In chapter 2, I describe a shift in millenarian "style" that I believe accounts for their increasing prominence. The traditional religious and secular-ideological styles have now been joined by a third variety, which I call the improvisational style. Religious and secular millennialism, however different they are from each other, have two common characteristics: each one's adherents consciously place it within a well-defined tradition, often positioning it as an alternative to some reigning orthodoxy; and each is centered on a body of canonical literature or teaching (e.g., the Bible or Marx's writings), whose exegesis is believed to illuminate the essence of history.

Religious and secular millennialism have certainly not been immune to conspiratorial ideas, but they have normally adopted only those grounded in the particular vocabulary of a specific tradition. Thus, Christian millennialists could develop conspiracy ideas by elaborating the scriptural Antichrist, while Marxists could develop notions of a capitalist plot. Neither religionists nor secularists, however, could easily construct conspiracy theories not already rooted in their own texts and traditions.

Improvisational millennialism, by contrast, has a much freer hand. It is by definition an act of bricolage, wherein disparate elements are drawn together in new combinations. An improvisational millenarian belief system might therefore draw simultaneously on Eastern and Western religion, New Age ideas and esotericism, and radical politics, without any sense that the resulting mélange contains incompatible elements. Such belief systems have become increasingly common since the 1960s, and freed as they are from the constraints of any single tradition, they may incorporate conspiracist motifs whatever their origin. As we shall see, this has given conspiracy theories an unprecedented mobility among a wide range of millenarian systems.

Conspiracy Beliefs and Folklore

Because improvisational millennialisms are bricolages, they can be treated both holistically and in terms of their constituent elements. The latter become particularly important, as they can appear simultaneously in a broad range of belief systems, having a slightly different significance in each, depending on the other elements with which they are combined. The chapters that follow examine a series of conspiratorial ideas both individually and in combination, among them concentration camps run by the Federal Emergency Management Agency (FEMA), implanted mind-control devices, and the Illuminati. Each can be separately traced, as well as related to other ideas with which it may appear, and each moves among different audiences. Because the dualism inherent in conspiracy ideas makes them ideal vehicles for apocalyptic anxieties, their prevalence in the years leading up to 2000 was scarcely surprising. "Ideas and images about the end of the world," Daniel Wojcik has said, "permeate American popular culture and folklore, as well as popular religion." [12]

The nature of conspiracy ideas can best be illuminated through the category of folklore known as the *urban legend*. According to one of its most prominent students, Jan Harold Brunvand, "Urban legends belong to the subclass of folk narratives, legends, that—unlike fairy tales—are believed, or at least believable, and that—unlike myths—are set in the recent past and involve normal human beings rather than ancient gods or demigods." These stories are almost always false, "but are always told as true." As Patricia A. Turner points out, urban legends—those that deal with distinctively modern themes—are closely related to rumors. Both purport to be true, or at least to be believable, and both circulate rapidly, though legends are likely to be more long-lived and complex. Beliefs that originally circulate as rumors may subsequently appear as elements of legends.[13]

There is, however, one complication in dealing with conspiracy beliefs as urban legends: the modes of transmission. The bias of folklorists is toward oral transmission as the primary medium. Legend texts are often secured in tape-recorded examples with accompanying data about the teller and how he or she learned the story. Conspiracy ideas clearly circulate widely in oral form, as evidenced by Turner's important study of conspiracy legends in the African American community; but the media-rich, technologically sophisticated society that exists in both the United States and other developed countries opens up new avenues for transmission.[14]

Brunvand, writing in 1981, conceded that "today's legends are also disseminated by the mass media." During the succeeding two decades, the Internet has emerged as a major new medium. Wojcik notes: "Folklore is not only transmitted through printed sources and electronic media but now through the Internet and e-mail, as members of global subcultures who never interact face-to-face exchange and create folklore in cyberspace. Despite predictions to the contrary, technology and industrialization have not necessarily destroyed traditions but have altered the ways that traditions are expressed and communicated, and have helped to generate and perpetuate new types of folklore." Such technological innovations are particularly important for the subcultures in which conspiracy theories have taken root.[15]

Conspiracy ideas are particularly prevalent in what I call the realm of stigmatized knowledge (see chapter 2)—knowledge claims that have not been validated by mainstream institutions. Subcultures dominated by belief in some form of stigmatized knowledge—such as those defined by commitments to political radicalism, occult and esoteric teaching, or UFOs and alien beings—are therefore most likely to nurture conspiracy ideas. These are also precisely the kinds of subcultures most attracted to the Internet.

The Internet is attractive because of its large potential audience, the low investment required for its use, and—most important—the absence of gatekeepers who might censor the content of messages. To some extent, of course, the subcultures referred to above have access to conventional mass media. They publish books and periodicals, though these are often restricted to distribution by mail or only the largest bookstores, which may also screen out overtly anti-Semitic or racist material. Access to radio and television appears limited to shortwave stations and community-access cable channels. There have been, to be sure, exceptions, such as the newspaper *The Spotlight*, once the right-wing publication with the largest circulation in the United States, and which ceased publication in 2001; and the Australian New Age–conspiracy magazine *Nexus*. For the most part, however, stigmatized knowledge subcultures are at a distinct disadvantage as far as mass media are concerned, for the latter are precisely the mainstream institutions best positioned to confer stigma on certain knowledge claims, including those that are overtly conspiracist. This contempt is reciprocated by conspiracists themselves. Not only do conspiracists distrust the mass media as distorters and concealers of the truth; they also regard them as part of the conspiracy, a tool controlled by the plotters in order to mislead the public.

Consequently, those whose worldview is built around conspiracy ideas find in the Internet virtual communities of the like-minded. Copyright and other issues of intellectual property appear to count for little among many who engage in Internet posting. Multiple versions of the same document are likely to appear in various places, some identical, some slightly different, some with annotations by the poster. The result is not unlike the variant accounts of urban legends that circulate by word of mouth. Unlike oral versions, however, all of the variants may in principle be simultaneously accessible to the Web surfer, who may then be tempted to judge the credibility of a story by the number of times it is told. Here repetition substitutes for direct evidence as a way of determining veracity. The dynamics of rumor provides a helpful analogy, for it is in the nature of rumors to appear precisely in those situations in which normal means of determining reliability are not available, so the potential consumer of rumors may end up determining truth on the basis of how widely a particular one circulates. This gives to rumors—and, by extension, to Internet conspiracy accounts—a self-validating quality. The more a story is told, and the more often people hear it, the more likely they are to believe it.

In a somewhat different way, search engines' placement of a page in a list of responses can reflect searchers' preferences. Google, for example, ranks pages produced in response to a search on the basis of both the page's content and the frequency with which it is linked to other pages. The more frequently other pages include it as a link, and the more prominent the pages that include the link, the higher the placement.

This communications milieu, in which self-validating rumors and urban legends can spread with unrivaled rapidity, has had particularly important implications for the spread of millenarian and apocalyptic beliefs. The result has been millennialism that is not only pervasive but increasingly varied in form. While many of the older religious and ideological forms remain—as, for example, among fundamentalist Protestants—these have been joined by many other varieties that resist easy classification. These are the examples I call improvisational millennialism, discussed in chapter 2, and it is to improvisational millennialism that conspiracists have most often been drawn.

CHAPTER 2

Millennialism, Conspiracy, and Stigmatized Knowledge

It has become a commonplace that America is in the throes of an unrivaled period of millenarian activity. In 1978, William McLoughlin spoke of a religious resurgence that constituted a new "great awakening." He expected it to end by about 1990. Instead, it intensified, driven in part by the proximity of the year 2000. Even the heyday of the Millerites, Shakers, Mormons, and Oneida Perfectionists in the 1830s and 1840s cannot compare to it. There is no sign that millenarian anticipation will diminish anytime soon. The uneventful passage from 1999 to 2000 has had little effect on many millenarians, who merely set the date of the apocalypse ever further in the future.[1]

What makes the present period an era of particular interest to observers of millennialism, however, is less the sheer volume of activity than its bewildering diversity. Attempts to map contemporary millennial ferment have become increasingly difficult and frustrating. The reason, I suggest, is not simply that there is so much "out there," but that old categories no longer fit well. Much of the proliferating millennialism is neither of the old religious variety, whose roots lie in the theological controversies of earlier centuries, nor a product of secular ideological battles that dominated the nineteenth and twentieth centuries. While neither of the latter strains of millennialism has vanished, they share the stage with a rapidly growing third variety, which is the subject of this chapter.

Religious and Secular Millennialism

The Christian idea of the millennium is rooted conceptually and etymo-logically in the New Testament passage that prophesies that at the end of time, the saved will "reign with Christ a thousand years" until the Last Judgment (Rev. 20:4). By extension, *millennialism*—belief in this end-time—came to mean any religious vision that saw history reaching its climax in a collective, this-worldly redemption. In this redeemed state, those who had once suffered would receive justice, and the poor and powerless would gain what had formerly been withheld from them. Although religious institutions often had a decidedly ambivalent atti-tude about this implied rejection of the status quo, the origin of millen-nialism in a canonical text insured its survival, and resilient strains of millenarian popular religion continue in Christianity into the present. They can be seen especially in the many contemporary religious funda-mentalisms, most of which contain millenarian elements.

By the late eighteenth century, however, a second form of millenni-alism was developing, unconnected to religious concepts. This consisted of secular visions of a perfect future—ideas propelled by faith in tran-scendent but not conventionally religious forces. These forces were sometimes identified with reason, and sometimes with science or his-tory. By the late nineteenth century, secular millenarian visions had be-come closely linked with political ideologies, especially those that grew out of ideas about nationality, class, and race. Hence the twentieth cen-tury was both dominated and scarred by Marxism, Nazism, and a host of nationalisms, all of which promised a millennial consummation to some group judged to be particularly worthy. Like earlier religious mil-lenarians, these secular ideologists linked the end-times with a great battle between the forces of good and evil—not a literal, biblical Arma-geddon, but a struggle of comparably cosmic importance.

Thus, by the mid- to late twentieth century, millenarian beliefs could be conveniently classified in either of these two broad categories. To be sure, disagreements might arise. The more religiously inclined might question whether any secular beliefs not grounded in sacred texts could be considered millenarian. Millenarians in the West sometimes disputed the application of the label to non-Christian belief systems, especially those in the non-Western world, such as the cargo cults of Melanesia. (Members of these South Pacific island sects claimed to possess secret knowledge, allegedly hidden from them by Christian missionaries. They believed the manipulation of this knowledge would bring them a utopia of unlimited manufactured goods of the kind introduced by their colonizers.) Some secular millenarians, notably Marxists, resented the application to themselves of any term that might associate them with religionists. These objections, however, tended to originate from believers rather than scholars, most of whom have been willing to apply *millenarian* to both secular and religious manifestations far outside the term's original Christian frame of reference.

A tacit consensus thus developed, at least in academic quarters, about the idea of two streams of millenarian beliefs, one flowing from religious traditions and the other from secular thought. This division provided a handy classificatory schema, especially for Western history, which seemed to move from an age of religious struggles to one of ideological warfare. This simple schema, however, does not work well any longer.

The reason has little to do with the relative health of religious and secular millennialism. Both have flourished. Although it was once believed that forces for secularization would inevitably marginalize religion, the last three or four decades of the twentieth century demonstrated the vitality of many religious traditions. This is particularly evident in the growth of fundamentalisms—religious movements that seek to restore what believers consider a pristine, uncorrupted tradition. Such movements are characterized by their emphasis on the literal reading of sacred texts and the drive to remold society in conformity with religious norms. Such movements—whether in Christianity, Judaism, Hinduism, or Islam—have demonstrated both rapid growth and the ability to mobilize to pursue political objectives. While not all fundamentalisms are millenarian, many, in their quest for doctrinal purity, give millenarian teachings a position of prominence.[2]

Secular millennialism has been less vital, a product of what Daniel Bell famously referred to as "the end of ideology." The great left-right battles that polarized Western politics for more than a century have largely died down. Whether the collapse of the Soviet empire was a cause or an effect of this process is a question beyond the scope of this inquiry. Nonetheless, the Soviet collapse seemed to some the definitive end of ideological battle, a point made with triumphalism by Francis Fukuyama in *The End of History and the Last Man*. Samuel Huntington, who reacted somewhat differently, argues that the resurgence of religion as a polarizing force was the result of the diminished salience of ideology. In any case, in the hands of ideologues, Cold War battles developed a significant millenarian dimension, seeming to pit the forces of light ("the free world") against the forces of darkness ("the evil empire"), with the prospect of nuclear Armageddon ahead.[3]

While it may seem that ideology has died out in a post–Cold War world, islands of secular millennialism remain. They appear in the resurgence of ethnic nationalism in many parts of the world, notably the Balkans, the Caucasus, and South Asia. They also appear in the racist and xenophobic movements that are prominent in Western and Central Europe and, to a lesser degree, in North America. Finally, they emerge in some antiglobalization rhetoric, with its implied nostalgia for a lost golden age of small, self-sufficient communities. Thus it would be incorrect to say that the older millennialisms, whether religious or secular, have disappeared; both can be found in numerous vital forms. Nonetheless, they have been joined by a third variety, which I call the improvisational millenarian style.

The Rise of Improvisational Millennialism

The improvisational millenarian style is distinctive for its independence from any single ideological tradition. Its predecessors—the religious and secular styles—consisted of variations on or deviations from some well-defined set of ideas, whether grounded in sacred texts, political ideologies, or philosophical teachings. By contrast, the improvisational style is characterized by relentless and seemingly indiscriminate borrowing. For example, Shoko Asahara, the leader of Aum Shinrikyo, drew not only on esoteric Buddhism but also on the New Testament Book of Revelation, Nostradamus, and anti-Semitic conspiracy theories. Aum Shinrikyo was the Japanese religious organization whose members tried to set off an apocalyptic war by releasing sarin gas in the Tokyo subway in 1993. In his indiscriminate combination of beliefs, Asahara was typical of contemporary millenarian entrepreneurs—by which I mean individuals who create apocalyptic belief systems outside of customary religious or secular traditions. In a similar vein, Elizabeth Clare Prophet, until 1999 the head of the Church Universal and Triumphant, joined Christianity with Theosophy, channeling, and conspiracy theory. Her Montana-based church, near Yellowstone National Park, built elaborate underground bomb shelters after Prophet became convinced that a Soviet nuclear attack was imminent. In 1990, hundreds of her followers took to the shelters, only to emerge eventually into the same world they had left.

These idiosyncratic combinations highlight the improvisational style's characteristic bricolage. Such odd conceptual structures are apt to contain elements from more than one religious tradition, together with ideas from the New Age, occultism, science, and radical politics. The combinations do not appear "natural," since the elements often come from seemingly unrelated domains, such as conspiracy theories and fringe science, or from domains that appear to be in opposition, such as fundamentalist religion and the New Age. "New Age" is clearly the most recent constituent, and its very recency poses definitional problems. For present purposes, I employ J. Gordon Melton's definition, which includes the following elements: mystical individual transformation; an awareness of new, nonmaterial realities; "the imposition of [a] personal vision onto society"; and belief in universally pervasive but invisible forms of energy.[4]

The appeal of these collages lies in their claim to provide holistic and comprehensive pictures of the world. The variety of their elements implies that the belief system can explain a comparably wide range of phenomena, from the spiritual to the scientific and the political. The combinations also suggest that apparent oppositions and contradictions can be resolved, and that an underlying unity transcends outward differences.

Such belief systems can flourish only in an environment in which two conditions are present. The first requirement is that a wide range of potential material—motifs that might be incorporated into a belief system—be easily accessible. The second is that existing authority structures be sufficiently weakened so that novel combinations of ideas can be proposed and taken seriously. The first condition, accessibility, has resulted from cultural exchanges now taken for granted, and from the communications infrastructure through which diverse messages move. New technologies and marketing devices have vastly increased the ease with which unusual and unpopular ideas may be spread. For print media, this has been facilitated by the ubiquitous availability of mass-market paperbacks through large bookstore chains, such as Borders and Barnes and Noble, and specialty stores catering to niche audiences such as evangelical Christians and New Age believers. Millenarian books have proved to be massive sellers—epitomized by the extraordinary success of the Left Behind series of millennialist novels by Tim La Haye and Jim Jenkins, which has sold more than fifty million copies. In addition, computer, photocopying, and other technologies have made possible the production of self-published print periodicals ('zines) by individuals and groups who previously had no access to this medium.[5]

But changes in electronic communication have been far more important. Cable television, including its legally mandated community access channels, has given exponents of fringe ideas who were traditionally relegated to subcultures entrée to mass audiences. Related technology permits the sale of videocassette recordings to the general public. A number of radio talk-shows cater to the conspiracist audience, sometimes stressing political plots, sometimes with an emphasis on the occult or what they consider "alternative science." The most prominent hosts include Art Bell, Hal Turner, and Alex Jones. In addition to spreading the "real news" through exposés, they also offer national platforms for the ideas of prominent conspiracy theorists through interviews. The influence of these media, however, pales beside that of the Internet.[6]

By the beginning of the year 2000, there were in excess of a billion Web pages in existence, as compared to only 1.3 million five years earlier. Besides the sheer volume of material it can accommodate, the Internet is the first mass medium without gatekeepers. No intermediaries, such as editors, publishers, or producers, stand between the content provider and the distribution of the message. In addition, the creation and dissemination of content require only a modest financial investment. Anyone can place a message before a potentially global audience.[7]

One effect of the Internet is to obscure the distinction between mainstream and fringe sources; another is to bind together individuals who hold fringe views. The validation that comes from seeing one's beliefs echoed by others provides a sense of connection for otherwise isolated individuals. Excessive claims have sometimes been made for "virtual community," but surely one effect of the Internet is to confirm and embolden those whose beliefs normally receive scant social reinforcement. The result insofar as millennialism is concerned is that the dissemination of a message is no longer linked to such traditional requirements as financial investment, popularity, or social acceptability. The bizarre, eccentric, and obscene appear on the same screen that might display the *Times* of London or CNN.com.

The second condition for the flourishing of improvisational millennialism, as mentioned earlier, is the erosion of existing authority structures. Even repressive governments find it difficult to block unwanted communications. Although secularization has not marginalized religion, it has weakened many traditional religious authority structures. Contributing factors to this decline have been the prestige of science and technology; population migration to diverse, media-rich urban areas; and the spread of compulsory secular education. Many religious authorities have responded by attempting to withdraw into enclaves, while others have tried to adapt their teachings to avoid conflicting with secular ideas. In either case, a reduction in power, scope of authority, and prestige have commonly resulted. Paradoxically, although science has contributed to the decline of religious authority, science too has seen its standing decline, especially in the last three decades of the twentieth century. The fruits of scientific research—whether they be nuclear weapons and nuclear power, the application of fossil fuels, or the manipulation of genetics—appear morally ambiguous. Hence science itself, instead of emerging as a surrogate for religion, has faced challenges to its authority, notably from those claiming access to nonrational forms of knowledge.

In short, many forms of authority that might in other circumstances have interfered with the ability of new belief systems to arise have proved unable to do so. Taken together, open communications and weakened authority create an environment favorable to millenarian entrepreneurs. Unconstrained by confessional traditions or ideological systems, they are free to engage in the kind of bricolage that distinguishes the improvisational millenarian style. They can borrow freely from many religious traditions, from occultism and the esoteric, from radical politics, and from both orthodox and fringe science.

In an environment in which authority has come into question, the very unclassifiability of these belief systems makes them attractive. Are they Christian or Buddhist, Western or non-Western, scientific or anti-scientific, religious or secular? The very questions and categories seem out of place when the belief systems themselves ignore such boundaries. In the act of ignoring boundaries, improvisational millenarians implicitly challenge orthodox conceptions of belief and knowledge. By picking and choosing among a variety of beliefs, improvisationalists convey the message that no single belief system, whether religious or secular, is authoritative. By implication, only the idiosyncratic combination associated with a particular leader or group is deemed to be valid. The millenarian entrepreneurs who construct such collages of beliefs assert that they alone possess insights that transcend conventional differences, whether among religious traditions, between religion and politics, or between science and esotericism. The result has been a dramatic proliferation of millenarian schemata, both in terms of the number of competing visions and in terms of their diversity.

The Sources of Improvisational Millennialism

Where does improvisational millennialism come from? The religious and secular forms of millennialism described earlier in this chapter have relatively unproblematic origins, because they rose out of well-defined bodies of religious and political ideas. Even systems of millenarian thought that are clearly heretical or deviant define themselves in opposition to a known orthodoxy. For instance, the more militant forms of late medieval Catholic millennialism emerged in opposition to the official Augustinian doctrine of the church, just as fringe Maoist revolutionary groups later placed themselves in opposition to more established custodians of Marxist thought.

Religious and secular millennialism are, to be sure, never absolutely pure types, emerging solely from within a single tradition with no outside influences. Soviet Marxist-Leninism surely absorbed and secularized some of the religious salvationism of the Russian Orthodox Church, and many in the Nazi inner circles combined racial pseudoscience with occultism. Nonetheless, neither participants nor observers have much difficulty in assigning most millenarian movements to some single, dominant category. A movement is religious or secular. If the former, it may be Catholic, Protestant, Jewish, Islamic, or some such; if the latter, racialist, socialist, et cetera. Classification problems can sometimes emerge concerning particular cases (to what secular category does one assign French revolutionary Jacobinism?), but it is rarely in much doubt that some appropriate category can be identified.

The belief systems with which this inquiry is concerned, however, permit no such easy pigeonholing. They are beholden to no dominant set of ideas. They are not the work of religious heretics rebelling against the constraints of orthodoxy; nor are they the product of deviationists defying received political doctrines. Instead, they combine elements so disparate that it is often impossible to determine what if any influence predominates. The practitioners of improvisational millennialism are not mere syncretists, hybridizing a few belief systems that happen to impinge on their consciousness. Rather, they construct wholly new creations out of bits and pieces acquired from astonishingly diverse and unrelated sources. It is as though there were some reservoir of motifs into which the new millenarians can dip, acquiring scraps of this or that ideology, idea, or creed. But what sort of reservoir is this that encompasses not only the familiar themes of religious and secular millenarians but also the more outré elements as well—Jesuit-Masonic conspiracies, Jewish cabals, sudden shifts in the polar axis, UFOs bearing alien emissaries, subterranean tunnel systems populated by strange races? This is a mélange that we may intuitively recognize as standing outside the boundaries of even most typical millenarian discourse.

Three ideas will help us to gain a clearer understanding of the reservoir from which improvisational millennialists draw their ideas: rejected knowledge, the cultic milieu, and stigmatized knowledge claims. *Rejected knowledge* is a concept developed by James Webb to aid in mapping the outer boundaries of the occult in Western culture. The closely related concept of the *cultic milieu* was devised by sociologist Colin Campbell to designate the sources from which many New Religious Movements draw their inspiration. Finally, in reaction to these ideas, I use the concept of *stigmatized knowledge claims* to designate a broader intellectual universe into which both rejected knowledge and the cultic milieu may be fitted.[8]

REJECTED KNOWLEDGE

In his histories of European occultism, Webb describes the occult as "rejected knowledge." This term refers less to the possible falsity of knowledge claims (though they may indeed be false) than to the relation between certain claims and the so-called Establishment—the dominant institutions associated with the spread of European Christianity. Christianity, in the course of achieving cultural hegemony, suppressed or ignored bodies of belief deemed to be irrelevant, erroneous, or outmoded. By the same token, those whose beliefs seem to conflict with dominant values sometimes choose to withdraw into subcultural undergrounds. The result is the creation of worldviews that exist in opposition to the prevailing ones and manifest in such forms as "Spiritualism, Theosophy, countless Eastern (and not so Eastern) cults; varieties of Christian sectarianism and the esoteric pursuits of magic, alchemy and astrology; also the pseudo-sciences."[9]

Such underground worldviews tend to be ill-defined potpourris in which are "jumbled together the droppings of all cultures, and occasional fragments of philosophy perhaps profound but almost certainly subversive to right living in the society in which the believer finds himself." This cultural dumping ground of the heretical, the scandalous, the unfashionable, and the dangerous received renewed interest in the nineteenth century, when at least some in the West became bored or disillusioned with rationalism. Such ideas were often presented under the

rubric of "ancient wisdom," the alleged recovery of a body of knowledge from the remote past supposedly superior to the scientific and rational knowledge more recently acquired.[10]

Webb's conception of the occult as rejected knowledge is not universally accepted by scholars of occultism, in part because not all traditions of sectarianism, mysticism, and deviant spirituality were rejected
by the mainstream. Until the end of the seventeenth century, and especially during the Renaissance, they enjoyed high levels of social acceptance. This quarrel among students of the occult need not detain us,
however, for our concern is with the present, not the past; and for
that purpose, rejected knowledge remains a useful idea. Improvisational
millenarians are frequently drawn to beliefs that have an occult prove-
nance—for example, the belief that a superior civilization on the continent of Atlantis before it sank constructed a global system of tunnels
connecting its cities to other parts of the world. Improvisationalists
do indeed seem attracted to precisely the kinds of ideas Webb had in
mind, those that have been discarded or whose believers have chosen
to withdraw into a secretive domain of their own. Cultural rejection is
clearly a powerful force that gives believing in the occult a certain fris-
son, and that same thrill of the forbidden is often found among conspiracy believers.[11]

THE CULTIC MILIEU

Attractive as the concept of rejected knowledge is, it has limitations,
and not only with regard to the place of occultism in earlier periods. A
more significant problem is its limited focus. Webb was concerned with
mapping the occult in the nineteenth and twentieth centuries, based on
a conventional understanding of what that term encompassed, including such subjects as spiritualism and Theosophy. But the domain of the
occult omits much of both millennialism and conspiracism. Improvisationalists are ideological omnivores. They draw on the "ancient wisdom" claimed by occultism, but they do not necessarily limit themselves to such sources; their reservoir of knowledge claims is partly but
not entirely defined by the concept of occult-as-rejected-knowledge.
Hidden knowledge may suffer not only from overt rejection but merely
from lack of attention. That is to say, it may never be addressed, even
negatively, by knowledge-validating institutions. Those who accept
knowledge claims that stand on the fringes often confuse inattention
with rejection. As far as they are concerned, those who do not address

their claims have in fact rejected them. To grasp the novel character of the improvisational style, therefore, requires a concept broader than rejected knowledge. Just such a concept is available in the form of the cultic milieu.

The term *cultic milieu* was introduced in the early 1970s by British sociologist Campbell. It was subsequently applied to some of the New Religious Movements that flourished during the period, but it remained little utilized until recently. Campbell was concerned with the process by which so-called cults develop; but he was not employing *cult* as the word is now commonly used. In keeping with predominant usage in the sociology of religion, Campbell did not regard the term as inherently pejorative. Thus, his use does not carry the conventional implications of violence, irrationality, or brainwashing currently associated with the term. Rather, he treated cults as loosely structured religious groups that make few demands on their members and that are often based on belief systems that deviate from the dominant culture. Unlike sects, they are not groups that have broken away from existing religious organizations over disputes about leadership, doctrine, or personality. Since they are not breakaway groups, Campbell sought to determine how they came into being, a question made more significant by the fact that cults constantly form and dissolve.[12]

Campbell argued that cults emerge out of a supportive social and ideological environment, which he called the cultic milieu. This cultural underground encompasses Webb's concept of rejected knowledge, but is broader in two ways. First, it includes "all deviant belief systems," not merely those that find their way into occultism, though the occult remains a major component of the cultic milieu. But that milieu also includes such areas as alternative medicine and healing, not normally considered part of the occult domain. Second, the cultic milieu includes not simply beliefs and ideas but also their related practices, "the collectivities, institutions, individuals and media of communication associated with these beliefs." There is, in other words, a world of persons, organizations, social interactions, and channels of communication that makes the cultic milieu a genuine subculture rather than a mere intellectual or religious phenomenon.[13]

The cultic milieu is by nature hostile to authority, both because it rejects the authority of such normative institutions as churches and universities, and because no single institution within the milieu has the authority to prescribe beliefs and practices for those within it. As diverse as the cultic milieu is, however, Campbell finds in it "unifying tenden-

cies." One such tendency is its opposition to "dominant cultural orthodoxies." This is a point I shall return to many times, for it is also a
major characteristic of the culture of conspiracy, within which the reigning presumption is that any widely accepted belief must necessarily be
false. The very oppositional situation of the cultic milieu makes it wary
of all claims to authoritative judgment. Its suspiciousness makes it in-
trinsically receptive to all forms of revisionism, whether in history, religion, science, or politics.[14]

If disdain for orthodoxy is one trait of the cultic milieu, another is its
fluidity. Ideas migrate easily from one part of the milieu to another,
their movement facilitated by both a general receptivity to the unorthodox and a communication system of publications, meetings, and (more
recently) interlinked Web sites. According to Campbell, "the literature
of particular groups and movements frequently devotes space to topics
outside its own orbit, includes reviews of one another's literature and
advertises one another's meetings. As a direct consequence of this individuals who 'enter' the milieu at any one point frequently travel rapidly
through a variety of movements and beliefs and by so doing constitute
yet another unifying force within the milieu." As we shall see in succeeding chapters, such currents can connect antigovernment, fundamentalist, and UFO subcultures, permitting both individuals and ideas to
move among them with astonishing rapidity.[15]

Campbell's essay is among the most acute and perceptive descriptions of the dynamics of contemporary religious experimentation. Its
major limitation lies in its concentration on religious movements to the
exclusion of other kinds of groups. Indeed, the very logic of the concept of the cultic milieu suggests that under certain circumstances,
a person's religion becomes indistinguishable from political ideology
and the occult. Thus, without discarding Campbell's valuable insights,
we need to extend the cultic milieu to encompass a broader range of
phenomena. This can be done through the concept I call stigmatized
knowledge claims.

STIGMATIZED KNOWLEDGE CLAIMS

By *stigmatized knowledge* I mean claims to truth that the claimants
regard as verified despite the marginalization of those claims by the institutions that conventionally distinguish between knowledge and error—universities, communities of scientific researchers, and the like. Although this definition encompasses rejected knowledge in both Webb's

and Campbell's senses, it also includes a broader range of outsider ideas. The domain of stigmatized knowledge claims may be divided into five varieties:

· *Forgotten knowledge:* knowledge once allegedly known but lost through faulty memory, cataclysm, or some other interrupting factor (e.g., beliefs about ancient wisdom once possessed by inhabitants of Atlantis).

· *Superseded knowledge:* claims that once were authoritatively recognized as knowledge but lost that status because they came to be regarded as false or less valid than other claims (e.g., astrology and alchemy).

· *Ignored knowledge:* knowledge claims that persist in low-prestige social groups but are not taken seriously by others (e.g., folk medicine).

· *Rejected knowledge:* knowledge claims that are explicitly rejected as false from the outset (e.g., UFO abductions).

· *Suppressed knowledge:* claims that are allegedly known to be valid by authoritative institutions but are suppressed because the institutions fear the consequences of public knowledge or have some evil or selfish motive for hiding the truth (e.g., the alien origins of UFOs and suppressed cancer cures).[16]

Two characteristics of the stigmatized knowledge domain require particular attention: the special place accorded to suppressed knowledge and the empirical nature of the claims. The suppressed knowledge category tends to absorb the others, because believers assume that when their own ideas about knowledge conflict with some orthodoxy, the forces of orthodoxy will necessarily try to perpetuate error out of self-interest or some other evil motive. The consequence is to attribute all forms of knowledge stigmatization to the machinations of a conspiracy.

Conspiracy theories therefore function both as a part of suppressed knowledge and as a basis for stigmatization. At one level, conspiracy theories are an example of suppressed knowledge, because those who believe in conspiracy theories are convinced that only they know the true manner in which power is held and decisions made. The conspiracy is believed to have used its power to keep the rest of the populace in ignorance. At another level, conspiracy theories explain why all forms of stigmatized knowledge claims have been marginalized—allegedly the conspiracy has utilized its power to keep the truth from being known.

So the distinction between hidden knowledge on the one hand, which is "true," and orthodoxy on the other, which is "false," acts to push believers in stigmatized knowledge claims toward beliefs about plots to suppress the truth, and hence in the direction of conspiracism.

Stigmatized knowledge appears compelling to believers not only because it possesses the cachet of the suppressed and forbidden, but because of its allegedly empirical basis. Some stigmatized knowledge appears to rest on nonempirical or antiempirical foundations—for example, knowledge claimed to derive from spiritual entities channeled through human intermediaries. To a striking extent, however, stigmatized knowledge rests on asserted empirical foundations: those who make the claims explicitly or by implication challenge others to test their facts against evidence. For example, people who traffic in conspiracy theories do not claim for their beliefs the status of revelation, nor do they ask that their beliefs be taken on faith. Yet the version of empiricism that operates in the domain of stigmatized knowledge has its own peculiar characteristics.

In the first place, stigmatization itself is taken to be evidence of truth—for why else would a belief be stigmatized if not to suppress the truth? Hence stigmatization, instead of making a truth claim appear problematic, is seen to give it credibility, by implying that some malign forces conspired to prevent its becoming known. A presumption of validity therefore attaches to stigmatized claims, which greatly facilitates the flow of such claims through the cultic milieu. As Campbell observed, beliefs in the cultic milieu tend to move and combine freely, so that individuals in the milieu quickly become exposed to previously unfamiliar ideas, which they often appear predisposed to accept. It seems to matter little whether the belief in question concerns the Kennedy assassination, Atlantis, Bigfoot, or UFOs. The belief must be true *because* it is stigmatized.

At the same time that stigmatization is employed as a virtual guarantee of truth, the literature of stigmatized knowledge enthusiastically mimics mainstream scholarship. It does so by appropriating the apparatus of scholarship in the form of elaborate citations and bibliographies. The most common manifestation of pedantry is a fondness for reciprocal citation, in which authors obligingly cite one another. The result is that the same sources are repeated over and over, which produces a kind of pseudoconfirmation. If a source is cited many times, it must be true. Because the claims made by conspiracy theorists are usually nonfalsifiable, the multiplication of sources may leave the impression of validation without actually putting any propositions to the test of evidence.

This pattern was noted almost thirty-five years ago by Richard Hofstadter in his examination of what he called the paranoid political style, discussed in more detail in chapter 1. He observed that the more sweeping the claims, the more " 'heroic' [the] strivings for 'evidence' to prove that the unbelievable is the only thing that can be believed." The result is a literature that, "if not wholly rational, [is] at least intensely rationalistic." Indeed, conspiracy theorists insist on being judged by the very canons of proof that are used in the world they despise and distrust, the world of academia and the intelligentsia. For all its claims to populism, conspiracy theory yearns to be admitted to the precincts where it imagines the conspirators themselves dwell.[17]

Fact-Fiction Reversals

The commonsense distinction between fact and fiction melts away in the conspiracist world. More than that, the two exchange places, so that in striking ways conspiracists often claim first that what the world at large regards as fact is actually fiction, and second that what seems to be fiction is really fact. The first belief is a direct result of the commitment to stigmatized knowledge claims, for the acceptance of those claims rests on the belief that authoritative institutions, such as universities, cannot be trusted. They are deemed to be the tools of whatever malevolent forces are in control. Hence the purported knowledge propagated by such institutions is meant to deceive rather than enlighten. The baroque conspiracy theories that are so much a part of the stigmatized knowledge milieu are presumed to be explanations that expose the misleading—and therefore fictional—character of public knowledge. Because stigmatized knowledge claims and conspiracism insist on the illusory character of what passes for knowledge in the larger society, the equation of fact with fiction seems relatively straightforward. The belief that fiction is actually fact, however, is less obvious.

Conspiracy literature is replete with instances in which manifestly fictional products, such as films and novels, are asserted to be accurate, factual representations of reality. In some cases, they are deemed to be encoded messages, originally intended for the inner circle of conspirators, that somehow became public. In other cases, truth is believed to have taken fictional form because the author was convinced that a direct representation of reality would be too disturbing and needed to be cloaked in fictional conventions. In still other instances, fictionalization is deemed to be part of the conspirators' campaign to indoctrinate or prepare a naive public for some momentous future development.

The most common fiction-is-fact assertions deal with films, and especially the science-fiction films that have played to an immense audience in recent years, such as the *Star Wars* cycle and *Close Encounters of the Third Kind*. In a 1987 press statement, John Lear, the estranged son of inventor William Lear, claimed not only that the U.S. government had close and continuing contacts with extraterrestrials, but that an inner circle of powerful officials had "subtly promoted" the films *E.T. the Extra-Terrestrial* and *Close Encounters of the Third Kind* so that the public would come to think of extraterrestrials as benevolent "space brothers." Somewhat similar claims were made by conspiracy writer Milton William Cooper, who said that the films were "thinly disguised" descriptions of contacts that took place in the early 1950s between extraterrestrials and the government. The most sweeping claims of this kind have been made by Michael Mannion, whose "mindshift hypothesis" asserts that the "shadow government," whose members know about aliens, has been systematically "re-educating" the American public. According to Mannion, this campaign has touched virtually every area of popular culture, from films and television programs to the lyrics of popular songs. Hence every fictional reference to UFOs and their occupants is actually a purposeful representation to serve the ends of the secret elite who deal with the aliens behind the scenes.[18]

Such views have been met with skepticism by some conspiracists, either because the use of motion pictures in this way would mean that too many people would know the "real truth," thus making secrecy harder to maintain; or on the grounds that films have as much potential to mislead as to enlighten or indoctrinate. Thus Jon King suggests that the prominence given to the mysterious Area 51 in the 1996 film *Independence Day* is a "smoke screen," for the most secret alien-related activities have actually been transferred elsewhere. Nevertheless, he still sees a sinister hand behind the film: "It is highly unlikely that any blockbuster movie focusing so heavily on Area 51 would be allowed out into the public domain unless sanctioned by an ulterior motive."[19]

John Todd, an itinerant evangelist who spread conspiracy theories through pentecostal churches in the 1970s, saw the *Star Wars* sequel *The Empire Strikes Back* as depicting a battle between satanism and the false Christianity of the Illuminati, while the Robert Redford film *Three Days of the Condor* contained a doubly encoded message. Todd believed the book on which Redford is working as a CIA analyst early in the film was Ayn Rand's novel *Atlas Shrugged,* itself an encoded conspiratorial work. According to Todd, Rand had been commissioned to write the novel by "Philip [*sic*] Rothschild," allegedly the leader of the Illuminati. Todd claimed that "[w]ithin the book is a step-by-step plan to take over the world by taking over the United States."[20]

Todd's bizarre claims about Rand's novel had a deep influence not only in fundamentalist churches, but in the Covenant, Sword and Arm of the Lord, a heavily armed commune in the Ozarks affiliated with the anti-Semitic and millennialist Christian Identity movement. Todd's ideas about *Atlas Shrugged* were incorporated into a CSA pamphlet titled "Witchcraft and the Illuminati." The community apparently learned about Todd's theory from the pamphlet's author, Kerry Noble, who had been given one of Todd's audiotapes by a friend in Texas. Noble went on to read Rand's massive novel (supposedly in only two days!), and belief that the novel was an Illuminati code book swept the CSA community. Indeed, Noble attributes CSA's program of arming and military training to the fears raised by Todd. The community dissolved shortly after a raid by federal law-enforcement agencies in 1985.[21]

As eccentric as Todd's ideas were, an even stranger example of fact-fiction transposition concerns literature about a subterranean world, according to which alien races inhabit caverns and tunnels below the earth's surface. The earliest fictional work to attract the attention of those in the stigmatized knowledge milieu was Edward George Bulwer-Lytton's 1871 novel, *The Coming Race.* Bulwer-Lytton (1803–1873) is far better known for having written what is said to be the worst opening line in English literature: "It was a dark and stormy night." Quite apart from his dubious literary talents, however, it is the substance of *The Coming Race* that commends it to devotees of stigmatized knowledge.

The Coming Race purports to describe the journey of a young American narrator into the bowels of the earth, where he discovers a hidden civilization whose members represent a hitherto unknown race. They lead a pleasant and harmonious life underground, made possible by their discovery of a mysterious and unlimited source of energy called vril. Bulwer-Lytton's novel obeyed the conventions of utopian fiction and, like many utopian novels, was a vehicle for social satire and commentary. Within a short time, however, it had acquired a different sort of reader, who insisted it was true.[22]

The transfer of *The Coming Race* from fiction to fact was facilitated by Bulwer-Lytton's own flirtations with occultism, which led some in the occult subculture to assume he had adopted the conventions of fiction to cloak an astonishing but hidden feature of the real world. His most influential occult reader proved to be Helena Petrovna Blavatsky (1831–1891), the cofounder (with Henry Steel Olcott) of the Theosophical Society. "The name vril may be fiction," she wrote, "[but] the force itself is doubted as little in India as the existence itself of their Rishis, since it is mentioned in all the secret works." While a contemporary writer on the occult, Alec Maclellan, also grants that Bulwer-Lytton may have yielded to some poetic license, he insists, "If, as an initiate, he concealed some of its [vril's] attributes this is understandable."[23]

Believers in vril and *The Coming Race* kept alive not only the idea of a pool of free energy, but also the idea of an underground world with its own species and civilizations, a concept that has ramified in ways Bulwer-Lytton could scarcely have imagined. As we shall see in chapter 7, one result has been a vast contemporary literature purporting to describe subterranean caverns, tunnels, and races and speculating that flying saucers come not from outer space but from this underground world, whence they allegedly reach us through hidden openings in the earth's surface.

The most influential examples of this genre are a set of science-fiction stories published in the pulp magazine *Amazing Stories* between 1945 and 1948. The stories and their surrounding circumstances came to be known as "the Shaver Mystery," after their principal author, Richard Shaver, a welder from Pennsylvania. Shaver claimed to have been in psychic communication with a subterranean race and to have once physically visited their underground civilization. The "mystery" deals in part with the basis of Shaver's bizarre claims, and in part with the question of authorship. Some have attributed much of the actual writing, and especially the use of the literary conventions of science fiction, to Shaver's editor, Raymond A. Palmer. Palmer himself claimed to have written the first Shaver story, based on a ten-thousand-word letter Shaver had sent to *Amazing Stories.* In an account written during Shaver's lifetime, Palmer claimed, "While it is true that a great deal of the actual writing of the stories published under Mr. Shaver's name have been written by me [*sic*], it has been in an editorial and revisional [*sic*] capacity, and although the words are different, the facts of the Shaver Mystery are the same and remain original with him." Shaver himself strongly disputed this account and claimed, "There is very little revision in any of my work, just cutting where it didn't fit."[24]

Regardless of who may have authored the published stories, they took on a life of their own and have come to be treated not as science fiction but as factual accounts. While some writers on the occult, such as Maclellan, regard Shaver's work as a hoax based on earlier writings such as Bulwer-Lytton's, an immense Shaver Mystery literature has proliferated, some of it in print but much on the Internet. It has fused with later claims about secret underground bases and tunnels, some of which are alleged to have been constructed by the government and others by alien races. As in so much of the literature from the stigmatized knowledge domain, complex patterns of cross-referencing and cross-citation have come to be taken as proof. Thus if a claim is made that a contemporary government tunnel system exists, that is deemed to be proof that Shaver was correct, and vice versa. By most accounts Shaver himself believed with absolute conviction in the truthfulness of his stories. This, combined with their appearance in a pulp-fiction venue, served further to blur the already uncertain boundary between fact and fiction.[25]

Stigmatized Knowledge and Popular Culture

The volume and influence of stigmatized knowledge have increased dramatically through the mediation of popular culture. Motifs, theories, and truth claims that once existed in hermetically sealed subcultures have begun to be recycled, often with great rapidity, through popular culture. Although this movement may be observed in a variety of forms, including television and mass-market fiction, the most important and visible venue has been film. Two particularly notable examples are *Conspiracy Theory* (1997) and *The X-Files* (1998).

The significance of *Conspiracy Theory* lies in both the construction of the protagonist and the surprising and dramatic denouement. The protagonist, played by Mel Gibson, gives every indication early in the film of being delusional to the point of paranoia. He lives in a fortresslike apartment, complete with an escape hatch and self-destruction capability. The rooms are a warren of securely locked spaces; even the refrigerator is padlocked. Surrounded as Gibson is by shadowy, imagined enemies, the viewer is surprised by the gradual realization that indeed, there is a conspiracy, one of whose aims is to destroy this lone eccentric who has stumbled across truths that have been successfully concealed from his supposedly normal fellow citizens. In the film's final frame, the sky above the conspiracy theorist fills with emblematic and all-too-real black helicopters.

The film's conversion of its seemingly lunatic central character into a seer illuminating the dark side of American life clearly resonated with at least one real-world conspiracy theorist. Michael A. Hoffman II, a Holocaust denier and exponent of multiple conspiracy theories, seemed to find personal vindication as well as a convincing conspiratorial message. The film was, he writes, "a new revelation . . . which restores credibility to the investigators and validates their concerns." He acknowledges Gibson's wild, delusional ideas but concentrates on the awareness that while "[m]uch of what he says is nonsense . . . the kernel of truth is so potentially lethal that it justifies his paranoia."[26]

If *Conspiracy Theory* implied that militia claims about black helicopters (discussed further in chapter 4) were grounded in reality, conspiratorial preoccupations were presented in a far more detailed and literal fashion in *The X-Files* motion picture. The film, which grossed $150 million worldwide, joined T-shirts and a veritable library of books and magazines as part of the industry generated by the original television series. While the film contains the expected quota of references to black helicopters and alien abduction, its most striking characteristic is its demonization of FEMA, the Federal Emergency Management Agency. Since the 1970s, FEMA has been a target of conspiracy theorists. The film's principal conspiracy theorist, the ill-fated Dr. Kurzweil, predicts that when the conspirators are ready to strike, the president will declare a "state of emergency . . . All federal agencies will come under the power of the Federal Emergency Management Agency—FEMA— the secret government." This belief, which has circulated widely on the radical right for decades unbeknownst to the general population, suddenly was presented to an audience of millions.[27]

The appearance of conspiracism in major motion pictures signals a major change in the relation between stigmatized and mainstream knowledge claims. The coteries within which stigmatized knowledge was refined and nurtured were traditionally insular and marginalized— the worlds of occultism, alternative science and medicine, sectarian religion, and radical politics among them. These domains were marginalized in part because they were so closely associated with stigmatized knowledge. At the same time, the reverse was also true—some knowledge claims were stigmatized because they were identified with marginal subcultures. Now, however, the boundary between the stigmatized and the mainstream has clearly become more permeable. Themes that once might have been found only in outsider literature or on the more outré Web sites have become the stuff of network television and multimillion-dollar motion pictures.

It may be, as Jodi Dean suggests, that such easy cross-boundary movement has erased any distinction between "consensus reality" (the version promulgated by powerful mainstream institutions) and deviant, alternative realities, including those in which conspiracies figure prominently. On the other hand, as Dean herself concedes, stigmas have not been wholly erased, giving to those who traffic in the forbidden the thrill of the taboo. Thus, for example, "the very stigma makes UFOs and alien abduction seductive, transgressive." The as-yet-unanswerable question is whether the partial absorption of these ideas by popular culture will increase or decrease their potency and appeal.[28]

Surely the appearance of conspiracy themes in popular culture at least partially destigmatizes those ideas, by associating them with admired stars and propagating them through the most important forms of mass entertainment. They are sometimes identified with stigmatized sources, as is the case with the strange cabdriver at the center of *Conspiracy Theory,* who clearly reads publications and pursues issues of which most people are unaware, making them part of his reclusive lifestyle. But at other times, as in *The X-Files,* the claims may appear strange, but their sources are never identified, other than through tipsters in the film such as Kurzweil. And even Kurzweil is literate, well-spoken, and far better dressed than his fugitive life would lead one to expect.

Popular culture can also reduce the potency of conspiratorial themes by depriving them of some of their allure. Once hidden, they are now revealed. Once intended only for the knowing few, they are now placed before the ignorant many. Once mysterious, they can now appear banal, the building blocks of not particularly distinguished popular entertainments. Those who frequent the domain of stigmatized knowledge do so in part because it confers feelings of chosenness: only we few know the truth. That sense of constituting an elite provides partial compensation for what might otherwise be insupportable feelings of powerlessness—the sense of being a minority in a world of scoffers. The popularity of conspiracy films does not inevitably translate into a feeling of empowerment for conspiracy theorists. To the extent that their common currency is placed in everybody's hands, it is devalued. It is also potentially trivialized, for there is no assurance that those watching a conspiracy film really believe it. It is, after all, only a story. So the popularization of conspiracism is tinged with ambivalence for conspiracists, combining a sense that they were right all along with a fear that the newly enlightened will not take the ideas seriously enough to act on them.

We can gain some sense of this ambivalence from a practice mentioned earlier: that of treating some films and novels as encoded messages created by the conspirators. That claim has apparently not yet been made about either *Conspiracy Theory* or *The X-Files,* but it has been made about numerous science-fiction films. The belief in hidden messages has two advantages. First, it locates a level of meaning in popular culture that the mass audience is unaware of but that the knowing few can read. Second, it maintains a consistent view of the world as controlled by powerful, hidden forces, since if the forces are as powerful as the conspiracists assert, then they would surely be able to control the content of movies and books.

As I have indicated, believers in stigmatized knowledge assume that any widely held belief must necessarily be false—the result of indoctrination, suppression of the truth, or some other insidious mind-control technique. As ideas from stigmatized knowledge migrate into popular culture, conspiracy theorists must burrow ever deeper to discover the truth hidden by appearances. One of the chief exemplars of this technique is Milton William Cooper, who became widely known for his 1991 "exposé" of the alien control of the American government, *Behold a Pale Horse.* By 1995, however, Cooper had decided that UFOs were a creation of an all-too-earthly conspiracy and that the revelations of ufologists were "intentional disinformation projects designed to promote the alien threat scenario while allowing for complete deniability on the part of government."[29]

Thus the larger audience that popular culture has given to the culture of conspiracy must be balanced against the loss of special knowledge that conspiracy believers suffer—the threat that conspiracy knowledge, once the ultimate secret, will become merely another artifact of mass entertainment. It is far too early to know which set of forces will turn out to be the more powerful. One possibility is that the normal politics of compromise, openness, and incrementalism will give way to an orthodoxy of conspiracist politics dominated by belief in secrecy, dissimulation, and covert control. Another possibility is that conspiracism will become a diverting convention, with no greater claim to realism than, say, the antics of James Bond.

A more radical approach lies in Dean's suggestion that, at least where political matters are concerned, there is no longer a consensus reality about the causes of events and the reliability of evidence. In such a situation of uncertainty, she argues, "conspiracy theory, far from a label dismissively attached to the lunatic fringe, may well be an appropriate vehicle for political contestation." She is at pains to make clear that "The sort of conspiracy theory I'm advocating here has nothing to do with anti-Semitism." That is no doubt the case; however, the desire to distinguish "good" conspiracy theories from "bad" ultimately founders.[30]

First, although Dean is clearly correct in suggesting that the domain of consensus reality has shrunk and that formerly stigmatized beliefs have joined the mainstream, the wish to possess secret knowledge unavailable to or shunned by the majority keeps regenerating. Even as parts of stigmatized knowledge get swallowed up by popular culture, novel forms of esotericism and the forbidden arise in their place. In chapter 6, I will show this process unfolding in the increasingly bizarre ideas about UFO aliens that sprang up in the 1990s.

Second, the relation between conspiracy theories and anti-Semitism is far more problematic than Dean indicates. There can certainly be conspiracy theories that are not anti-Semitic; some are described in chapters 3 and 4. But contemporary conspiracy theories manifest a dynamics of expansion—the movement from event conspiracies to systemic conspiracies to superconspiracies described in chapter 1. As this progression occurs, two characteristics appear. First, the more a conspiracy theory seeks to explain, the larger its domain of evil; the conspiracy includes more and more malevolent agents. Second, the more inclusive the conspiracy theory, the less susceptible it is to disproof, for skeptics and their evidence are increasingly identified with the powers of evil.

The result of these processes is that the villains who populate conspiracy theories tend to multiply rapidly. Conspiracists find it difficult to keep out new putative evildoers. As succeeding chapters will demonstrate, ufologists—the very subculture on which Dean focuses—began with conspiracy theories that had nothing to do with anti-Semitism, yet in some cases ended up testifying to the veracity of *The Protocols of the Elders of Zion*.

Whichever path becomes dominant, it seems unlikely that the domain of stigmatized knowledge claims will disappear. Some will, no doubt, become the victims of their own success; that is, they will become so widely accepted that they will lose their stigma and become indistinguishable from the mainstream ideas they challenged. To a great extent, that has already happened to alternative medicine, now the beneficiary of government funding, with at least some access to conventional medical journals. Notwithstanding the increased permeability of boundaries, however, a domain of stigmatized knowledge seems likely to remain stigmatized, if only because it reflects the alienation and suspicions that some continue to direct toward government, science, higher education, and mainstream religion. As long as those suspicions remain, so too will the belief in a realm of hidden or forbidden knowledge. As ideas pass across the border that separates the world of the stigmatized from the world of the accepted, the world of the stigmatized must be reinforced with new additions. If the past is any guide, the cultic milieu provides a seemingly bottomless reservoir from which new knowledge claims can be drawn. Thus the attractions of the taboo and proscribed can always be met by visions of ever darker plots and ever more shocking revelations.

The existence of a self-perpetuating domain of stigmatized knowledge means that the raw material for improvisational millennialism will remain plentiful. We can see the flourishing undergrowth of improvisationalism in the development of increasingly complex beliefs about conspiracies. Although belief in malevolent plots has a long history in American culture, it is safe to say that no period has evinced so strong an appetite for conspiracism as the last twenty-five or thirty years of the twentieth century. Conspiracism increasingly manifests itself in depictions of plots so vast that they can be undone only in an Armageddonlike conflict. Small wonder, then, that so much improvisational millennialism revolves around visions of conspiracy that purport to describe a coming diabolical New World Order—the focus of the next two chapters.

CHAPTER 3

New World Order Conspiracies I

The New World Order and the Illuminati

Although styles of millenarian thought have become increasingly diverse, the result has not been the cacophony one might expect. Despite the unprecedented millenarian pluralism in contemporary America, the varieties described in the preceding chapter—religious, secular, and improvisational—have been integrated by the wide acceptance of a unifying conspiracy theory commonly denoted by the phrase *New World Order*. This theory may be found in religious, secular, and improvisational versions. In this chapter I examine its disparate origins, for it appears to have developed separately out of religious and secular ideas that subsequently converged.

New World Order theories claim that both past and present events must be understood as the outcome of efforts by an immensely powerful but secret group to seize control of the world. Most commonly, these theories now include some or all of the following elements: the systematic subversion of republican institutions by a federal government utilizing emergency powers; the gradual subordination of the United States to a world government operating through the United Nations; the creation of sinister new military and paramilitary forces, including governmental mobilization of urban youth gangs; the permanent stationing of foreign troops on U.S. soil; the widespread use of black helicopters to transport the tyranny's operatives; the confiscation of privately owned guns; the incarceration of so-called patriots in concentration camps run by FEMA; the implantation of microchips and other advanced technology for surveillance and mind control; the replacement of Christianity with a New Age world religion; and, finally, the manipulation of the entire apparatus by a hidden hierarchy of conspirators operating through secret societies.

These concepts were, of course, far removed from what President George H. W. Bush had in mind when he popularized the phrase *new world order* at the time of the Gulf War of 1991. He drew on a quite different tradition, which went back many decades and referred to a new and more stable international system associated with effective mechanisms for collective security. This distinction, however, is not one that New World Order writers have found persuasive. Indeed, considering Bush's past associations with such organizations as Skull and Bones (a secret society at Yale University), the United Nations, and the CIA, it was easy for conspiracists to view his new world order references as messages to his fellow plotters. While Bush no doubt thought the phrase suggested a reassuring entry into a post–Cold War world, those who saw conspiracies everywhere saw his open use of the term as evidence of the cabal's newfound brazenness.[1]

Thus by the early 1990s, what most regarded as innocuous political rhetoric was seen by others as a sign of onrushing calamity. They did so not only because they distrusted Bush's patrician origins but because, unbeknownst to him, the New World Order was already a well-consolidated element in the thinking of both religious millenarians and those on the extreme political right. It is not clear how far back these sectarian usages go, but they certainly antedate Bush's use by decades.

The idea of the New World Order as a sinister development draws on two distinct streams of ideas that evolved separately but eventually converged. One source is millenarian Christianity, embedded in fundamentalist Protestantism. Its speculations about the end-times, when history would reach its climax and termination, led to scenarios in which a diabolical figure—the Antichrist—would fasten his grip upon the world. The other, secular source, less easily categorized, consists of a body of historical and political pseudoscholarship that purported to explain major events in terms of the machinations of secret societies. They, rather than governments, were said to be the real holders of power. The eventual aim of these shadowy plotters was nothing less than world domination—the imposition of a New World Order.

The Reign of the Antichrist

The term *antichrist* itself appears only a few times in the New Testament, relegated to the First and Second Epistles of John. It is invoked almost in passing, but always with the sense that the person or persons referred to are "deceivers" and "false prophets" who will appear as adversaries in the last days. The sparse scriptural citations speak sometimes of a single Antichrist, and sometimes of many: "Little children, it is the last hour: and as ye heard that antichrist cometh, even now have there arisen many antichrists; whereby we know that it is the last hour" (1 John 2:18). Other than suggesting a capacity for deceiving the faithful, these passages say little about what such a person or persons will do. The vagueness of the concept, however, allowed it to be filled out with whatever content believers wished, particularly as time passed and it became evident that the Christ's return was to be indefinitely delayed.[2]

Two strategies eventually developed for the elaboration of the concept. The most common was to seek the Antichrist's identifying characteristics, the better to recognize him when the time came. Eventually, this quest produced a massive literature, especially among Anglo-American Protestants, aimed at determining who the Antichrist was, and always assuming that there was only one. The second strategy, which seems to have developed later, joined the figure of the Antichrist to an organization or institution through which he was to impose his will on the faithful.[3]

The Antichrist's eschatological role was significantly increased by the rise of dispensational premillennialism in the late nineteenth century. The dispensational system, devised by British evangelical John Nelson Darby (1800–1882), quickly became the dominant form of millenarianism among Protestant fundamentalists and remains so today. Premillennialists believe the millennium will not begin until after Christ's return and the events associated with it. Postmillennialists, on the other hand, regard the Second Coming as an event that will not take place until the millennium itself has ended. As a result, premillennialists conceive the end-times in terms of high drama and the catastrophic demise of the present order, while postmillennialists are far more apt to view the millennium as a state to be achieved through the gradual perfection of the world. Darby produced an elaborated version of premillennialism, in which sacred history was divided into periods or "dispensations," concluding with a complicated sequence immediately before the Second Coming. He argued that the end-times would commence with a seven-year period called the Tribulation. At the outset of the Tribulation, the saved would be Raptured, "caught up in the air" to be with Christ in heaven until his return. For the unsaved, however, the seven years of the Tribulation would be a time of increasing violence, persecution, and terror, much of it at the Antichrist's hands.

According to Darby's system, the Antichrist would become the leader of a global dictatorship after three and a half years, at the midpoint of the Tribulation, and seek to secure the world for Satan until the battle of Armageddon signaled Christ's return. The leading dispensationalist theologian, John Walvoord, says of this period, "This man's absolute control of the world politically, economically, and religiously will give him power such as no man has ever had in human history. His brilliance as a leader will be superhuman, for he will be dominated and directed by Satan himself." This scenario might well be dismissed as merely idle speculation, were it not for the conviction of many contemporary millennialists that the Tribulation will begin soon. In keeping with Darby's belief that the prophetic clock would begin to run only after scriptural prophecies concerning the Jews were fulfilled, Christian millennialists see in the creation and expansion of the state of Israel indisputable evidence that their end-time expectations are about to be fulfilled.[4]

While some millenarians concentrated on the Antichrist's personal characteristics, the better to identify him, others began to speculate about his apparatus of control—for if, indeed, the second half of the Tribulation was to be dominated by a world dictatorship, then surely that would require a formidable governmental and administrative structure. Because his rule was to constitute a resuscitated Roman Empire, there had to be an organizational as well as a personal component. This train of thought was evident as early as the 1920s, when some American millennialists regarded the new League of Nations as the institution awaiting the Antichrist's controlling hand.[5]

The interwar period provided fertile ground for Antichrist speculation, not only because of the League but also because of the emergence of European dictators. Hitler and, especially, Mussolini lent themselves to the scenarios of millenarians. For once, Mussolini seemed to trump his German ally because—at least insofar as the Antichrist was concerned—his identification appeared to be firmer. He reached an agreement with the pope, he ruled from Rome, and he made no secret of his desire to revive the Roman Empire. Among the most enthusiastic exponents of this theory was American Nazi sympathizer and anti-Semite Gerald Winrod (1900–1957).[6]

Winrod was of two minds concerning the Antichrist. On the one hand, like many of his contemporaries, he saw Mussolini as a natural candidate. On the other, his intense anti-Semitism dictated that the Antichrist be a Jew. The two positions could be harmonized by making the Jews the Antichrist's allies, or by manufacturing a Jewish ancestry for

Mussolini. Unlike the typical dispensationalist, Winrod felt compelled to draw Jews into the Antichrist system. He did so most extensively in a 1936 pamphlet, "Antichrist and the Tribe of Dan."[7]

In that pamphlet, Winrod brushed aside the issue of Mussolini's family background. Indeed, it was not necessary to establish his Jewish roots in order to identify him as the Antichrist; quite the contrary. For Winrod, "If it developed that Mussolini is the Antichrist, the rumors concerning his Jewish ancestry would be confirmed." The issue, in any case, was not Mussolini but the organizational structure behind him, for Winrod saw the Antichrist as merely the instrument of an invisible Jewish conspiracy: "A Jewish Antichrist, in the end of this age, pre-supposes an international system of Jewish government. There can be little doubt that such a system, based upon the Jewish Money Power, has already been created—and is ready to step into the open and assume control of world affairs as soon as the time is ripe." Winrod did not abandon the concept of a personified Antichrist, but he joined it so closely to a conspiracist view of history that the man and the organization became inseparable.[8]

The anti-Semitic implications of the Antichrist suddenly reemerged more than sixty years later when, in January 1999, the Reverend Jerry Falwell asserted that the Antichrist was probably already alive and was certainly a Jew. He seemed genuinely taken aback when many called the claim anti-Semitic. In a press statement, Falwell asserted, "Since Jesus came to earth . . . as a Jewish male, many evangelicals believe the Antichrist will, by necessity, be a Jewish male." Saying that he himself is "strongly pro-Jewish and pro-Israel," he denied any anti-Semitic intent, and agreed in hindsight that it would have been better never to have made the claim.[9]

As Falwell's comments suggest, Winrod's views were hardly typical of evangelicals—he was even tried for sedition during World War II. But his linkage of the person of the Antichrist with a satanic organization later reappeared in other forms. In this manner, the Antichrist suspicions originally attached to the League of Nations came to rest on the United Nations after 1945. The UN was a more tempting target for American millenarians, for although the United States had rejected membership in the League, it was a prime mover in the new organization. In the postwar era, Antichrist fears on the organizational level confronted, as it were, an embarrassment of riches, for in addition to the UN, the creation of the European Common Market (later the European Union) offered yet another potential venue for the Antichrist's machinations. Because the Antichrist's domain was widely regarded as successor to the Roman Empire, a Western European superstate was a particularly attractive candidate.

In addition to these organizational developments, Antichrist writers were encouraged by technological ones. The Antichrist folklore consistently emphasized his capacity for deception and control; indeed, it became an unquestioned tenet of dispensationalism that the world would initially welcome the Antichrist as a charismatic peacemaker whose diabolical designs would remain hidden until he had achieved total power. Modern technology appeared to equip the Antichrist with hitherto unavailable capacities for misrepresentation and domination. Electronic communications, especially television, could create instant global celebrity, while computers and microelectronics offered the means to monitor and control behavior and commerce. In fact, for some the Antichrist and the computer came to be virtually interchangeable.[10]

Paul Boyer notes, "Several [religious] popularizers even suggested that Antichrist would *be* a computer." The most common version of this legend is that a giant computer in Brussels, the headquarters of the Common Market/European Union, would keep track of everyone in the world. Because the Book of Revelation says that the mark of the beast would be required for anyone to buy and sell during the Antichrist's reign, such concentrated power could theoretically control the world. In another, more baroque version of the computer-as-Antichrist, the Brussels machine was said to be at the center of a global network of 365 computers that would keep track of the Antichrist's minions in their various secret, conspiratorial organizations. So prevalent did these beliefs become after about 1980 that a 1994 tract on computers and the Antichrist explicitly repudiated them: "False reports and silly rumors only damage the credibility of one of the most powerful prophetic passages in Scripture."[11]

An important result of these developments was an increasing tendency among fundamentalist millenarians to view the Antichrist as part of a system of control rather than simply an evil and deceitful individual. The figure of the Antichrist became enmeshed in a complex of related ideas: the mark of the beast as a satanic device to control economic activity; the universal bar code and implanted microchips as precursors of the literal mark; credit and debit cards as ways of habituating people to an economy without tangible money; and vast computer systems tracking the details of daily life. Although these were real and in some cases disturbing developments, the manner in which Antichrist writers treated them carried the seeds of a conspiracist view of the world. They saw in them an insidious plan for satanic control. As Grant Jeffrey says:

The prophecies of the Bible tell us a world government will arise in the last days led by the Antichrist, the world's last dictator . . . The prophets also foretold that money would cease to exist in the last days. It would be replaced by a cashless society that will use numbers instead of currency to allow you "to buy and sell." We are now rapidly approaching the moment when these ancient Bible prophecies can be fulfilled through the introduction of the 666-Mark of the Beast financial system of the Antichrist.[12]

Fundamentalist millenarians saw President Bush's uttering of the phrase "new world order" as a sign that the network of Antichrist forces had advanced so far that they could risk speaking about it publicly. To those already habituated to thinking about the Antichrist not simply in individual terms but as a system that drew in the UN, computers, and the global economy, the public invocation of the New World Order could only mean that the days of the Tribulation were imminent.

Thus, *New World Order* came to connote an impending world dictatorship in which the Antichrist would seize control through a combination of co-opted international organizations and marvels of electronic surveillance. But simultaneously, a second conception of the New World Order had arisen, growing in this case from secular roots.

The Illuminati

The secular version of the New World Order foresaw an equally bleak future, also dominated by expanding tyranny. In this case, however, the source of domination was not the power of Satan but an evil cabal that sought absolute power over the world's people and resources for its own selfish reasons. Although many secret societies were deemed to be carriers of the conspiracy, the one most often invoked was also the most shadowy and obscure, the Illuminati.

Richard Hofstadter began his seminal essay "The Paranoid Style in American Politics" with an example probably unfamiliar to most of his readers—the belief in late-eighteenth- and early-nineteenth-century America that the new nation was about to be taken over by the Bavarian Illuminati. The fear of a plot by this secret Masonic society had been stoked by an earlier literature that sought to portray the French Revolution as the result of an Illuminatist conspiracy. The two key works on this revolutionary conspiracism were John Robison's *Proofs of a Conspiracy* (1798) and Abbé Barruel's *Memoirs, Illustrating the History of Jacobinism* (1803). Although the alleged doings of Illuminatist plotters in America seemed credible to some prominent New England clerics and academics, the panic peaked by the turn of the nineteenth century, after which it became increasingly clear that the Illuminati lived mostly in Robison's fantasy life. Hofstadter himself disposed of the topic by noting that it may have opened the way for the anti-Masonic movement of the 1820s and 1830s, but he then proceeded to better-known examples of the "paranoid style" such as anti-Catholic nativism. The Illuminati were relegated to the role of the progenitors of a conspiracist strand in American life that was to take other forms in the future.[13]

In fact, however, the Illuminati—or at least the *image* of the Illuminati—had just begun to spread by the 1830s. Both Robison's and Barruel's books continued to be reprinted, and both are featured works currently sold by the John Birch Society's book service. Its catalog touts Barruel's work as "The most comprehensive expose of a Master Conspiracy to rule the world," while offering Robison's book as a description of "this secret group, whose select members became part of a conspiracy to enslave all people in Europe and America." By way of updating Robison's scenario, his current American publisher asserts that the Illuminati "have long since discarded Freemasonry as their vehicle," preferring to operate in "universities, tax-free foundations, mass media communication systems, government bureaus such as the State Department, and a myriad of private organizations such as the Council on Foreign Relations."[14]

So much mythology has encrusted the Illuminati that their actual history has been obscured, even by scholars. This is a case of the image having achieved greater prominence than the reality of the organization itself—an ultimate though dubious tribute to the influence of the genre begun by Robison and Barruel. Distinguishing the image from what it purports to represent is made more difficult by the Illuminati's own penchant for secrecy, its small size, and its brief lifespan. Nonetheless, the broad outlines of its history are reasonably clear.

The Bavarian Illuminati (formally, the Order of Illuminists) was established by a Bavarian canon-law professor, Adam Weishaupt, on May 1, 1776. Utilizing organizational models taken from both the Jesuits and the Masons, Weishaupt created a secular organization whose aim was to free the world "from all established religious and political authority." An elaborate apparatus of secrecy and ritual was designed not only to protect the organization from state penetration but to mold its members into an elite capable of achieving Weishaupt's grandiose objective. By the early 1780s, it had acquired a peak membership of approximately 2,500, most in German-speaking areas. The organization's aims and its clandestine methods (for example, the infiltration of some Masonic lodges) attracted unwelcome government attention, which proved potent enough to bypass even the order's security measures. By 1787, the Illuminati had been dissolved, but its sweeping goals, attention to secrecy, and insistence on unswerving personal dedication made it a model for a sizable number of early-nineteenth-century revolutionary organizations, much in the manner of the Paris Commune in the next century.[15]

In short, the Illuminati influenced subsequent revolutionaries, albeit indirectly, even though the organization seems on the most reliable evidence to have lasted no more than eleven or twelve years. Yet the irony is that if its sympathizers were eager to preserve its legacy and to achieve the total liberation that had eluded Weishaupt, its enemies were even more eager to keep it alive. They insisted that it had never died, that its dissolution was only apparent, and that in the ultimate act of clandestinity, it had survived its own death. The fact that the order had been dissolved even *before* the French Revolution began made allegations of its survival all the more attractive, for how better to explain an unprecedented upheaval than by fastening on an unprecedentedly cunning cabal? Hence by an act of reductionist self-deception, opponents of the revolution could both explain its occurrence and resuscitate the Illuminati. And so began the convoluted tale of an evil conspiracy that was said to move from country to country, and century to century, setting off revolutionary conflagrations wherever it appeared.

THE ILLUMINATI IN THE TWENTIETH CENTURY

Illuminati literature took a major leap in the interwar period of the twentieth century, when the legend of Weishaupt's group came to be placed within a far more complex and ambitious conception of history. This transformation was mainly the work of two English writers, Nesta Webster (1876–1960) and Lady Queenborough, also known as Edith Starr Miller (d. 1933), each responsible for remarkably similar syntheses of the Illuminati literature. It is scarcely hyperbole to say, as Nicholas Goodrick-Clarke does, that without Webster "few Americans today would have heard of the Illuminati." The women shared an unshakable

faith in Robison's and Barruel's notion that the Illuminati were responsible for the French Revolution, and like the earlier authors, they insisted that the Illuminati had not disappeared in the late 1780s but
had gone on causing mayhem for decades thereafter. More important,
Webster and Queenborough added two ideas that turned out to be immensely influential in later years: first, that world history could be correctly understood only as the product of the machinations of secret
societies; and second, that Jews were central to these activities. By ele-
vating secret societies to the role of prime movers in world history,
they left the French Revolution behind, extending the Illuminati's field
of action into the present, including above all a catalytic role in the
Russian Revolution. By linking Illuminism with the Jews, Webster and
Queenborough gained access to a whole new body of conspiracy ideas,
which they quickly appropriated.[16]

The problem they both confronted was that of fitting an organization that had not been founded until 1776 and that appeared to have
fizzled out about 1787 into a conspiracist historiography. Building such
a theory, while at the same time giving the Illuminati their due, required
them to sweep in a whole raft of other organizations as ancestors, suc-
cessors, affiliates, or subsidiaries of the Illuminati. In the end, Webster
and Queenborough included, among many others, the Knights Templar, the kabbalists, the Rosicrucians, and the Carbonari, postulating or
claiming to demonstrate all manner of linkages among dozens of clandestine groups. Thus was born the concept of a kind of interlocking di-
rectorate of conspirators who operate through a network of secret societies. The fact that there had actually been secret societies that had
played a modest role in channeling European political dissent from
about 1790 until the middle of the nineteenth century gave a surface
plausibility to some of these claims, but scarcely provided justification
for the wildly inflated charges made by Webster and Queenborough.[17]

Webster, writing in 1924, concluded that the world's ills were attributable to anti-Christian Illuminati, to "Pan-German Power" (she was,
after all, writing shortly after World War I), and to "the Jewish power."
She was unsure exactly how these three forces were intertwined, but
proposed the following scenarios:

If . . . one inner circle exists, composed of Illuminati animated by a purely de-
structive purpose it is conceivable that they might find support in those Ger-
mans who desire to disintegrate the countries of the Allies with a view to future
conquest, and in those Jews who hope to establish their empire on the ruins of
Christian civilization . . . On the other hand it may be that the hidden center

consists in a circle of Jews located in the background of the Grand Orient [Masonry] working in accord and using both Pan-Germans and Gentile Illuminati as their tools.

She ended up unsure which was the more likely, though she clearly leaned toward the second possibility. In any case, who was using whom scarcely mattered, since the three forces differed only marginally in their capacity for evil.[18]

Lady Queenborough's view of the world was much the same: a complex of secret societies acted in concert to control the world and corrupt its values through their domination of the arts, political parties, the press, crime, and a host of other forces. But for her the ultimate lever was money, because money could buy control. "This power," she concluded, "is wholly in the hands of international Jewish financiers." She had less difficulty than Webster in figuring out the relation between the Illuminati and the Jews; as far as she was concerned, the Illuminati was simply one tentacle of the Jewish world conspiracy: "Illuminism represented the efforts of the heads of the powerful Jewish Kahal [sic] which has ever striven for the attainment of political, financial, economic and moral world domination."[19]

Webster's and Queenborough's ideas quickly crossed the Atlantic. Once again, the main channel for their dissemination in America appears to have been Gerald Winrod. His 1935 pamphlet, "Adam Weishaupt, a Human Devil," drew explicitly on Webster and Queenborough, as well as on Barruel and Robison. Paraphrasing Queenborough, Winrod concluded, "The real conspirators behind the Illuminati were Jews." As far as he was concerned, communism in the Soviet Union was merely Illuminism's most recent manifestation. "Karl Marx . . . edited [sic] his teaching out of the writings of Adam Weishaupt." As if that were not sufficient, Winrod proceeded to lay out a series of resemblances between the Illuminati and the Bolsheviks, ranging from alleged ideological parallels to their common penchant for changing their names. He concluded "that the Illuminati was Jewish. In like manner the Moscow dictatorship is Jewish." Hence to fight Jews was simultaneously to fight both communism and the Illuminati, who now merged into a single entity.[20]

Anti-Illuminism thus became a staple of the American far right, particularly in that variant that linked the Illuminati to a worldwide Jewish conspiracy. This tendency was doubtless reinforced by the wide circulation given in the 1920s to Victor Marsden's English translation of *The*

Protocols of the Elders of Zion, whose contents were disseminated in the United States through Henry Ford's weekly newspaper, *The Dearborn Independent.* The *Protocols* purports to be the transcripts of speeches given to an assembly of Jewish "Elders" who collectively conspire to rule the world. It takes the form of twenty-four brief addresses that explain the techniques Jews and their Masonic allies will employ to subvert governments and institutions. As journalists and scholars quickly discovered, it was plagiarized from two sources: Maurice Joly's *A Dialogue in Hell: Conversations between Machiavelli and Montesquieu about Power and Right,* a polemic directed against Napoleon III and having nothing to do with Jews; and an anti-Semitic novel, *Biarritz,* by "Sir John Retcliffe" (a.k.a. Hermann Goedsche).[21]

After World War II, however, the situation had seemingly changed. *The Protocols* had long been discredited as a forgery, anti-Semitism had begun what was to be a long and steady decline, and the fixation on the origins of the Russian Revolution, so strong in the interwar period, gave way to the predictable mutual hostilities of the Cold War. Indeed, one may speculate that this combination of factors explains the manner in which Hofstadter treated the Illuminati literature. Writing in the depths of the Cold War and preoccupied with the Red Scare of the 1950s, he treated the Illuminati literature not as a living part of American mythology but as an artifact of the early 1800s, interesting largely as a precursor of the paranoid political style. If Hofstadter was aware of the links among Webster, Queenborough, and Winrod, he chose not to mention them.

In fact, Illuminism was of more than merely antiquarian interest, for the American right was on the threshold of an Illuminati explosion. Much of the stimulus for this renewed interest came from the John Birch Society, founded by Robert Welch in 1958. Welch himself picked up the strands of Robison's argument even as Hofstadter was writing in 1964, and it remained a staple of the society's view of history after Welch's death.[22]

A recent systematic statement of Birch Society conspiracy theory blends traditional sources—Barruel and Robison—with modern scholarship on the Illuminati. It dismisses the supposed suppression of the order as meaningless, contending that it was soon transplanted to both the United States and other parts of Europe, where it gave rise to the *Communist Manifesto* and the revolts of 1848. The Birchite retelling attributes to the Illuminati the creation of movements as varied as "the Marxian and 'utopian' socialist movements; anarchism; syndicalism; Pan

Slavism; Irish, Italian and German 'Nationalism'; German Imperialism; the Paris Commune; British 'New Imperialism'; Fabian Socialism; and Leninist Bolshevism."[23]

CONTEMPORARY ILLUMINATI LITERATURE

The post-1965 Illuminati literature became so vast that only a sampling can be discussed here, drawn from both secular and religious sources. Larry Abraham's *Call It Conspiracy,* first published in 1971, claims to expose a conspiracy of "Insiders" bent on world domination: "After the *Insiders* have established the United Socialist States of America (in fact if not in name), the next step is the Great Merger of all nations of the world into a dictatorial world government." Although his roster of Insiders is drawn from the usual reservoir—the Council on Foreign Relations and the Trilateral Commission (discussed in chapter 4)—their roots are claimed to be in the late-eighteenth-century Illuminati: "The role of Weishaupt's Illuminists in such horrors as the Reign of Terror is unquestioned, and the techniques of the Illuminati have long been recognized as models for Communist methodology."[24]

While Abraham avoids the overt anti-Semitism of Webster and Queenborough, he treads perilously close to an anti-Semitic theory of history, in which Jews sit at the center of a conspiratorial web. "Anti-Semites," he claims, "have played into the hands of the conspiracy by trying to portray the entire conspiracy as Jewish. Nothing could be farther from the truth." Nonetheless, he places the Rothschilds at the conspiracy's heart, and calls the Anti-Defamation League of B'nai B'rith an instrument created by "the Jewish members of the conspiracy" to "stifle . . . almost all honest scholarship on international bankers" through "highly professional smear jobs." The Rothschild family established banks in Frankfurt, Vienna, Paris, and London. Their prominence as international bankers peaked in the early nineteenth century and waned thereafter as national governments became increasingly adept at raising funds without recourse to private bankers. Nonetheless, the specter of Rothschild power continued to grow even as the family's real influence declined. Although this type of speculation was widespread throughout anti-Semitic circles in the late nineteenth and twentieth centuries, it was notably strong in the United States, where radicals of every stripe seemed obsessed by financial conspiracies. The Rothschilds, who combined Jewishness, banking, and international ties, presented an attractive target.[25]

A more openly anti-Semitic version of Illuminati theory came in 1984 from the pen of Eustace Mullins, a protégé of Ezra Pound. Like his mentor, Mullins sees the world's evil as a product of financial manipulation, in which Jews play a central role. But as an explanation of world, as opposed to modern, history, his conspiracist vision makes the Illuminati merely a link in a much longer chain that extends back to the ancient Near East and forward to the nascent communist movement of the early Marx. Weishaupt himself is portrayed as a mere figurehead. As Queenborough and Winrod had claimed half a century earlier, Mullins sees the Illuminati as really run by Jews, in this case a Jewish banker who worked for the Illuminati's "corresponding branch in Italy."[26]

A slightly different set of emphases informed William T. Still's 1990 book, *New World Order: The Ancient Plan of Secret Societies.* Here, too, the link between the Illuminati and the Rothschilds is of prime importance. By the time Weishaupt and his key followers were forced to flee Bavaria, "the Illuminati had taken root among the rich and powerful of Europe, including, possibly, the wealthiest of all, the first international bankers and railway kings, the German brothers Rothschild." Weishaupt's infiltration of the Masonic movement, together with the Rothschilds' money, made possible the manipulation of the French Revolution. But Still parts company with many earlier writers in concentrating on Masonry as the key to understanding the conspiracy's reach. Jewish bankers may supply the conspiracy's capital, but its camouflage comes from its control of the Masonic movement. Nevertheless, Still is willing to concede that in the twentieth century, the plotters have found alternative homes in such organizations as the Council on Foreign Relations.[27]

Religious concerns hover in the background of much recent Illuminati literature; the Illuminatists' deism tends to be regarded as anti-Christian agitation if not outright satanism. In the majority of the literature, the alleged Illuminatist attack on revealed religion is a secondary motif, but in the works of Texe Marrs and Pat Robertson, it emerges as the central theme.

Unlike almost all others who have written about the Illuminati, Texe Marrs detaches the idea from any historic roots. While deeply suspicious and fearful of Masonry, Marrs, a Texas-based evangelist, has no particular interest in Weishaupt, whom he barely mentions, or in the actual Illuminati order. Instead, *the Illuminati* becomes an umbrella category under which he can subsume everything from the Knights of Malta and Skull and Bones to the Aspen Institute and the Trilateral Commission:

"All of these groups—and many more which we will expose—are part of one gigantic, unified, global network known collectively as the *Secret Brotherhood*. In the past they have also been identified as the Illuminati." Although its members are anti-Christian, their demonic religion is itself part of God's plan, a sign of the nearness of the millennial end-times. "The unseen men who rule the world are determined to bring in their New World Order by the magical year 2000—the advent of a New Millennium." The chaos this portends "will fulfill Bible prophecy, for our Lord warned us the time would come when the very denizens of hell would lash out and attempt to destroy God's people." The Illuminati, by whatever name, are none other than the beast of the Book of Revelation.[28]

No work on the Illuminati published in recent decades—whether secular or religious—has matched the influence of Pat Robertson's *The New World Order*, which first appeared in 1991. With several hundred thousand copies in print, it turns up in mainstream bookstores and airport paperback racks, as well as at outlets that cater to evangelicals. Robertson's secret plotters aim to create a world government, simultaneously attacking Christian religion and American liberties, and setting in motion the final struggle between the forces of good and evil that will bring history to a close.

In the course of laying out this scheme, Robertson presents a picture familiar to readers of Illuminati literature: Weishaupt's order prepared the way for the French Revolution, then became the source for global communism, producing in time the Russian Revolution. These efforts were financed at key points by Jewish international bankers: the Rothschilds; the firm of Kuhn, Loeb; Jacob Schiff; and the Warburgs.[29]

This is scarcely an original scenario. Its significance lies not in its content but in its authorship, for Robertson is the first modern religious and political figure of national stature to embrace a belief in an Illuminatist conspiracy. Oddly enough, Robertson's views passed nearly unnoticed by the mainstream press for four years, until they became the subject of two lengthy and critical articles in *The New York Review of Books* in 1995. The articles' authors, Michael Lind and Jacob Heilbrun, pointed out that Robertson had drawn heavily on the work of both Webster and Mullins, and that in fact he was recycling their anti-Semitic theory of history. The essays appeared at a time that Robertson's political organization, the Christian Coalition, was reaching out beyond evangelical Protestants to other "people of faith," including Jews. Stung by the Lind and Heilbrun articles, Robertson and the coalition's then director, Ralph Reed, apologized to the Jewish community and denied holding anti-Semitic views. Nonetheless, Robertson has never explained why he employed sources such as Webster and Mullins, and his book has continued to circulate widely.[30]

Authors such as Abraham, Still, Mullins, Marrs, and Robertson represent a widely diffused form of Illuminati conspiracy theory, but theirs is not the only version. They have done little more than produce variations on the synthesis developed by Webster and Queenborough. Simultaneously with this derivative literature, however, a second form of Illuminati material began to appear—what might best be described as *superconspiracy theories.* In these theories, a single line of secret-society plotters spawned by Illuminism is replaced by extraordinarily complex structures of plots layered within one another, like Russian nested dolls, or linked together in complex combinations. Beginning in the 1970s, increasingly complex scenarios of Illuminati plots began to circulate, first on the fringes of evangelical Protestantism, and subsequently in some New Age circles. Both varieties, for reasons that will become clear, quickly spread into the radical right.

Among the earliest descriptions of a superconspiracy was Des Griffin's *Fourth Reich of the Rich,* which appeared in 1976. While Griffin accepts and builds on the work of Robison, Barruel, and Webster, he gives their traditional attack on the Illuminati a significant theological twist, for he projects the origins of the Illuminati back to before the creation of the world. He accomplishes this by fusing the original idea of an Illuminati conspiracy with the far older story of Lucifer's rebellion against God.[31]

Griffin believes the earth was originally populated by Lucifer and his fallen angels, after the failure of their rebellion in heaven—a view held by others on the radical right, such as Christian Identity preacher Wesley Swift. Although Adam had the opportunity to undo Satan's earthly crimes, his and Eve's sin in the Garden eliminated that option. A satanic system was eventually institutionalized in Babylon by the shadowy Nimrod (a figure sufficiently obscure to be utilized freely by those seeking to reconstruct the antediluvian past). According to Griffin, Nimrod created a satanic religion that not only survived the Flood but eventually infiltrated and captured the Catholic Church. Griffin owes this strange argument to a Scottish divine, Alexander Hislop (1807–1865), who presented an almost identical view in his book *The Two Babylons,* published in the 1850s.[32]

The novelty of Griffin's work lies in his fusion of this version of sacred history with conspiracist explanations of modern politics. Thus in addition to their seizure of the Catholic Church, he claims, satanic forces also lay behind the founding of the Illuminati, which was to become the master instrument in Lucifer's scheme to regain full control of the earth. Even the Illuminati's apparent dissolution in the late 1780s was part of the plan, the better to conceal the conspirators' nefarious activities: "This lie [concerning the dissolution of the Illuminati] has been perpetuated ever since by 'historians' anxious to cover the truth about the Illuminati's subsequent activities." [33]

These activities took familiar forms: the French and Russian revolutions, the establishment of the Federal Reserve, and the advancement of a global dictatorship. In thus linking the Illuminati with both an obscure Luciferian past and a revolutionary future, Griffin made possible a form of anti-Semitism far more sweeping than that which had appeared in the interwar synthesis. He did so by bringing into prominence a theme that had been subordinate in Webster's writing about *The Protocols of the Elders of Zion*. While Webster was inclined to regard *The Protocols* as an authentic document of some kind, she was not entirely sure what kind it was—not surprising in light of the fact that her own book, *Secret Societies and Subversive Movements,* was published only a few years after the forgery had been exposed. [34]

Griffin, writing more than half a century later, has no such reservations. Indeed, he asserts that *The Protocols* is none other than "the 'Long Range Master Plan' by which this comparatively small group of immensely wealthy, diabolically crafty and extremely influential men [the leaders of the Illuminati] plan to subvert and pervert the leadership in all strata of society in order to attain their goal." As for the Jews, they are important participants in the plot, but *The Protocols* was deliberately given a Jewish cast so that its Illuminati origins could be better concealed. Griffin reprints most of *The Protocols* verbatim—launching (as discussed in chapters 6 and 9) what was to become a staple of conspiracism in the 1990s, the idea of the "Illuminati *Protocols*." [35]

At the same time that Griffin was laying out his superconspiracy, tales of an equally involved Illuminati plot were sweeping through churches, mainly Pentecostal ones. From 1976 to 1979, itinerant evangelist John Todd began to present through personal appearances and audiotapes a strange tale of Illuminati intrigues. Todd claimed to have been raised by a witch mother and trained as a witch since his early teens. He had allegedly progressed through an occult hierarchy until he was made a "Grand Druid High Priest" and "a member of the Druid Council of Thirteen," the instrumentality through which he claimed the Illuminati implemented their designs. [36]

Todd was a shadowy figure who moved around frequently, but the basic outlines of his career as an evangelist have been reconstructed. He appeared first as a storefront preacher in Phoenix, Arizona, in 1968. He was then nineteen and already claimed to have been a witch before his born-again experience. He appears to have been in the army from 1969 until sometime in the early 1970s. He had psychiatric problems in the military, though it is not clear whether they led to his discharge. He reemerged in the Phoenix Pentecostal subculture in 1973 with much-elaborated tales of his witchcraft days. He left for Dayton, Ohio, the next year, where instead of rejoining Christian organizations, he opened an occult store, the Witches Cauldron. He apparently engaged in sex with minors during this period, for which he received a sentence of six months in jail. Released after two months and placed on probation, he quickly violated his parole by returning to the Phoenix Pentecostal community, though he may have continued to dabble in the occult. He next appeared in California as a Christian evangelist. During at least some of this time, he appeared to gravitate toward fundamentalism and attacked Pentecostals. Within a few years, his itinerant preaching and tapes of his sermons began to spread widely among conservative Christians.[37]

Todd's superconspiracy was remarkably detailed, so much so that there seemed to be more institutions within the conspiracy than outside it. Todd was less concerned with reconstructing history than with laying out the conspiracy's structure. In place of discussions of the French and Russian revolutions, he substituted elaborate diagrams of conspiratorial hierarchies, which he passed out at church meetings. The Illuminati allegedly worked its will largely by wielding financial power, led by the Rothschilds but aided by, among others, the Rockefeller, Kennedy, and Dupont families; the central banks of England, France, and the United States; the world copper market; and many major corporations. The Council of 13, of which Todd claimed to have been a member, executed decisions of the Rothschild tribunal through its control of churches, political institutions, and voluntary associations. Thus, among its lackeys were the World Council of Churches, the Anti-Defamation League, the Council of Foreign Affairs [sic], the UN, the FBI, the CIA, the Communist Party, the John Birch Society, the ACLU, the Masons, and the Knights of Columbus. In his hands, the Illuminati became Satan's coordinating mechanism, through which diabolical forces insinuated themselves into virtually every aspect of American life.[38]

Todd not only exposed the depth of the Illuminati's penetration, he also claimed to know its "Plan for World Takeover." It involved removing the Republicans from control, repealing the tax exemption for churches, criminalization of genocide (which Todd interpreted as meaning that converting someone from one religion to another could result in a murder charge), awarding martial-law powers to the president, and passage of an antihoarding act. At the same time, Israel would cause World War III, and the financial machinations of the Rothschilds would leave all Americans at their mercy. Todd even incorporated Charles Manson's "helter-skelter" plan, in which the country would be terrorized by motorcycle gangs.[39]

By the late 1970s, Todd's increasingly strident attacks on other Christian religious leaders had begun to erode his support. During these years, he predicted that the Illuminati's plan would begin to be implemented in fall 1979. Whether because of the former or the latter, he disappeared from view in that year, and "according to reliable sources he is currently in Montana selling freeze-dried food." Though out of sight, he was clearly not out of mind; as mentioned earlier, he left his mark on the Covenant, Sword and Arm of the Lord, which adopted his conspiracy theory wholesale in a 1981 pamphlet.[40]

The penetration of Illuminati superconspiracy theories into fundamentalist and right-wing circles was predictable. The former found them a vivid demonstration of the devil's doings, while the latter used them to conceptualize a cunning, shape-changing literature of the "New Age." The *New Age* is a construct variously described in terms of the counterculture, self-actualization, neo-paganism, and inner spirituality. The appearance of Illuminati themes in this amorphous area has, however, been limited to a relatively well-defined segment of the literature— specifically, that concerned with UFOs and extraterrestrials.[41]

One of the earliest attempts to link the Illuminati with UFOs came in 1978 from Stan Deyo, an American expatriate in Australia. His book *The Cosmic Conspiracy* fused Illuminati theory with dispensational premillennialism and a variety of UFO speculation generally referred to as Alternative 3. Alternative 3 (discussed in detail in chapter 5) began as a 1977 British television program of the same name that purported to expose a plot in which a secret organization of the superrich kidnapped and exploited scientists in order to create a clandestine space colonization program that would allow them to escape the earth before pollution and overpopulation reached catastrophic levels. Though widely considered a hoax, both the television program and a subsequent book quickly came to be accepted as fact by many conspiracy theorists.[42]

Deyo's book is not entirely coherent, but the basic argument may be reconstructed as follows. The Illuminati's remote origins lay in the "mystery school of Moses," whose esoteric teachings were amplified and transmitted by Solomon and the master masons who built Solomon's temple. In time, however, these "mysticists" split into two factions, one religious and one antireligious. The Illuminati provided the leadership for the "perverted," antireligious faction.[43]

The Illuminati went underground after the French Revolution (Deyo, not surprisingly, cites Robison), but their hand remained visible in subsequent upheavals: "modern 'observers' must surely concede that the most daring and diabolical social experiments in the history of man are presently illustrating the basic tenets of Weishaupt's school in both Russia and China." Far from limiting their activities to Europe and Asia, however, the Illuminati have insinuated themselves into centers of power in America. Indeed, according to Deyo, the Great Seal of the United States is full of Illuminati symbolism (a theme commonly found in conspiracist literature). The fixation on the seal emphasizes its reverse side. Conspiracists like Deyo insist that the pyramid capped by a single eye is an Illuminati symbol, and they translate the motto, "Novus ordo seclorum," not as "A new order of the ages" but as "New world order." He concludes that from a scriptural point of view, "America is either a pawn of the modern Babylonian mystery school or the seat of the 'new Babylon' mentioned in Christian prophecy." The Illuminati's power structure is made up of familiar elements: the Council on Foreign Relations, the UN, the Trilateral Commission, the Bilderbergers (an organization of European and North American movers and shakers, discussed further below), the Club of Rome (a private international organization of civil servants, academics, and business people devoted to the study of global problems), and the Royal Institute of International Affairs (a London-based foreign policy think tank founded in 1920).[44]

To this point, there is little in Deyo's arguments to differentiate them from theories already introduced by Robison, Webster, Griffin, and others. He enters new territory, however, with the appearance of his variation on Alternative 3. Powerful though the Illuminati are, their ultimate goal, "the establishment of a dictatorial world government," has remained just out of reach. It could be achieved, Deyo speculates, only in a sufficiently charged atmosphere of global crisis. A crisis of unimaginable dimensions could both maintain cohesion within the Illuminatist forces and induce the population to accept unprecedented regimentation. What might induce people to give up their freedom? Deyo suggests that an appropriate catalyst would be an invasion by UFOs, in either of two scenarios. One envisions a fake extraterrestrial invasion, in which conspirators on earth produce an armada of seemingly alien flying saucers manned by human impostors, in order to create an artificial common enemy against which humanity could unite under a world government—an idea similar to that proposed by André Maurois in his 1923 tale, *The War against the Moon.*[45]

But Deyo seems more attracted to a scenario drawn from *Alternative 3,* in which cascading deprivations lead an increasingly desperate humanity to accept the leadership of seemingly benevolent "space brothers," who are in reality the conspirators in disguise:

I can see it now . . . frozen in an energy crisis, saddened by the Watergates of the world, dying from environmental pollution, starving from food shortages, frightened of a global nuclear war, sick of the moral decay, afraid of the daily news, bankrupted by global monetary fluctuations, unemployed from economic depressions, crowded by the ever present birth rate, frightened by the suspicion that a global weather catastrophe was about to happen . . . mankind . . . would have been ready for "Alternative Three."

In Deyo's variation, the conspirators bring in spacecraft manned by "teams of highly-trained actors" who offer their leadership in "the greatest attempted deception of all history." The Illuminati, having discovered the secret of antigravity propulsion, can now use their fleet of flying saucers first to control the earth and then, if circumstances require, to leave it.[46]

Deyo then takes this strange idea one step further by linking it to dispensational premillennialism, in a manner not unlike that of Marrs and Robertson. God's plan for the end of history requires seven years of the Tribulation before Christ's Second Coming can inaugurate the millennial age. Essential to the Tribulation is a "New World Order" ruled by the Antichrist and his forces, whose control has been made possible by the appearance of the false extraterrestrials. Presumably, the saved will be spared the severities of Illuminati rule, having been rescued in the Rapture of the Church, a disappearance made plausible to those who remain by the presence of UFOs. On this point, however, Deyo is ambiguous, for he closes his book with the survivalist admonition that all opponents of the Illuminati should "[a]cquire warm clothing, good walking boots, means of procuring food from the land, a basic medical kit, and a Bible."[47]

THE CONSPIRACISM OF MILTON WILLIAM COOPER

The most elaborate and convoluted such theory, however, has come from Milton William Cooper, characterized by one scholar of apocalypticism, Daniel Wojcik, as "perhaps the most infamous UFO conspiracy theorist." Regardless of whether this accurately characterizes Cooper, his 1991 book *Behold a Pale Horse* is not only among the most complex superconspiracy theories, it is also among the most influential, widely available in mainstream bookstores but also much read in both UFO and militia circles. What little is known about his life prior to his career as a conspiracist came from Cooper himself. He claimed to have been raised in a military family, to have served first in the air force and then in the navy (the latter in Vietnam), and to have been discharged in 1975. After graduating from a junior college in California, he worked for several technical and vocational schools. He burst onto the ufology scene in 1988 with dramatic revelations of government involvement with extraterrestrials, charges he repeated in *Behold a Pale Horse*.[48]

Cooper projected the Illuminati back to remote origins as the manifestation of a long-simmering Luciferian plot. Far from having been founded by Weishaupt, the Illuminati were an outgrowth of the sinister activities of the medieval Knights Templar. Weishaupt merely established a new and particularly evil outpost of this order, financed by the Rothschilds. Although Cooper denied any anti-Semitic intent, he followed his predecessors in linking the Illuminati to Jewish influences. As Griffin had earlier, he asserted that *The Protocols of the Elders of Zion* was an Illuminatist tract. Indeed, he reprinted the entire text, with the somewhat disingenuous prefatory note that "This [*The Protocols*] has been written intentionally to deceive people. For clear understanding, the word 'Zion' should be 'Sion'; any reference to Jews should be replaced with the word 'Illuminati'; and the word 'goyim' should be replaced with the word 'cattle.'"[49]

American members of the Illuminati became so emboldened, Cooper said, that they felt free to incorporate Illuminatist and Luciferian themes into the Great Seal of the United States, and he repeated the common claim that the phrase "Novus ordo seclorum" on the seal really means "New world order." The Illuminati, however, are allegedly not an American but an international organization, whose inner circle is the Bilderbergers. The Bilderberg group, an organization of European and North American businessmen, academics, and lawyers, was founded in 1952 and—like its offshoot, the Trilateral Commission—has been a favorite of conspiracy theorists seeking to identify the secret holders of power. Cooper claimed that together with a dizzying array of other secret societies and front organizations—including the Knights of Columbus, the Jesuits, the Masons, the Communist Party, the Nazi Party, the Council on Foreign Relations, the Vatican, and Skull and

Bones—the Illuminati and the Bilderbergers "all work toward the same ultimate goal, a New World Order." When the conspirators feel ready, their minions in the federal government will swoop down on "patriots," probably on a national holiday, and incarcerate them in detention centers run by FEMA, removing the last sources of resistance.[50]

To this point, Cooper's theory resembles the speculations of earlier conspiracists such as Todd. But UFO themes eventually emerged as central to Cooper's view of the world. Indeed, he presented not one but two Illuminati-UFO superconspiracy theories, both of which he alleged to be true. The first, like Deyo's, assumed that the conspirators capitalize on fear of catastrophe by inventing an alien threat in order to arrange their own rescue. The second claimed that actual extraterrestrials are acting in concert with human plotters to take over the world.

According to the first version, Illuminatists have been working on an invasion-from-outer-space hoax since 1917, the better to bring the New World Order into being. The Cold War was no hindrance, as the Soviet leaders were active participants in the conspiracy. Cooper claimed to have seen documents showing that once a year, U.S. and Soviet nuclear submarines met under the polar ice, connected their airlocks, and hosted a meeting of the Bilderberg policy committee to advance "combined efforts in the secret space programs governing Alternative 3"—surely as bizarre a gathering as one can find in a literature replete with strange meetings.[51]

Such astonishing efforts were necessary, according to Cooper, because "the elite" had learned that the future of the human race was grim in the absence of dictatorial regimentation:

They were told that by or shortly after the year 2000 the total collapse of civilization as we know it and the possible extinction of the human race could occur . . . They were told that the only things that could stop these predicted events would be severe cutbacks of the human population, the cessation or retardation of technological and economic growth, the elimination of meat in the human diet, strict control of future human reproduction, a total commitment to preserving the environment, the colonization of space, and a paradigm shift in the evolutionary consciousness of man.

Only the New World Order can accomplish this. Even Cooper conceded that it may be necessary: "The New World Order is evil but very much needed if man is to survive long enough to plant his seed amongst the stars."[52]

But while at one level Cooper ruefully conceded that the New World Order is a grim necessity, at another he was prepared to do battle with evil. That other level concerned the aliens, for even though Cooper sometimes believed Illuminati circles would invent an extraterrestrial threat in order to provide a pretext for the seizure of power, at other times he was certain that the ETs have already arrived.

Cooper was one of the first to link Illuminati theory with some of the stranger beliefs about extraterrestrials that began to appear in ufology circles in the late 1980s. In Cooper's version, sixteen alien spacecraft crashed in the United States during the Truman administration, leading the inner circles of government to fear an imminent invasion from space. According to Cooper, the next president, Dwight Eisenhower, decided that the safest path was a negotiated treaty with the aliens, and one was allegedly signed on February 20, 1954, by Eisenhower and "our first alien ambassador from outer space." In order to regulate relations with the aliens while keeping their presence secret, an inner circle was established within the U.S. government, consisting of individuals involved with and controlled by the Illuminati. Although the aliens have proved to be slippery allies, routinely violating the treaty, they have been a boon to the Illuminati, who could now pursue an *Alternative 3*–style escape from the earth's coming calamities, thanks to the space travel technology they acquired.[53]

In the end, Cooper gave the aliens the last word; he told us that the Illuminati are really not so powerful after all. In fact, the conspirators are little more than the unknowing tools of extraterrestrial masters: "aliens have manipulated and/or ruled the human race through various secret societies, religions, magic, witchcraft, and the occult." The Illuminati, seemingly at the pinnacle of the world's power hierarchy, are exposed as the dupes of a strange and evil alien race.[54]

The New World Order as a Post–Cold War Phenomenon

As we have seen, by the early 1990s, both the Antichrist and the Illuminati literatures had identified their respective subjects with an imminent tyranny most often subsumed under the New World Order rubric. The two literatures had also begun partially to overlap, so that religious students of the Antichrist like Robertson experienced no difficulty in drawing the Illuminati into their speculations. The two might have different origins, but they were not mutually exclusive. Thus New World Order theory came to constitute a common ground for religious and secular conspiracy theorists.

The internal logic of Antichrist and Illuminati ideas might explain their compatibility, but it did not explain their rise to prominence in the early 1990s. Notwithstanding right-wing suspicions about George Bush and his patrician connections, his use of the phrase is not sufficient to explain its currency among outsider and antigovernment groups. More important than Bush's rhetoric was the dramatic change in the international political landscape produced by the dissolution of the Soviet Union and the end of the Cold War. This development removed suddenly from mental maps a defining element of the post-1945 period: the figure of an adversary. The Soviet Union was not simply an enemy, it was *the* enemy, the evil empire against which all American and "free-world" resources were marshaled. It was also a visible opponent, with a physical presence and location. Although themes of invisible communist subversion were prevalent in the 1950s, these spectral agents could ultimately be linked to the visible symbol of the Soviet state. Finally, Americans saw Soviet communism as a conspiracy, a plot using various devious means to take by stealth what could not be acquired by direct confrontation. The Sino-Soviet split, the USSR's increasing economic difficulties, and the sclerotic Soviet leadership made conspiracy theories less persuasive. Nonetheless, as long as the Soviet Union and its Warsaw Pact client states held together, their vast nuclear arsenal and their stated aim of subduing the West imposed a kind of Manichaean moral order on the American consciousness. The world was a battleground between light and darkness.

Between 1989 and 1991, that organizing conception abruptly vanished. The Soviet Union disappeared, the Warsaw Pact dissolved, and the Russian Federation teetered on the brink of economic and political collapse. While undoubtedly these developments had strategic benefits for the United States, they carried a psychological price. The dualistic worldview that had existed since the end of World War II, with its clearly delineated struggle between good and evil, was suddenly no longer viable. And the mind abhors a vacuum where conceptions of moral order are concerned.

It was a particularly confusing period for Protestant premillennialists. Under the influence of dispensationalism, they had looked primarily to foreign affairs for signs of the imminence of the end-times. Popularizers such as Hal Lindsey had developed elaborate scenarios of the international conflicts that would bring on and define the Tribulation. In all of them, two factors were paramount. First, the Soviet Union would take a central role. Second, the crucial events would take place as a result of war in the Middle East that involved Israel.[55]

The post–Cold War period made this vision increasingly untenable. Although some millenarians insisted that the fragmentation of the Soviet Union was a sham to deceive the West, over time the decay of the former Soviet states became undeniable. The centrality of the Middle East became more and more problematic as well. The Gulf War in 1991 temporarily reinvigorated conceptions of an ultimate world conflict in the Middle East, but the war's rapid conclusion dashed such hopes. In addition, a major war involving Israel became less likely, thanks to both peace negotiations between Israel and the Palestinians and the end of Soviet aid to anti-Israel client states. Thus the loss of the traditional enemy was felt most acutely by millennialists.

The New World Order came to fill this vacuum for premillennialists and for many on the far right. As this chapter has indicated, the sources for New World Order ideas can be traced back many decades, whether in the Antichrist version or in the secret-society/Illuminati version; yet despite the concept's significant historical roots, it had always been a subsidiary motif. It did not appear as the central organizing concept for significant numbers of fundamentalists and right-wing ideologues until about 1990.

In fulfilling its role as a central moral vision, the New World Order had significant advantages. First, precisely because it had roots in the past, it could be put forward as a legitimate moral vision rather than an innovation. As Boyer has noted, millenarians are nothing if not adaptable, and they have a long history of bringing formerly secondary themes to the fore when circumstances require. Second, the New World Order is by its very nature invisible, always cloaked in garb that disguises its true nature, whether it takes the form of the UN, philanthropic foundations, or academic organizations. This gives it a resiliency that makes New World Order theory virtually unfalsifiable. No event or set of events can reliably be taken as disconfirming evidence, for in the view of conspiracy theorists, nothing is as it seems. Finally, New World Order theory seemed to provide a graceful way of exiting the domain of international relations and refocusing upon domestic politics. Although the forces of the New World Order are international, they are assumed to be concentrating on domestic agendas, particularly the alleged destruction of American liberties. In an era no longer dominated by chronic international conflict, the New World Order allows its devotees to rebuild their Manichaean worldview in a new venue.[56]

CHAPTER 4

New World Order Conspiracies II

A World of Black Helicopters

In broad outline, New World Order theory claimed to provide an overarching explanation for contemporary politics by fitting all events into a single scenario: a diabolically clever and unscrupulous secret organization was in the process of seizing control of the world. As the preceding chapter showed, this scenario appealed to both religionists and secularists. The former saw in it the end-time events associated with the Antichrist, while the latter regarded it as confirmation of their fears of elite domination. To the extent that both groups found such ideas compelling, New World Order became a generic, "ecumenical" conspiracy theory, which—at least in its overall configuration—could be shared across the religious-secular boundary.

As these ideas were developed in the 1990s, the picture of the New World Order became increasingly detailed. Instead of simply positing conquest by an evil cabal, the New World Order came to include highly specific claims about both the identities of the conspirators and the means they would employ to seize power and defeat their opponents. Among the latter techniques, three allegations were particularly significant: that black helicopters are tangible evidence of the conspiracy's existence, that a network of concentration camps is being readied to incarcerate dissenters, and that a technology of mind control has been developed in order to make the rest of the population docile and malleable. The significance of these claims lies in their relative novelty. While other elements of New World Order theory, such as the Illuminati, have roots that go back centuries, the black helicopter, concentration camp, and mind-control charges are extremely recent. They first took shape in the 1970s, and did not become linked for another two decades.

The Conspiracy's Members

The largest subset of the literature concerns the identity of the New World Order's masters. Conspiracists, convinced that their truths are empirically verifiable, are rarely satisfied simply to posit a vague other. They seem obsessed by the need to break the cabal into its constituent parts, in terms of both organizations and individuals. This push to identify the conspirators has bifurcated into a modest approach, in which the conspiracy is identified with a single organization, and an ambitious approach, in which the conspiracy operates through a network of linked organizations. The ambitious versions, referred to here as superconspiracies, appear to be proliferating, driving out or absorbing the simpler plots.

The modest version of conspiracy theory concentrates on one or two well-defined groups, whose individual members are identifiable. Most commonly, the groups selected are composed of elites such as the Council on Foreign Relations or the Trilateral Commission. They have only slightly overlapping memberships, but the involvement of the Rockefeller family in both has made them attractive targets.

The Council on Foreign Relations—by far the better known of the two—is particularly identified with its influential publication, *Foreign Affairs*. The council was organized in 1921, "dedicated to increasing America's understanding of the world and contributing ideas to U.S. foreign policy." At the time, isolationist sentiment was strong, especially in the Midwest. In reaction to World War I and the establishment of the League of Nations, many Americans sought to reduce if not eliminate American involvement in conflicts outside the United States. Those who by conviction or need felt that American national interest was bound up with the rest of the world were concentrated in eastern urban centers. Seeking ways to shape American foreign policy, these internationalists founded the council. The sons of John D. Rockefeller, Sr., with far-flung business ventures and deep personal commitments to international cooperation, were catalysts in its establishment, as they were later with the Trilateral Commission. Anti-internationalists frequently characterized their adversaries as part of an eastern "elite" conspiracy, a stereotype to which the Rockefeller family's international business activities lent themselves.[1]

An even stronger current of antielitism drives hostility toward the Trilateral Commission. The commission was itself a by-product of an older elite group, the Bilderbergers, founded in 1952 to bring together

European and American political and business leaders. Between 1954 and 1978, slightly more than nine hundred people attended the Bilderbergers' closed meetings, whose aim was to develop common transatlantic policies. By the early 1970s, some within the Bilderberg group felt the need to reinvigorate their efforts in response to the economic rise of Japan (excluded from Bilderberg) and European opposition to President Richard Nixon's foreign and economic policies. The Trilateral Commission was organized in 1972, under the leadership of David Rockefeller, with members drawn from not only the Bilderberg group but also academic, business, and governmental institutions.[2]

The prospect of identifying a list of names of the true rulers of the world is heady stuff for conspiracists. John McManus, president of the John Birch Society, calls Council on Foreign Relations and Trilateral Commission members "Architects of the New World Order" and devotes one-fifth of his book, *The Insiders,* to membership lists. Interestingly, McManus omits the names of the Trilateral Commission's European and Japanese members, implying that they are mere tools of their American colleagues. Larry Abraham's *Call It Conspiracy* also includes a Council on Foreign Relations membership roster—seventeen closely printed pages—and adds charts that graphically depict the conspiracy.[3]

Abraham's diagrams reflect the tendency of conspiracy theorists to think increasingly in terms of complex, interlinked plots. He includes a diagram of the "World Supra-Government," with the Council on Foreign Relations at its center and an array of spokes that connect to international banks, the Royal Institute of International Affairs, major foundations, the U.S. government's executive branch, think tanks, major media organizations, and large corporations. While Abraham is clearly of the political right—preoccupied with tales of the communist conspiracy—his suspicion of these institutions is based on antipathy toward wealth and corporate power. People on both the left and the right who share this antipathy have found the Trilateral Commission and similar organizations attractive targets. In addition to laying out the components of the "supra-government," Abraham includes an elaborate 1984 chart, attributed to Johnny Stewart of Waco, Texas, titled "The C.F.R./Trilateral Connection." The same chart reappears in many conspiracist works. It deconstructs the lists by placing members under such headings as "Media," "House & Senate CFR/TC Members," and "U.S. Military." At the diagram's pinnacle, flanked by the Federal Reserve and the Treasury, sits David Rockefeller. The implications are clear: although the conspirators are few in number, they have managed to infiltrate and control every significant social institution, so that understanding their evil designs requires not merely possession of the membership list, but also an appreciation of the complex interconnections. Indeed, Stewart suggests that membership lists alone are misleading, for he points out that some members are merely careerists or have been added for "window dressing," and thus presumably are not members of the conspiracy.[4]

Not surprisingly, these organizational components can easily be connected to the Illuminati. Because for all practical purposes the Illuminati ceased to exist nearly two hundred years earlier, those who insist on its continued vitality have had free rein in identifying Illuminatist conspirators. Any charge may safely be made, particularly inasmuch as the Illuminati are said to possess extraordinary talents for disguise. And this fascination with linkages leads to the superconspiracies, the ambitious version of conspiracist theories of politics and history. John Coleman's widely cited 1992 book, *Conspirators' Hierarchy: The Story of the Committee of 300,* manages to connect this international elite not only with such obvious targets as the UN and the Trilateralists, but also with the drug trade, the royal families of the Persian Gulf states, Freemasonry, and what he calls the "One World Government Church." Similarly, conspiracy-minded evangelist Texe Marrs includes a list of conspirators conveniently coded to identify members of the council, the commission, the Bilderbergers, and the Masons (though he notes that the Illuminati's inner circle is also connected with "Skull & Bones Society, Aspen Institute, Knights of Malta, *Opus Dei,* Club of Rome, Bohemian Grove, World Economic Forum, World Federalists, and many others").[5]

The logic of conspiracy theory, with its premise that everything is connected to everything else, ultimately leads to theories in which the conspiracy includes virtually everyone but the writer and his or her intended readers. The notion of an inclusive conspiracy may seem oxymoronic, but it has become increasingly common. British author David Icke (discussed in detail in chapter 6), who commands significant New Age and right-wing audiences, manages to construct a conspiracy whose categories include mind manipulation, tax-exempt foundations, elite military, the drugs and arms trades, religion, and politics—dragging in, along with the Bilderbergers, Illuminati, and other standard players, the Vatican, Christianity, Judaism, Islam, capitalism, fascism, communism, and Zionism, among others. In much the same manner, John Todd found room for virtually every major corporation, fraternal order, intelligence agency, and communications medium. In what is perhaps the mother of all superconspiracies, UFO writer Val Valerian includes so many organizations in the conspiracy that he requires six pages merely to provide a condensed, diagrammatic representation.[6]

The generation of ever-broader superconspiracies reinforces the intrinsic resistance of conspiracy theory to falsification, for if everyone besides the conspiracist and the reader is complicit, then no information outside conspiracist literature itself can be relied on. Indeed, in the reductio ad absurdum to which this kind of thinking leads, conspiracy theorists often turn on one another with accusations of disinformation and infiltration. Thus, Milton William Cooper accused James "Bo" Gritz, a celebrity in "patriot" circles, of being "a 32nd Degree Freemason, . . . an FBI Informant, and . . . an active undercover agent for the Special Operations Group of the Department of Defense." The very vagueness of the term *New World Order* (referring only to some type of secret global control) allows it to accommodate a bewildering variety of conspiracist constructs, ranging from modest attacks on the Council on Foreign Relations to systems so sweeping as to appear delusional. Yet it is their very sweep that makes them attractive, for they appear to explain everything.[7]

Black Helicopters

As newspaper readers discovered after the bombing of the Oklahoma City federal building in 1995, no element of New World Order theories is mentioned more often than black helicopters. They were quickly recycled into popular culture, as exemplified by the final scene of the film *Conspiracy Theory*. Although some debate persists among members of the antigovernment right about the function of these allegedly ubiquitous aircraft, they have become emblematic of the New World Order conspiracy. Although there are some skeptics (the John Birch Society is one), for the most part militia members, conspiracists, and survivalists believe that the presence of black helicopters signals the conspirators' presence, penchant for secrecy, and hostile intentions.

Two of Jim Keith's books, *Black Helicopters over America: Strikeforce for the New World Order* (1994), and *Black Helicopters II: The End Game Strategy* (1997), constitute the most systematic and influential treatment of the subject. The former was endorsed by no less a figure than John Trochmann, founder of the Militia of Montana, on a militia videotape. Keith claims to have records of sightings as early as 1971, though he could find none between 1985 and 1993. He links the pre-1993 sightings to reports of western cattle mutilations but claims that those thereafter "more often were seen in urban settings and flying in formation, or in the context of covert military maneuvers." [8]

Keith is convinced that black helicopters are the advance guard of the New World Order forces who, barring organized opposition, will shortly take over the United States. His earlier book relies heavily on the videotapes and shortwave-radio broadcasts of Mark Koernke, known as Mark from Michigan, an influential figure in Michigan and Ohio militia circles. For Koernke, fleets of black helicopters that allegedly rush back and forth across the U.S.-Canadian border operate in support of the large detachments of UN-commanded foreign troops he believes to be already stationed in the United States. Unless something is done, writes Keith, "By the year 2000 America will be merged into a Socialist New World Order, and the world will be split into three functional divisions: European, North American, and the Pacific Rim power structure." In 1997, he added to his fear of the UN the prediction that New World Order–minded American leaders were being manipulated by expansionist Russian policymakers, who only appeared to be weak and conciliatory, the better to lull Americans into complacency. [9]

Not surprisingly, Keith finds a place in this scenario for the concentration-camp legend, though its precise connection to the black helicopters is not made clear. Nonetheless, he presents lists of alleged locations, one that shows twenty-three camps, and another that lists fifty-four. Some are too general to be of much interest ("Chicago, Illinois"), but others carefully specify the nearest town and interstate highway. Keith, like many others, thus employs the image of the black helicopter as a handy symbol for a conspiracy he sees spreading through American public life. [10]

A less sweeping but no less significant approach to black helicopters was taken by Linda Thompson, head of the Indianapolis-based American Justice Federation. Thompson, conspicuous in militia circles, is best known for her two videotapes on the Waco standoff, *Waco: The Big Lie* and *Waco: The Big Lie II*, in which she charges that the government intentionally killed the Branch Davidians. She believes that black helicopters come from an army special-operations unit drawn from "CIA-sponsored thugs" with close ties to law enforcement groups dealing with drugs and organized crime. For its masters, the unit constitutes a "private mafia" that is engaged in "what amounts to a military takeover in this country, through a combination of drug running, gun running, lobbying [*sic*], blackmailing congressmen, and terrorism." [11]

Although there may be disagreements about exactly whose black helicopters they are and what functions they perform, there is widespread agreement that they are important and evil. At least two Web sites are primarily devoted simply to providing links to other black helicopter Web sites. The Internet repertoire of black helicopter material extends over more than two thousand pages.[12]

The principal dissenting voice about black helicopters among those who fear a New World Order is the John Birch Society, which dismisses them as an annoying distraction. Tales such as Keith's are examples of "why naiveté, rashness, and hysteria can lead to embarrassment for the people directly involved in disseminating dubious conspiracy stories." Worse, such stories might serve as a pretext for ridicule from "the establishment media." The society concedes that black helicopters exist, but dismisses them as elements of regular army units and law enforcement agencies rather than of sinister invasion forces. Such restraint, however, has done little to reduce the frequency with which those on the extreme right invoke the black helicopter symbol.[13]

Black helicopters have a combination of advantages. On one level, they appear concrete and empirically demonstrable, and indeed the helicopter literature is replete with reports of sightings giving precise dates and locations (not unlike the UFO literature—a similarity to which I will return). On another level, however, black helicopters are elusive, not only because they move away from the place they were sighted, but because they are allegedly unmarked and cannot be traced to points of takeoff and landing. Further, their blackness reinforces their association with death and evil. Hence the believer or viewer can project onto them whatever manner of villainy seems most suitable, making them an all-purpose object for fears and anxieties. Stories of government concentration camps hold much the same appeal.

Concentration Camps

Among the claims made by New World Order writers, surely the most sensational is the assertion that the federal government has prepared a national network of concentration camps in which dissenters and other undesirables will eventually be confined. The concentration-camp legend appears to have grown out of a cluster of actual government activities in the 1970s and 1980s, when various proposals, contingency plans, exercises, and executive orders were developed, aimed at managing future emergencies. These were for the most part responses to the civil

disorders that had begun in the mid 1960s. As those disorders proliferated, some in the federal government feared that local law enforcement lacked the training, discipline, and resources to deal with them
effectively.[14]

Belief in the existence of American concentration camps is now
closely associated with the extreme right, but the original critics of federal efforts to quell civil disturbances came most often from the left. The
leading leftist exponent of these ideas was Daniel Sheehan, chief coun-
sel of the Christic Institute. Sheehan saw then–attorney general Edwin
Meese as the architect of mass internment plans. His view is hardly
surprising in light of the groups frequently identified with rioting and
demonstrations during the 1960s and 1970s: inner-city blacks, university students protesting the Vietnam War, and to a lesser extent, Native
American militants. In addition, federal involvement in quelling disturbances suggested potentially significant deprivation of civil liberties, including freedom of speech and of assembly, and the violation of privacy
through illicit intelligence gathering. Indeed, with only a few significant
exceptions, it was conservatives who sought an expanded federal role in
law enforcement, and liberals who opposed it. Over time, however, with
the passing of a sense of crisis, left-liberal critics moved on to other issues, while those on the right found more and more to fear.

The unusual involvement of ideological adversaries in this set of issues suggests the extent to which at least certain New World Order concerns appear to cut across the traditional left-right divide. Nevertheless,
the left and right had different ideas about what was dangerous about
federal antiviolence activities. In general, those on the left emphasized
activities that might have a chilling effect on political speech and protest, such as intelligence gathering and the creation of lists identifying
allegedly dangerous persons. Those on the right, by contrast, became
obsessively concerned with the risk of their own incarceration, creating
in the process the concentration-camp legend.

Congress authorized emergency detention in the Internal Security
Act of 1950, passed over President Harry Truman's veto; but the detention provision was repealed in 1971—ironically, just at the time that, according to the concentration-camp legend, the creation of a series of
permanent detention facilities was getting under way. Beginning in
the mid-1960s, the army, in conjunction with local and federal law-enforcement agencies, developed a series of civil-disturbance contingency
plans and exercises. Consistent with standard military practice, these
bore code names—Garden Plot, Lantern Spike, Cable Splicer. Their

existence, not generally known at the time they were developed, became a matter of public knowledge in the mid 1970s. Those on the left were concerned primarily with two features of the plans: the use of military personnel for law enforcement, and the covert collection of intelligence on the political views of citizens.[15]

Concern about alleged facilities for the mass detention of American citizens was apparently first raised by William Pabst of Houston. Pabst produced a tape recording titled "Concentration Camp Plans for U.S. Citizens." The version in extant transcripts speaks of it as "my 1979 updated report," implying the existence of an earlier version whose date is not given. A considerably abbreviated version is posted on the Internet, on a Web page last revised in June 1998. Pabst claims to have filed suit against the government in April 1976 in an attempt to expose and challenge the "Concentration Camp Program," at the same time that liberal publications were voicing concern about civil-disturbance contingency plans.[16]

While Pabst, too, discusses Garden Plot and Cable Splicer, most of his attention is directed at alleged federal detention facilities. He claims that the 1971 repeal of the detention provision was a sham, and that identical provisions in other legislation remained on the books: "The public was in fact tricked by the congress of the United States!" He goes on to give the location of a dozen such facilities, some of which are existing federal penal facilities and military bases. In Pabst's view, this alleged network of "concentration camps" is not merely contingency plans run amok; rather, it constitutes "the enforcement arm of the conspiracy," though exactly who the conspirators are remains vague. Nonetheless, Pabst is certain that unless action is taken, "your country and way of life [will be] replaced by a system in which you will be a slave in a concentration camp."[17]

In all but one respect, the Pabst report served as the template for subsequent right-wing concentration-camp literature: that exception is the government agency regarded as the locus of responsibility for the tyranny in progress. In Pabst's view, that agency is the Law Enforcement Assistance Administration, which was particularly active in the 1970s. Within a few years, however, the conspiracists' bête noire became FEMA, and the Law Enforcement Assistance Administration passed out of the literature.[18]

The concentration-camp story soon took on a life of its own, and subsequent versions often failed to mention Pabst's original. In April 1984, *The Spotlight*—a periodical associated with the Liberty Lobby, and the closest thing the radical right has had to a mass-circulation newspaper—claimed that President Ronald Reagan was about to establish "10 huge prison camps at key defense commands located across the nation," under an operation called Rex 84. *The Spotlight*'s list of locations was entirely different from Pabst's, but this report, like his, took on a surface plausibility by virtue of the specificity of the charges. According to *The Spotlight*, these "concentration camps" would be used not only for "subversives and draft resisters," but also for "a citizen [who] subscribes to the wrong newsletter" and for tax resisters.[19]

By this time, responsibility for such facilities had passed to FEMA, "an agency that stands ready to assume control of the U.S. government." By 1995, the FEMA concentration-camp legend had expanded still further to encompass a network of "43 internment camps already built and operational," each able to house between thirty-five thousand and forty-five thousand prisoners, plus "hundreds of secondary facilities." This astonishing claim, suggesting the capacity to incarcerate secretly more than 1.5 million Americans, seemed plausible enough to those who trafficked in such stories, because it had by then circulated for more than fifteen years, becoming more threatening and detailed with each retelling. Indeed, the theme of FEMA as the country's secret government eventually received Hollywood's imprimatur when the phrase was placed in the mouth of a sympathetic character in the 1998 film *The X-Files*.[20]

The attraction of the concentration-camp legend, similar to that of the black helicopters, lies in its combination of specificity and vagueness. On the one hand, the maps and lists of place-names that routinely accompany such stories suggest unimpeachable validity. As Richard Hofstadter long ago noted, this emphasis on detailed factual claims is part of the conspiracists' insistent claim of empiricism. For the same reason, many of the accounts contain not only highly specific charges but a pseudoscholarly apparatus of footnotes as well. On the other hand, concrete though the claims are, they turn out to be miragelike in their tendency first to blur and then to vanish. In this case, almost all of the locations labeled concentration camps turn out to be existing federal facilities, military or correctional, to which the general public does not have routine access. Hence nefarious activities can be attributed to them with little likelihood that the claims will be quickly rebutted, and the same security arrangements that shield them from public view may be blamed for the public's supposed ignorance of their true purpose.

Mind Control

The inclusion of so-called mind control in descriptions of the New World Order had its origins in research funded by the CIA from 1949 to 1973. The research was for the most part conducted by scientists at leading institutions in the United States and Canada under cover of foundation sponsorship. The subjects were patients or prisoners who were not informed of the experiments' purposes and who therefore did not provide informed consent. Between 1975 and 1977, efforts by Senate committees, journalists, and CIA administrators led to the disclosure of many of these activities, though by that time the agency had destroyed many relevant files. In 1984, a private citizen sued under the Freedom of Information Act to force the CIA to reveal the names of those involved in the research, but the agency's claim of confidentiality was eventually upheld by the Supreme Court. Four years later, in 1988, a civil lawsuit by a group of surviving experimental subjects resulted in a cash settlement by the government.[21]

This story was attractive to conspiracy theorists for three reasons. First, there was sufficient mystery as a result of withheld or destroyed documents to encourage unrestrained speculation. Second, the horrific nature of the experiments suggested that those in the government who sponsored them lacked any moral scruples—though in fact the CIA developed elaborate justifications based on Cold War tensions at the time. Finally, the existence of such an elaborate research program led conspiracists to assert that it created an entire technology of behavioral manipulation and mind control that allowed the controllers to produce any behavior they desired in their subjects. In fact, this assertion appears to be entirely unsupported. All of the extant documentation, as well as the information uncovered by journalists, suggests that despite its heavy funding, the program was singularly unproductive: its sponsors did not achieve mastery over brainwashing, as they had hoped. Nonetheless, the research was pursued for almost twenty-five years in the belief that the Soviets were engaged in similar, but more successful, activities.

The research cited most frequently by conspiracists is the MK-ULTRA project of the 1950s, in which researchers at or funded by the CIA sought mind control through chemical means. In the most infamous experiments, LSD was given to unknowing subjects. The best-known case is that of Frank Olson—ironically a CIA scientist—who died under circumstances that remain unclear. In 1984 this research was the subject of a Freedom of Information Act lawsuit. More recently, it was used in the film *Conspiracy Theory,* whose central character learns that he had been an MK-ULTRA subject. MK-ULTRA has provided material for both the left and the right. To a writer on the left, Jonathan Vankin, its motive was "the establishment's need to rip apart the fabric of progressive politics" by flooding the youth culture with LSD—a notion similar to the allegation that the CIA introduced crack cocaine into the African American community. To an anonymous self-described patriot on the right, MK-ULTRA continues to operate as part of the "psychological Warfare Mind War that has been waged against humanity by the few power brokers in control of the world."[22]

Like much else in the complex of New World Order ideas, mind-control charges grow from a kernel of truth. By the 1970s, the existence and scope of, and ethical violations in, CIA behavioral research had become part of the public record, but the clandestine nature of the research kept some aspects of it from being fully documented, and some existing documentation was almost certainly purposely destroyed. While this makes impossible any definitive evaluation of MK-ULTRA and similar programs, no credible evidence exists that successful techniques of mind control were ever developed.[23]

The limitations of the evidence concerning CIA activities during the Cold War have encouraged the extension of the mind-control literature into areas for which there is no substantiation. The most sensational of these tales revolves around Project Monarch, a supposed CIA program known only through the revelations of a purported victim, Cathy O'Brien. Under hypnosis performed by her deprogrammer husband, Mark Phillips, O'Brien allegedly recovered repressed memories of her training as a sex slave and drug courier for the CIA, during which time, she reports, she was sexually abused by a who's who of American public life, including President George H. W. Bush and then–first lady Hillary Clinton. O'Brien's indoctrination into a life of sexual submission allegedly began with childhood abuse by family members and Catholic priests.[24]

The O'Brien-Phillips account—sensational even by the standards of conspiracy literature—has generated a mixed response. On the one hand, Oregon-based evangelist and deprogrammer Fritz Springmeier calls it "one of the best kept secrets in history." On the other, even the normally credulous Jim Keith (of black helicopter fame) considers it fraudulent or delusional. What is clear is that similar stories have circulated sufficiently to call into being a community of self-described victims, who allege that as a result of torture, abuse, or implanted elec-

tronic devices, they were enslaved by a government that had taken possession of their minds. Phillips asserts that "a wave of transgenerational
occult mind control victims are [sic] so numerous within our general
population that the U.S. government has launched . . . misinformation
campaigns to cover-up this source of pure evil." Nevertheless, scholarly
and journalistic treatments of MK-ULTRA and related projects make
no mention of a Project Monarch. Ufologist Martin Cannon, willing
to look sympathetically at O'Brien and Phillips's claims, ended his
inquiry in frustration, irritated that their accusations "never came
backed by hard evidence" and unable to resolve contradictions in their
stories.[25]

In any case, enough individuals believe they have undergone such
experiences to constitute themselves a community of victims, complete
with the apparatus of self-help groups and hypnotic regression that
is evident in other victim populations. Indeed, self-described mind-
control victims tend to resemble other, better-known groups, including
those who consider themselves victims of childhood sexual abuse, satanic ritual abuse, and abduction by extraterrestrials. One finds the same
motifs of sexual violation and the disbelief of others. To these woes the
people focused on mind-control traumas add a repertoire of technologically sophisticated tortures and body implants that allegedly made
them robotic servants of the New World Order. Although they have escaped, they warn that millions of others walk among us in an enslaved
condition, ready to do the bidding of their invisible masters. Rumors
about satanic cults ritually abusing children arose contemporaneously
with New World Order conspiracies and UFO abduction tales in the
1980s, peaking at the end of the decade. Bill Ellis's claim that "abductees . . . report memories of child abuse and trauma on [sic] a significantly higher rate than the general population" is worth noting.
Gareth Medway points out that "In both cases, usually the alleged victim had a traumatic experience at the hands of unearthly beings, aliens
or Satanists, and then forgot about it until treated by a therapist spe-
cializing in recovering such memories." These highly conventionalized
victim accounts not only tie together outwardly dissimilar groups but
also link different historical epochs. Such stories have notable prece-
dents in an earlier America; they resemble the fraudulent nineteenth-
century confessional literature attributed to escaped Catholic nuns and
Mormon plural wives.[26]

Mind-control speculation rapidly acquired similarities to the speculation about the Antichrist discussed in chapter 3. This convergence oc-

curred because recent writers on the Antichrist have fastened on modern technology as the means by which this diabolical ruler will achieve global control. Antichrist scenarios centered on microelectronics emphasize the possibility of implanting devices in the human body. This claim is an obvious by-product of a long tradition that has sought to elucidate the meaning of the mark of the beast biblical passage of Rev. 13:16–17.

In the 1980s, Mary Relfe predicted that the bar code read by optical readers at checkout counters was the precursor to the beast's mark, which would consist of a bar code implanted in an individual's hand. This idea also appealed to Texe Marrs, who began to consider the possibility of an implanted microchip rather than a bar code. Such a chip could not merely track an individual's purchases but also manipulate his mind: "The implantable biochip provides incredible potential for the Illuminati and their stooges to gain absolute, permanent control over the minds of men." Implanted chips would convert human beings into manipulable robots. The bits and pieces of information on MK-ULTRA and other government initiatives fitted perfectly into this description of conspiratorial control.[27]

New World Order theory consequently took shape as an integrated whole, in which such elements as black helicopters and mind control became part of the enemy's arsenal. New World Order beliefs had the special advantage of speaking with equal force to both the religiously and the secularly inclined. They could accommodate the end-time preoccupations of fundamentalists as well as the obsessive fear of tyranny and invasion among those on the secular right.

This breadth of appeal turned out to be greater than anyone had anticipated. The attraction of religionists was predictable because of the Antichrist tradition, and that of secularists as a result of the Illuminati literature; but the presence of a large new audience, UFO believers, was far less obvious, and it is to this migration of ideas that we now turn.

CHAPTER 5

UFO Conspiracy Theories, 1975–1990

Immediately after the Oklahoma City bombing in the spring of 1995, mainstream Americans suddenly became aware of a radical political subculture in their midst. With the arrest of Timothy McVeigh and Terry Nichols and the media coverage of their lives, attitudes, and associations, the public was abruptly introduced to the previously insular world of militias, antigovernment shortwave-radio broadcasts, and racist literature. A racist novel (written by Andrew Macdonald, also known as William Pierce), *The Turner Diaries*—unobtainable through conventional bookstores—became an object of intense interest once it became known that McVeigh had read and recommended it and that the novel contained an episode strikingly similar to the federal building bombing. An avalanche of television, magazine, and newspaper stories uncovered the existence of conspiracy believers obsessed with black helicopters and armed against what they believed to be an imminent invasion by forces of the New World Order.[1]

More than any other single event, the Oklahoma City bombing brought New World Order ideas to the public's attention. But New World Order ideas had begun to seep into broader segments of the American consciousness even earlier. Pat Robertson had published his book *The New World Order* in 1991. Robertson's version of the conspiracy (what might be termed "New World Order lite") is mild compared to that of such militia figures as Mark Koernke; nevertheless, his book is filled with ominous warnings: "The New Age religions, the beliefs of the Illuminati, and Illuminated Freemasonry all seem to move along parallel tracks with world communism and world finance. Their appeals vary somewhat, but essentially they are striving for the same very frightening vision." Robertson claims that an elite network of the superrich, operating through secret societies, is on the verge of taking undisputed control of the world. At the same time, references to the New World Order were also beginning to appear in the speeches of another conspicuous public figure, Pat Buchanan, who linked such concerns with threats to America's economic independence.[2]

Thus in the early 1990s New World Order conspiracy theories ceased to be beliefs that circulated only in an obscure political underground and began to penetrate some channels of mainstream discourse. In fact, however, the most dramatic New World Order penetration came not from Robertson, Buchanan, or coverage of the Oklahoma City bombers. Rather, it occurred earlier, in a segment of American culture that straddles the divide between "mainstream" and "deviant" and encompasses millions of people—the UFO community. Those who are interested in UFOs, believe in them, or claim to have been contacted or abducted by them form a subculture knitted together by lecture circuits, Web sites, magazines, and conventions. Depending on how it is defined, it is also a subculture of immense size.

UFOs and Public Opinion

The number of Americans who actually participate in the UFO subculture—by buying books, magazines, and videotapes; attending conferences; visiting Web sites; and engaging in similar activities—cannot be precisely estimated. But survey data make clear that those who do participate represent merely a fraction of a vast number of people interested in the subject. Whether they are open-minded or simply credulous, it remains the case that millions of Americans view UFOs with considerably less skepticism than do the government and the academy.

Within a few months of the first modern claim of a flying saucer sighting in June 1947, polls showed that 90 percent of the population had heard of them. By 1966, that figure had risen to 96 percent, and, more important, 46 percent of all Americans believed UFOs actually existed. More than a decade later—in 1978—30 percent of college graduates believed they existed. At that time, the number of Americans who believed UFOs were real reached its highest level, 57 percent. The number fell to 47 percent in 1990 but was still at 48 percent in a 1996 Gallup poll, nearly half a century after the first sighting.[3]

The Yankelovich polling organization interviewed 1,546 adults in mid-January 2000 for *Life* magazine. Forty-three percent of respondents believed UFOs were real as opposed to "the product of people's imaginations," and 30 percent thought intelligent beings from other planets had visited the earth. Six percent had seen a UFO, and 13 percent knew someone who had. Seven percent claimed to have "had an encounter with beings from another planet" or knew someone who had.[4]

A 1997 *Time*-CNN poll (presumably commissioned in connection with the fiftieth anniversary of the Roswell, New Mexico, UFO "crash") indicated that 17 percent of Americans believed in alien abduction. An even stranger result had appeared in a 1992 Roper survey, which suggested that 2 percent of Americans (roughly 3.7 million) believed they themselves had been abducted. While the Roper result is almost certainly inflated, a number even half as large would be extraordinary.[5]

Two aspects of these figures are particularly striking. First, they have remained astonishingly stable over a fifty-year period. What might have been an early Cold War fad clearly came to occupy a semipermanent niche in the American psyche. Second, the level of belief was not only relatively stable; it was extraordinarily high, regardless of when the survey was taken or by which polling organization. Even if one compensates for problems of sampling or the wording of questions, tens of millions of Americans accept the reality of UFOs. In a survey of 765 members of the UFO community, Brenda Denzler found her respondents to be anything but "fringe." They were predominantly white, male, middle-class college graduates, with incomes just slightly below the national median.[6]

At the same time, attitudes about UFOs contain the seeds of conspiracist thinking, for public attitudes are clearly at variance with the official position that there is no credible evidence that UFOs exist. Indeed, in the 1996 Gallup survey, when subjects were asked, "In your opinion, does the U.S. government know more about UFOs than they are telling us?" 71 percent answered yes. In the Yankelovich poll in 2000, 49 percent believed that the government was withholding information about UFOs.[7]

Thus an extremely large number of people hold beliefs that contradict official government positions and believe that government concealment explains the discrepancy. Belief in a government cover-up runs deep in the ufology community, especially among those who are professional or full-time UFO writers or investigators. Because government investigations have failed to satisfy believers, the existence of a cover-up appears logical to them. Even so, early ufologists did not generally advance a broader political agenda. While steadfastly maintaining that military and intelligence organizations were concealing the truth from the public, they did not extend that suspicion to embrace any larger ideology of conspiracy. In short, ufology's early political program did not extend beyond a general desire to see revealed what was believed to be concealed.

But by the late 1980s, elements of the UFO community began to link their interest in explaining flying saucers with a larger political vision. Receptivity to New World Order ideas in some UFO circles was facilitated by two legends peculiar to the ufology milieu: the "men in black" story and the tale of underground bases.

The legend of the men in black originated in the early and mid 1950s and quickly became a staple of UFO folklore. According to this legend, people whose experiences or research brought them too close to the truth were apt to be stalked, harassed, or even killed by small groups of men—usually two or three—in dark suits who did not identify themselves. Their ambiguous appearance has led to a number of explanations: to some, they are secret government operatives; to others, representatives of a conspiracy that controls the government; to still others, they are aliens whose appearance is close enough to that of humans to allow them to pass. In any case, their appearance and demeanor make them a potent symbol of mysterious but pervasive evil.[8]

The underground-bases legend is part of a larger complex of beliefs about secret installations where (depending on the version) captured or crashed alien craft or aliens themselves may be kept. In the most dramatic versions, the aliens actually control parts of the installation, either by themselves or in concert with secret government agencies. The most famous base is Area 51, also known as Groom Lake and Dreamland, north of Las Vegas, Nevada; but the most elaborate tales involve labyrinthine subterranean caverns, tunnels, and chambers such as those allegedly near the town of Dulce, New Mexico. These stories have led to belief in a hidden world variously inhabited by alien beings or evil human forces, in which conspirators can both conceal their enterprises and seek safety when disasters overtake the earth's surface.[9]

UFOs and the New World Order

Gradually, parts of the UFO community began to adopt elements of the conspiracy theories described in the previous two chapters, and by the end of the 1980s virtually all of the radical right's ideas about the New World Order had found their way into UFO literature. Ufology's adoption of the New World Order was by no means universal, but those who have found it attractive have been able to create a version of New World Order theory with some distinct political advantages.

The most immediate advantage for New World Order ideas of being placed in a UFO context has been a reduction in stigma. Although UFO ideas have often been the target of ridicule, the enormous size of the UFO-accepting public has made it impossible to stigmatize UFO beliefs so completely that they are banned from public discussion. Far from it—UFO ideas have ready access to such avenues of distribution as cable television, mainstream bookstores, and magazine publishers. They fall into the realm of stigmatized knowledge discussed in chapter 2, in that they are rejected by science, universities, and government, but the level of stigmatization has not been so great as to exclude them from popular culture.

By contrast, the views of the radical right have been so excluded, through an unstated yet powerful pattern of self-censorship on the part of the mainstream. This voluntary silence has denied access to beliefs deemed racist, bigoted, completely unfounded, or likely to justify or promote violence. Tales of secret Illuminati conspiracies, imminent UN invasions, and Jewish, Masonic, or Jesuit plots, for example, have been informally banned from media, classrooms, and other mechanisms of knowledge distribution. Unlike beliefs about flying saucers, considered eccentric but socially harmless, many conspiracy ideas deemed both false and dangerous have been banished from the mainstream discourse.

The linkage of New World Order ideas with UFOs gave the former a bridge to the territory of semirespectable beliefs. Ufology became, as it were, the vehicle for the New World Order to reach audiences otherwise unavailable to it. To be sure, New World Order ideas occasionally reached mass audiences, as the cases of Pat Robertson and Pat Buchanan have shown. In both cases, however, the conspiracies were presented in highly diluted versions; and in Robertson's case, even his weak version produced significant political problems.

The story of the New World Order–UFO connection is a story of ideas moving in two directions, not one. In the initial movement (examined later in this chapter), New World Order beliefs became entwined with UFO beliefs. A second migration followed in the 1990s, in which New World Order ideas with their new UFO add-ons returned to the right-wing milieu in which they had first developed. In that milieu, the combination led to the development of two diametrically opposed syntheses. In one, exemplified by British writer and lecturer David Icke (discussed at length in chapter 6), the human conspirators feared by the radical right are actually doing the bidding of malevolent extra-terrestrial forces whose ultimate aim is control of the earth. In the other, epitomized by the views of Milton William Cooper at the end of his life (addressed later in this chapter), there are in fact no aliens at all. The appearance of an alien assault on the earth is being manufactured by human conspirators to provide a pretext for the assumption of global dictatorial powers.

The first movement, when New World Order ideas left the hermetic world of the extreme right and began to seep into ufology, is the more significant of the two. As the preceding discussion suggests, there were factors in ufology that made this penetration seem logical, but it was not inevitable. It does not seem to have been consciously undertaken by conspiracists or done for opportunistic reasons, even though in the end it provided a large new audience. Rather, it began in a disorganized, piecemeal fashion, and it provides a case study in the migration of deviant ideas.

UFO Conspiracism: The First Phase

The development of New World Order conspiracy theories within ufology can best be understood as the product of two separate phases. The first—from roughly 1975 to 1980—introduced increasingly conspiratorial motifs into UFO speculation, but without any discernible links to the conspiracy ideas that were prevalent on the extreme right. There seem to have been two separate conspiracist tracks that developed independently of each other. This lack of connection between the two is all the more striking because the late 1970s were a period of substantial right-wing activity, with the growth of such movements as Christian Identity and the Posse Comitatus. The Posse was an antigovernment movement made up of local paramilitary groups active in the West and Midwest during the 1970s and 1980s. They believed the only legitimate governmental authority to be the county sheriff's posse, in the form of the armed adult males of a community. There is no evidence that ufologists were aware of, interested in, or sympathetic to those tendencies.

During this initial phase, some important themes emerged in the UFO literature that were eventually integrated into more elaborate conspiratorial structures. One of these concerned small devices allegedly implanted in the bodies of UFO abductees. Although such stories were not numerous, they implied the existence of a powerful technology for monitoring and controlling victims' behavior. Thomas Bullard's detailed analysis of 270 abduction stories (most of them dating between the 1940s and 1980) reveals only thirteen cases of reported implants—barely 5 percent. These were almost uniformly distributed among the 1950s, 1960s, and 1970s. Despite their small numbers, however, the implant stories contained two points of potential connection with the independently developed New World Order conspiracy theories described earlier. First, they offered apparent confirmation of the mark of the beast associated with the Antichrist. Second, they also appeared to validate the mind-control fears of more secular conspiracists.[10]

About the same time, in 1976, a Toronto-based neo-Nazi and Holocaust denier, Ernst Zundel, published the first of several reports linking flying saucers with the Nazis. In the strangest version of this tale, Nazis, not aliens, had invented flying saucers and, with the regime's defeat, had fled to subterranean bases in Antarctica with their invention. The suggestion that flying saucers had been under development by the Third Reich and were spirited out of Germany appears to have emerged first among German nationalists in the 1950s. It was quickly assimilated into legends of Hitler's supposed escape to South America or the Antarctic. By 1960, comparable tales were circulating in English, though their full elaboration had to await the efforts of Zundel and other neo-Nazis a decade and a half later. While this scenario begged the question of how so technologically advanced a government could manage to lose the war, it was a story that turned out to have a long life for two reasons. First, it introduced the idea that a secret group of human beings might in some conspiratorial fashion develop such devices. Second, it established a link between UFOs and the much older occultic tradition of an "inner world" beneath the earth, discussed in detail in chapter 7.[11]

The year 1976 was also the year that some ufologists began to link UFOs with cattle mutilations. Stories of mutilated cattle, mostly in western states, began to appear in the late 1960s and became numerous and the subject of national media coverage by the mid 1970s. Although they were occasionally connected to reports of UFO sightings, a number of alternative explanations were offered, including satanic rituals, "hippies," and natural enemies. The carcasses were often missing portions of soft tissue, and some reports claimed that cuts were made with a precision inconsistent with animal predators.[12]

In 1979, Linda Moulton Howe, a Denver filmmaker, began work on a documentary that alleged a mutilation-UFO connection. The film, *A Strange Harvest,* was broadcast in 1980. She later stated that "I am convinced that one or more alien intelligences are affecting this planet. I would like to know who they are, what they want and why the government is silent." Howe and others, influenced by her film and subsequent publications, began to speculate that aliens mutilated cattle in order to secure body parts or biological substances they needed for their own survival, and that the U.S. government was complicit in these efforts. The idea that aliens were engaged in some obscure effort to "harvest" or otherwise retrieve biological substances from the earth has turned out to be a fertile subject for speculation, which eventually came to include such suggestions as the breeding of alien-human hybrids. The ease with which stories of cattle mutilation were assimilated into the UFO literature was a paradigmatic case of fusing disparate forms of stigmatized knowledge. If cattle mutilations and alien spaceships could be connected, why not other stigmatized knowledge claims as well? [13]

Speculations about an alien harvest soon coalesced with aspects of the abduction stories. Nearly half of the abduction tales examined by Bullard featured invasive, often painful physical examinations. A number of accounts included examinations of reproductive organs, and about half a dozen individuals reported sexual intercourse with alien beings. Out of this body of narratives came suggestions that aliens were seeking either to harvest substances from human bodies or to create a race of alien-human hybrids. Because the "other" here was alien in every sense, it was easy to blur the distinction between procedures performed on cattle and those performed on human beings; in the more sinister interpretation, it suggested that human beings were being treated like breeding stock, presumably to compensate for some biological defect in the aliens.[14]

In 1977, UFO speculation took a different turn with the broadcast by Anglia TV in Great Britain of the strange purported documentary *Alternative 3. Alternative 3* claimed to expose a secret plan, approved at the highest levels of the U.S. and Soviet governments, to launch a program of space colonization that would allow a select few to flee the earth before environmental calamities made the planet uninhabitable. The show strongly implied that a secret joint base already existed on the far side of the moon, that another existed or would shortly be established on Mars, and that the Martian surface, contrary to general belief, was hospitable to human life.[15]

Alternative 3 was clearly a hoax—and not only because it was broad-

cast on April Fool's Day. The interviews with supposed scientists, astronauts, and others were far too dramatically polished to have been
spontaneous, and in any case the program's closing credits named the
actors who took the roles of interviewees and correspondents. Though
artfully produced, the show's counterfeit documentary style could
scarcely have been expected to fool many. As an Anglia TV spokes-
man put it, "We felt viewers would be fairly sophisticated about it."
They apparently were not; television and newspaper switchboards were
swamped after the broadcast. Anglia found it prudent to sell off the
book rights. The 1978 book version, by Leslie Watkins, continued the
pretense of factuality. It also reached countries, including the United
States, where the broadcast had not been aired. Whenever the book was
unavailable, believers attributed its absence to the conspirators' attempts at suppression. This type of quasiparanoid fear is a particularly
strong tendency in the United States. And the story lent itself to conspiracist interpretations—who were the elite the secret space program
was intended to save? Even those willing to acknowledge that *Alternative 3* was trumped up insisted that its core argument might very well be
true—another instance of the demolition of the fact-fiction boundary
discussed in chapter 2.[16]

Alternative 3 does not mention UFOs or aliens. As discussed in
chapter 6, its role in the growth of conspiracy theory lay in a later permutation, according to which UFOs and the threat of an alien invasion
of the earth are believed to have been invented by the shadowy elite in
order to gather sufficient power and resources to complete the space-
colonization enterprise. When the scenario of Alternative 3 came to be
enfolded within ufological conspiracism, it suggested that UFO conspiracy theories could go in two different directions. The first insisted
on the reality of a threat from outer space, with human conspirators involved as the aliens' lackeys or collaborators. The other direction, following the Alternative 3 suggestion, claimed that UFOs from outer
space were a deception concocted by the conspirators for their own
malevolent purposes, in order to deflect attention from the real evil.

UFO Conspiracism: The Second Phase

The first phase in the growth of UFO conspiracy theories extended
through the late 1970s. It was characterized by a fragmentation of
themes, whether of abductees' implants, cattle mutilations, or Nazi

bases. The only product of the period that purported to offer an integral conspiracy theory was the fictional *Alternative 3* broadcast, which had not mentioned UFOs at all. By contrast, the second phase, which began in the mid 1980s, was marked both by the broader scope of conspiracy allegations and by the convergence of UFO plots with the better-developed conspiracism of the extreme right.

The first full published statement of such a theory appeared in 1986, in George C. Andrews's book *Extra-Terrestrials among Us*. Although Andrews's conspiracy theory appears in bits and pieces strewn throughout the volume, it can be reconstructed roughly as follows. A race of evil extraterrestrials is using a "privileged elite caste" of humans to manipulate and control the masses. As far as the United States is concerned, the principal mechanism for political control is the CIA, a "government within the government," implementing a form of "corporate fascism." Andrews accuses the CIA of having assassinated John F. Kennedy, and he cites William Pabst's pamphlet claiming that a network of concentration camps is being readied for dissenters. He fears that martial law is about to be declared, bringing an end to American democracy. The explicit use of Pabst's work, warnings about the Rex 84 exercise (discussed in chapter 4), and repeated claims that the Constitution is in imminent danger make Andrews's political views almost indistinguishable from those associated with militias. Only his placement of extraterrestrials at the pinnacle of the conspiracies identifies him as a ufologist.[17]

The publication of *Extra-Terrestrials among Us* marked the beginning of a feverish period of UFO conspiracism, from 1986 to 1989. Much of the literature of this period was based on the concept of a secret governing apparatus, unknown and unaccountable, not unlike Andrews's notion of the CIA as a "government within the government." The idea of a hidden government received its most significant boost in 1987 with the publication of the so-called MJ-12 papers.

MJ-12—sometimes referred to as Magestic-12 or Majic-12—purports to be a document prepared for President Dwight Eisenhower, to which was attached a memo from President Harry Truman to his defense secretary, James Forrestal. Though made public in 1987, MJ-12 had a history that went back to 1984.

According to those involved, on December 11, 1984, Jaime Shandera, a film producer, received a package anonymously sent from Albuquerque, New Mexico, containing an undeveloped roll of film. He and UFO writer William Moore developed the film, which they said contained images of the MJ-12 documents. Although the documents were not made public until June 1987, when they were revealed at a UFO conference in Washington, D.C., UFO publications referred to them as early as 1985. Facsimile copies were reproduced in the British edition (and later the American edition) of Timothy Good's *Above Top Secret*, and have appeared elsewhere many times since.[18]

The MJ-12 documents take the form of a briefing paper for the newly elected president, informing him of the existence of a supersecret group of the same name, allegedly established during the Truman administration, that consists of a dozen high military and scientific figures. The documents describe crashes of UFOs and the recovery of their occupants' bodies, which established them as of indisputably extraterrestrial origin.

MJ-12 immediately polarized the UFO community into believers and skeptics. Among the skeptics was Jacques Vallee, who compared the incident to the activities of "Deep Throat" during the Watergate scandal. He suggested that the documents' sender was more likely interested in disinformation than in whistle-blowing, and implied that the documents were forged. Even more dismissive was Philip J. Klass, a longtime debunker of UFO hoaxes, who argued that the format and language of the documents pointed to forgery.[19]

In the years since the MJ-12 papers became widely known, they have taken on a life of their own. Additional, related documents periodically appear, some as recently as 1998. Just as with the Kennedy assassination, MJ-12 has generated a cottage industry of commentators, authenticators, and critics. More broadly, MJ-12 laid the foundation for elaborate conspiracy theories by suggesting that UFOs were of extraterrestrial origin, that the federal government was aware of them as early as the late 1940s, and that a secret bureaucracy had been created to study and control the situation. These claims allowed some ufologists to shift from observation of flying saucers to attempts to unravel alleged government machinations. The proliferation of MJ-12 documents and theories not only identified the enemy as a segment of the government, but—inasmuch as this "secret government" was supposed to have hidden all relevant information—allowed great latitude in what might be "revealed." It mattered little whether publicly available evidence confirmed a claim; its author could always respond, "The government knows it, but won't tell you."[20]

The first such revelation occurred on December 29, 1987, a few months after the release of the MJ-12 papers. It took the form of a statement by John Lear, estranged son of inventor William Lear. Building upon the original MJ-12 documents, Lear constructs a far more elaborate edifice of intrigue and dissimulation. The Lear statement narrates the purported history of the relationship between the MJ-12 group and the extraterrestrials from 1947 to 1987. Although Lear cites few sources and offers no documentation, his statement, like many conspiracy narratives, is striking in its specificity.

The "horrible truth" to which MJ-12 was allegedly privy was so frightening that it drove at least one member—Secretary of Defense Forrestal—to suicide, his death disguised as the result of mental illness. According to Lear, the U.S. government began to hold meetings with the aliens on April 30, 1964, and by 1971 had negotiated a "deal." Its terms called for transfer of the aliens' technology to the government, in exchange for which the government would acquiesce in cattle mutilations and in the temporary abduction of American citizens. The abductees would be implanted with tracking and control devices, given posthypnotic suggestions, sometimes used as guinea pigs in genetic engineering and cross-breeding programs, and occasionally killed.[21]

Lear's text alleged that the "EBEs" (extraterrestrial biological entities) have a "genetic disorder" that has caused their digestive system to atrophy. They can survive only by ingesting biological substances obtained from cows or humans, or by creating an alien-human cross-bred race. This need led to the construction, under government auspices, of gigantic laboratories, not only to receive the aliens' technology but also to allow them to conduct biological experiments. These laboratories included Groom Lake, Nevada (better known in the ufology literature as Area 51 or Dreamland), and several in New Mexico, notably near the small town of Dulce. There, Lear claims, a joint CIA-alien laboratory provides facilities for unspeakable experiments on abducted subjects. Indeed, the aliens' behavior was so repugnant that in 1979 a subterranean battle supposedly took place between them and U.S. military personnel, in which sixty-six U.S. troops were killed.[22]

The battle at Dulce was the beginning of a crisis for MJ-12, which gradually became aware of the "Grand Deception"—namely, the failure of the aliens to live up to their agreement. Their technology turned out to be only partially usable, they were abducting far more Americans than they had agreed to, and they were mistreating them. Faced with this situation, MJ-12 supposedly decided it was foolhardy to attempt immediate resistance and instead opted to develop weapons that might permit effective resistance at some later time. This weapons development program was the Strategic Defense Initiative, disguised as a Cold War project.[23]

The Lear statement is brief—only seven printed pages—but dizzying in its claims. It elevates MJ-12 to a conspiratorial position nowhere hinted at in the original papers themselves. It implies a web of subsidiary conspiracies—to silence the news media and the academic community, and to mislead the UFO community as well. According to Lear, ufologist William Moore, the figure most identified with the MJ-12 papers, was probably himself a disinformation agent in the hire of MJ-12. The statement ends with a litany of rhetorical questions—a common device in conspiracy literature—all implying that the aliens' ultimate aim is the conquest of the earth, and that the conspirators in government, centered in MJ-12, are powerless to prevent it.[24]

Although Lear did not employ the term *New World Order,* he managed to bring together a number of elements compatible with New World Order theory, including mind-control implants, a government within the government, and the kidnapping of hundreds of thousands of Americans. Lear's claim of having been a CIA pilot only added to the sense that this was an insider's view, notwithstanding the paucity of evidence.[25]

If Lear had been alone in his bizarre allegations, they would have disappeared from view. But they were quickly taken up and amplified by a figure who was to prove central to the convergence of UFO and militia positions: Milton William Cooper, the most famous of UFO conspiracists. Cooper also had a military background, having served in the air force and later the navy, from which he was discharged in 1975. Between his discharge and his ufology debut, he apparently received some training and experience in photography as well as working at administrative jobs in vocational colleges. Best known in ufology circles for his bitter conflicts with rivals and critics, his conspiracist reputation rests primarily on his 1991 book, *Behold a Pale Horse.* While it may not be, as Cooper's Web site biography claims, "the best selling underground book of all time," it is widely available and, apparently, widely read in ufology, conspiracy, and antigovernment circles.[26]

THE COOPER NARRATIVE

Cooper presented his own MJ-12 account in a series of related documents released between December 1988 and the end of 1989. Coming as they did immediately after both the MJ-12 release and the Lear statement, Cooper's claims caused a sensation in ufology circles. In a series of Internet postings and in an appearance at the Mutual UFO Network (MUFON) symposium in Las Vegas in July 1989, Cooper claimed to have seen an astonishing array of secret UFO documents during his naval career. His earliest accounts, from December 1988 and January

1989, closely parallel the MJ-12 papers and the Lear statement, yet they mention neither Moore nor Lear. Instead, Cooper claimed independent knowledge, asserting that in 1972, while in the navy, he was shown sets of documents and photographs dealing with UFOs, their extraterrestrial passengers, and relations between the extraterrestrials and the federal government.[27]

The earliest statement of Cooper's views—"Top Secret/Majic"—was, according to Linda Moulton Howe, posted on the CompuServe and Paranet networks on December 18, 1988. It purports to summarize the material Cooper says he saw sixteen years previously. While the substance is closely related to the MJ-12 and Lear materials, the structure of Cooper's statement is quite different. It is neither a set of primary documents nor a narrative. Most of it consists of brief sections, often no more than a paragraph, each of which describes or defines a name or term Cooper said he encountered in the original navy material. Many are names of projects or operations allegedly initiated by the government to deal with extraterrestrials, giving the entire statement a decidedly bureaucratic tinge.[28]

Several details of Cooper's account are noteworthy, either in the manner in which they distance themselves from Moore and Lear or by suggesting new political implications. The latter are particularly important, because in the 1990s Cooper emerged as the most conspicuous link between UFO conspiracists and militia circles.

The Cooper variations, while small, increased the congruence between UFO conspiracies and the tales of plots circulating on the extreme right, though there is no explicit evidence that Cooper was familiar with right-wing literature at the time. In his version, the MJ-12 group is a relatively small part of a much larger government enterprise directed at understanding the aliens, dealing with them, and keeping knowledge from reaching the general public. Not surprisingly, the CIA is described as central to the enterprise, a claim also made in Andrews's 1986 description of the conspiracy. Black helicopters make an appearance as well, allegedly accompanying test flights of recovered alien craft over the Nevada desert. Although Andrews had not mentioned *black* helicopters specifically, he did report transformations in which saucers turned into helicopters and vice versa.[29]

Cooper did not mention the Trilateral Commission, but he introduced motifs that were to make its future inclusion appear natural. He referred to teams called Delta that, he claimed, provide security for all projects related to the aliens and whose members in fact are the legendary men in black. Later on, others more explicitly identified this group with the well-known Delta Force counterterrorism organization. Cooper's references to Delta are closely related to his lengthy discussion of what he called "a TRILATERAL INSIGNIA" allegedly found on alien spacecraft. He claimed that the Delta security guards wear red badges with a black triangle, similar to the "alien flag" of a triangle divided by parallel lines. His linking of the terms *delta, trilateral,* and *men in black* offered the possibility of conspiracy in which U.S. military forces, aliens, and the Trilateral Commission collude.[30]

Like Lear, Cooper alleged that the aliens came to earth not out of mere curiosity but because some biological flaw made them dependent on substances, including blood, that could be obtained from human and animal bodies. According to Cooper, they might have evolved from plants, because they use chlorophyll to convert food into energy and excrete waste products through the skin. How this mechanism related to the need for human and animal blood was not explained.[31]

In early 1989, Cooper issued a revised version of this document. It has since been frequently posted on the Internet. Not all versions, however, are identical. As is often the case with Internet documents, there is no way to determine definitively if changes have been made since the date the document bears.[32]

Notwithstanding these difficulties, the later Cooper document is interesting in its own right. In the first place, Cooper attributed the differences between this and the earlier version to his having undergone "hypnotic regression in order to make the information as accurate as possible." He did not indicate who performed the hypnosis, when, or under what conditions. The second version also contains a much elaborated description of the MJ-12 group itself. It allegedly consists of the twelve senior members of a thirty-two-member secret society called the Jason Society, which was "commissioned" by President Eisenhower to "find the truth of the alien question."[33]

Identifying a complete and accurate text of the second Cooper document is difficult. Howe's published version contains elisions. An Internet version is considerably longer and places material in a somewhat different order. It is also more overtly political, with references to the Kennedy assassination, the Rockefeller family, black helicopters, and the trilateral insignia; and it charges that the activities described violate the Constitution, as well as "the human rights of every citizen of the world." This longer text may well have been written as early as the printed one (i.e., January 10, 1989), but the technology of the Internet makes the date impossible to verify.[34]

Cooper's claims in the second document regarding abductee implants and concentration camps were equally sweeping. One in every forty Americans has allegedly been implanted, which would amount to several million individuals. The concentration camps are part of a plan in which, under the pretext of a terrorist nuclear threat, martial law would be declared and the media nationalized.[35]

Cooper's next text, dated May 23, 1989, was an Internet document made public at a UFO symposium in Las Vegas on July 2 of that year. It subsequently formed part of a chapter in *Behold a Pale Horse*. Here, too, the political element was conspicuously present: the CIA was created to deal with the alien threat, Secretary of Defense Forrestal was an abductee, and the presidents were kept in ignorance.[36]

Up to this point, Cooper had suggested little in the way of political action beyond recommending that Congress be informed. Sometime in 1989, however, he associated himself with an anonymous document labeled "Petition to Indict." In his undated accompanying letter, Cooper spoke of "Many other signatures . . . on the original copy," presumably in addition to his own. He begged Congress to act on the petition, but "not to trust any other government agency with these matters because this conspiracy runs deep within the government." [37]

The "Petition to Indict," which runs somewhat more than four typed pages, appears in some places to be addressed simply to "the government," at others more specifically to Congress. It charges that "the government" entered into "a secret treaty with an Alien Nation" in violation of the Constitution. In addition to repeating many of the points already made by Lear and Cooper, it charges that the resources to fund secret, alien-related projects came from CIA involvement in the international drug trade.[38]

The petition is also significant for its lengthy references to the involvement of then-president George H. W. Bush. Calling Bush "the most powerful and dangerous criminal in the history of the world," the petition charges that Bush's involvement in the international drug trade went back to his days in the oil business and continued throughout his tenure as CIA director. Bush's associations with Skull and Bones and the Trilateral Commission have made him a favorite target of conspiracy theorists.[39]

Because the petition asks full disclosure of government plots by May 30, 1989, it can reasonably be dated to early that year, that is to say, roughly contemporaneous with the revised version of the Cooper document. The petition is vague about what might happen if no government action is taken on its charges. But it warns that failure to act will make every member of the House and Senate "accessories to the conspiracy and the crimes outlined in this document," and the signatories "swear on the Constitution" to bring "all guilty parties . . . to justice." How they might do this is not specified.[40]

The "Petition to Indict" bears some similarities to the "Constructive Notices" sent in 1986 to a judge and to Internal Revenue Service personnel in Nevada. The "Constructive Notices" were purported indictments issued by the Committee of the States, an entity created by Christian Identity preacher and tax protestor William Potter Gale. The "Constructive Notices" threatened the lives of the recipients, and in October 1987, Gale and his associates were tried and convicted of interfering in the administration of the tax laws. In retrospect, it can be seen that the Committee of the States affair anticipated such developments as so-called common-law courts among antigovernment groups in the 1990s. There is no direct evidence that Cooper or the anonymous drafter or drafters of the "Petition to Indict" were familiar with Gale's activities. Nonetheless, like the Committee of the States and many subsequent examples of right-wing shadow legal institutions, the petition implies the authority to bring malefactors to justice if formal legal institutions do not.[41]

By the late 1990s, Cooper had moved away from the ufology community, where he had first appeared a decade earlier, to the subculture of militias and other antigovernment groups. His Web site circulated conspiracist versions of the Oklahoma City bombing, and he spoke in the name of a shadowy organization called the Second Continental Army of the Republic (Militia), about which little is known. As Gale had, Cooper also took on the Internal Revenue Service.[42]

Cooper became convinced that he had been targeted by "The Illuminati Socialist President of the United States of America, William Jefferson Clinton" as well as "by the bogus and unconstitutional Internal Revenue Service." His conflict with the latter resulted in an arrest warrant issued in July 1998. As of fall 2000, it still had not been executed, which resulted in Cooper's being named a "major fugitive" by the U.S. Marshals Service. The government's reluctance to arrest Cooper was apparently a reflection of his conflict-laden rhetoric: "We are formed as the Constitutional and Lawful unorganized Militia of the State of Arizona and the united [sic] States of America . . . By invading the Sovereign jurisdiction of the State of Arizona to attack the Citizens of the State of Arizona the United States has declared war upon the Citizens of the Several States of the Union . . . We have drawn our line in the sand." The warrant was never served, because Cooper was shot and killed by sheriff's deputies in November 2001 as a result of an incident unrelated to his tax problems. This bizarre conclusion to a strange life is described more fully in chapter 10.[43]

Cooper was not the only figure in the UFO subculture who was elaborating politically charged conspiracy theories by the end of the 1980s. The year 1989 marked the beginning of the activities of John Grace, also known as Val Germann and Val (or Valdamar) Valerian. Grace was an air force enlisted man stationed at Nellis Air Force Base near Las Vegas, where he apparently came into contact with Lear. About 1988, Grace-Valerian founded the Nevada Aerial Research Group in Las Vegas, but soon relocated it to Yelm, Washington, under the name Leading Edge Research Group. He has been an extraordinarily prolific writer and publisher, claiming to have issued tens of thousands of pages. His central works are the massive, ongoing series of *Matrix* volumes, of which at least six have appeared, and the serial publication *The Leading Edge*.[44]

It is impossible to summarize Valerian's system. Indeed, it may well be one of the most complex superconspiracy theories ever constructed. Scarcely any major organization or institution escapes inclusion. One diagrammatic representation requires six pages to lay out the connections among elements of the plot, including the Gestapo, the Mafia, and the Wobblies (IWW). Valerian ranges not only across the usual UFO and conspiracist terrain but across politics, religion, science, and history. He clearly regards his system not merely as an explanation of flying saucers or contemporary politics but as a synoptic vision of all knowledge.[45]

Cooper edged gradually toward more ambitious conspiratorial schemes, but even at his most sweeping he never sought to cover areas such as the sciences (about which, in fact, he claimed ignorance). Valerian, by contrast, takes conspiracism to its logical conclusion by suggesting that all true knowledge has been deliberately hidden, and that attempts to reveal it in one area will inevitably reveal the entire structure, if only one digs widely and deeply enough. Anything that is available and obvious is false, while what is hidden has to be true; its hiddenness can have occurred only because those who truly know do not wish it to be revealed. As Valerian puts it, "As a result of the suppression and compartmentalization of information, cultures have been fragmented into several distinct groups and mind sets which both co-exist and oppose each other." He clearly believes that he has discovered the suppressed synthesis.[46]

Leading Edge's location, Yelm, Washington, is also the home of J. Z. Knight, a channeler who claims to be the medium transmitting the words of a 35,000-year-old warrior named Ramtha. The Ramtha School of Enlightenment in Yelm was founded in 1988 or 1989, about the time Valerian arrived. There appear to be no direct links between Valerian's organization and Knight's, but they do share common themes. Ramtha asserts that the UFOs carry aliens who are "your higher brothers." Valerian, like Knight, employs the *entity* terminology standard in channeling circles, and he includes favorable material about Ramtha in the *Matrix* volumes. There are some differences: for instance, like many conspiracy-minded ufologists, Valerian believes that there are many alien races, some of which are malevolent. For their part, Knight and Ramtha identify evil with a conspiracy of international bankers who include the Rothschilds and the Federal Reserve. The Ramtha School's book service sells works by Cooper, David Icke, and Jim Keith, and the Ramtha newsletter has published lengthy interviews with Mark Phillips and Cathy O'Brien, with their tales of CIA mind-controlled sex slaves. Notwithstanding the lack of formal connections, Valerian and Knight clearly seem to tap into the same cultic milieu.[47]

By the early 1990s, therefore, at least some of the ufology literature had gone through several transformations. It had become intensely politicized. It insisted that powerful elements in the U.S. government were in continuing collaboration with an evil, alien race. And it claimed that in order to protect this information, the secret government was prepared to destroy American liberties. From 1986 to about 1990, the activities of Andrews, Lear, Cooper, and Valerian created a conspiracist form of UFO speculation, which Jerome Clark refers to as ufology's "dark side."[48]

Much of this material was either strikingly similar to or compatible with the conspiracy ideas simultaneously circulating in the militia and militant antigovernment subculture. The mythology of concentration camps, secret government security forces, wholesale violation of the Constitution, and control of the state by a hidden elite are themes prominent in both domains. Yet any link between them in the 1980s appears circumstantial. The UFO conspiracists were especially active in the West, where the extreme right was particularly evident; even so, no evidence exists at this time of direct contact between them. But convergent ideas are bound to meet, and as the next chapter shows, this occurred in the early 1990s.

CHAPTER 6

UFOs Meet the New World Order

Jim Keith and David Icke

New World Order ideas about a coming global tyranny coalesced with UFO conspiracist theories in the 1990s. Their union was exemplified in the works of two conspiracists, Jim Keith and David Icke. Although they both absorbed the New World Order beliefs of the Christian patriot subculture and increasingly linked the New World Order to UFOs, their approaches were not identical.

Indeed, a comparison of Keith and Icke is instructive not simply to demonstrate their similarities but also to illuminate their differences. Those differences begin with nationality (Keith was American, Icke is British), but go on to encompass their starting points and audiences. Keith was for all practical purposes a professional conspiracy theorist, writing for an audience of conspiracists. His initial interest lay in unraveling the plots that allegedly drove history. He can be placed in the conspiracist milieu that emerged after John F. Kennedy's assassination. Although Keith was only fourteen when the assassination occurred, he found a niche in the cottage industry of conspiracy theorists that flourished during succeeding decades. He was in no sense a person of the radical right, but the deeper he plunged into conspiracism, the readier he became to adopt the Christian patriot worldview. Similarly, he came to UFOs late and after long involvement with conspiracism, but at the end of his life, UFOs lay at the center of his concerns.

Icke, by contrast, began his journey to conspiracism in environmental politics and the New Age. *New Age* has always been a vague concept, but one finds in Icke many of its familiar themes—the search for spiritual enlightenment, the belief in transcendent, nonmaterial levels of reality, and the notion of a world that may be transformed by invisible forces, if only those forces can be identified and mobilized. Icke's rise is indicative of what Nicholas Goodrick-Clarke has called the "endemic spread of conspiracy theories in the New Age milieu," which he associates with a variety of pressures: the failure to bring about spiritual transformation in the 1970s, the economic stresses of globalization and job loss on the middle class, and a backlash against affirmative action and so-called political correctness. Whatever the causes, Icke has found a ready audience among those drawn to the promise of personal and societal redemption. He came early to the belief that world transformation was being blocked by evil elements, which he increasingly identified with the New World Order, and eventually with malevolent extraterrestrials. Like Keith, he did not start out on the political right (quite the contrary), but in time he came to accept much of the Christian patriot position. And like Keith, he did not emerge from ufology, but eventually accepted many of its most extreme positions.[1]

Jim Keith: UFOs and the Professional Conspiracist

Jim Keith (1949–1999) began writing for fringe publications as a child, in the mid 1950s, though his early works have been impossible to trace. He joined the Church of Scientology in 1972, at the age of twenty-three, and remained in it for a decade. He embarked on this career as a conspiracist writer ten years after that, in 1992, through his association with *Steamshovel Press.*[2]

Steamshovel Press is a conspiracy periodical published by Kenn Thomas. Thomas traces its origins to the influence of the aging members of the Beat Generation in the early 1980s. Indeed, the first issue of what was to become *Steamshovel* contained the transcript of an interview with Ram Dass, the former Richard Alpert, who collaborated with Timothy Leary in experiments with LSD. After a few intermittent issues, the regular publication began with issue number 4 in 1992. The Kennedy assassination was a major concern of the journal, but many other plots were covered, ranging from UFOs and the Vatican to Wilhelm Reich. Keith contributed to the first issue and to many subsequent ones. It was commonplace for *Steamshovel* to include sections on both the Kennedy assassination and UFOs, but Keith wrote across a wide range of subject matter. He was in no sense a UFO specialist.[3]

Keith began publishing books in 1992 and continued, sometimes releasing as many as three or four a year, until 1999. Nearly half the volumes deal with UFO-related subjects. Many of the others address issues familiar to New World Order conspiracists, including black helicopters and mind control. Indeed, Keith's 1994 book, *Black Helicopters over America: Strikeforce for the New World Order,* revised in 1997, became the central work on the subject.[4]

Just as conspiracism dominated Keith's writing career, so it dominated reactions to his sudden death. He died September 7, 1999, in a Reno, Nevada, hospital as a result of complications from a fall three days earlier. But fellow conspiracists hinted darkly of "mysterious circumstances" after a postsurgical blood clot proved fatal. Thomas remarked, "And if Jim Keith did not die as a result of a conspiracy, then I'm sure he would want us to make it look that way!" There were reports shortly after his death that in addition to writing under his own name, he had also been the pseudonymous Commander X, a writer whose baroque plots involving Freemasons and the Vatican are described in later chapters. Others who knew Keith denied that he was Commander X or had ever assisted the mysterious author.[5]

Keith remained consistent in his belief that the world was in imminent danger of falling into the grasp of a malevolent global elite: "This elite is composed of the financial controllers of the world, the Rockefellers, the Rothschilds, and their ilk, along with their allied social stratum." Operating through the UN, he wrote in 1994, they were planning a world takeover for the year 2000. His malefactors were not only financiers but included a supporting cast of the Trilateral Commission, Skull and Bones, the Council on Foreign Relations, the Knights of Malta, and Masonry, together with the Mafia, major intelligence services, what he called the "Nazi International," and more. They all allegedly did the bidding of "New World Order controllers."[6]

By 1999, the year of his death, Keith had brought his antielitism within the darker confines of an occultic conspiracy, dominated by the Illuminati and the Masons. In the omnivorous manner of those drawn to what I call superconspiracy theories, Keith absorbed diverse ideas, including those of Michael Baigent. Baigent's theories—widely publicized in occult and New Age circles—include the assertion that Jesus did not die on the cross, but fled to Europe with Mary Magdalene; that they married and had children; and that their blood descendants established European royal families and hope one day to enthrone a "World King" in Jerusalem. This contention led Keith to predict that the year 2000, with its millennial associations, would provide the perfect time to unveil such a global pretender. Because superconspiracy theories are structured in the manner of nested Russian dolls, Keith could add this innermost circle of intrigue without sacrificing his previous interest in such relatively banal conspirators as the CIA and the Bilderbergers.[7]

By the mid 1990s, Keith had begun to draw on the entire paraphernalia of New World Order conspiracy theories. He published three lists of FEMA concentration-camp locations, together with a map. As for the likely camp inmates, he speculated that "This group might include prison overflow, unbending patriots, random dissidents, anti-New World Order loudmouths, and the politically incorrect, but most particularly . . . groups and individuals who are not willing to go along with the next 'baby step' of totalitarian control in the United States." In the latter category, he placed "individuals . . . not . . . willing to surrender their guns." Keith also became preoccupied with the possibility of mind control through electronic implants. He believed that the CIA had developed techniques for surveillance and behavioral control using implanted microchips, and he suggested that Timothy McVeigh's story about suffering such an implant was probably true.[8]

One of the stranger stories circulating in militia circles in the 1990s was that numerical sequences on road signs, instead of carrying such prosaic information as maintenance data, were coded instructions to direct foreign, UN-commanded troops when their New World Order masters signaled the final takeover of America. Keith clearly believed this was the case, and devoted an entire chapter of *Black Helicopters II* to explicating the code.[9]

As Keith's work more and more closely tracked the orthodoxies of the Christian patriot right, he began to employ increasingly tainted sources. These included William Pabst, who did much to spread the concentration-camp theory; as well as Mark Koernke, spinner of the most recondite conspiracy theories on the extreme right. Although there was no explicit anti-Semitism in Keith's work, he drew on a range of anti-Semitic sources, both past and present. The former included Nesta Webster, the British writer of the 1920s (discussed in chapter 3), Willis Carto's newspaper *The Spotlight*, and the writings of Eustace Mullins.[10]

In all of this, UFOs, alien abductions, and related themes played a subordinate role, but as time went on Keith gave them increasing attention. On the one hand, he seems never to have seriously suggested that UFOs did not exist. On the other, he was unwilling to attribute them to extraterrestrials. As early as 1992, he speculated that they were a creation of "those at the top" who were actually running things, utilizing secret technologies for their own purposes.[11]

As far as alien-abduction experiences were concerned, Keith was convinced that although the "abductees" believed they had been seized by aliens, they were in fact victims of more mundane forces. In his view, they were in fact guinea pigs in CIA mind-control research who were made to believe that they had been kidnapped by extraterrestrials. These false impressions helped to conceal the government's nefarious "brainwashing" activities. At the same time, the government allegedly spread disinformation in the ufology community in order to make the concept of alien abduction appear more credible.[12]

Given Keith's conspiracist predilections, it is scarcely surprising that he frequently drew on the *Alternative 3* broadcast discussed in chapter 5. Like Milton William Cooper, Keith could fit the UFO invasion scenario into an Alternative 3 frame. How better for the elite to exert total control over the world than by counterfeiting an extraterrestrial invasion? He was aware that the broadcast had all the earmarks of a hoax; but in view of the conspiracist principle that nothing is as it seems, even the hoax bore the signs of elite control, because it was a way of discrediting ufologists and muddying the waters about topics like planetary survival. In short, one could believe *Alternative 3* or disbelieve it; the conspiracy was behind it either way.[13]

From 1997 until his death in 1999, Keith took a somewhat different tack on alien matters. While he had no intention of rejecting New World Order theory, he began to suggest a more complex set of possibilities. The additional possibilities were made feasible by a different epistemological approach—specifically, a willingness to consider the existence of other, perhaps nonmaterial realities. Thus in his later work Keith suggested the actual existence of both aliens and government-induced alien experiences. In his last book, provocatively titled *Saucers of the Illuminati,* he speculated that the Illuminati might have discovered forms of magic that allowed UFOs to appear. Similarly, the so-called men in black (the sinister trios who allegedly harass those who threaten to reveal too much about UFOs) could be, he said, either occultists or denizens of some supernatural realm. In a 1998 lecture, he suggested that far from being bound to physical reality, human beings could travel disembodied through space and time in the manner of occultists' "astral projection."[14]

In short, by the time he died, Keith had not only absorbed virtually all of the New World Order ideas from the Christian patriot–militia subculture; he had also opted for multiple epistemologies that could accommodate virtually any views on aliens and UFOs. They might be "real" or counterfeit, terrestrial or extraterrestrial, harmless or malevolent, or all simultaneously.

David Icke: New Age Conspiracist

David Icke (1952–) is a far more flamboyant figure. He achieved a measure of celebrity in Britain prior to his association with either conspiracy theories or aliens, and his gift for self-promotion has extended his audience throughout the English-speaking world. He had already had two public careers prior to the involvements that make him a significant figure among conspiracists. He first achieved notice as a sportscaster on the BBC-2 television network. After he and the BBC parted on unfriendly terms, Icke became public spokesperson for the Green Party in Great Britain. His flair for the dramatic led *The Observer* newspaper to characterize him as "the Greens' Tony Blair."[15]

Icke's life took a dramatic turn in 1990 when he consulted a psychic healer to alleviate the symptoms of rheumatoid arthritis. During an early healing session, the healer began transmitting spirit messages that proclaimed Icke "a healer who is here to heal the earth and he will be world famous." Stimulated by this prophecy, in 1991 he felt an "enormous urge" to visit Peru—a locale long favored by occultists for the supposed strength of its spiritual forces. Not surprisingly, Icke claimed to have undergone an intense experience there during which "Energy was pouring from my hands with fantastic power . . . My feet continued to burn and vibrate for some 24 hours." The immediate effect of the Peruvian vision was to motivate him to a form of New Age missionizing uncongenial to both the BBC and the Green Party. Shortly thereafter, he began a new career as a writer and lecturer.[16]

Icke's evolving worldview took the form of a New Age conspiracism, outlined in four books published in a seven-year period: *The Robots' Rebellion* (1994), . . . *And the Truth Shall Set You Free* (1995), *The Biggest Secret* (1999), and *Children of the Matrix* (2001). Although they appeared within a few years of one another, and all described a purported cabal of world-dominating evildoers, the volumes contain significant differences. In particular, Icke's characterization of the evil forces changed, with an increasing emphasis on the role of nonhumans.

The conspiracy theory in *The Robots' Rebellion* did not differ significantly from what might be described as a generic New World Order concept: humanity is in thrall to "manipulators" who keep us from reaching a condition of full freedom. Icke refers to these plotters as "the Brotherhood." The Brotherhood consists of "an enormous network of secret societies" at whose apex stand the Illuminati. This set of nested conspiracies achieves its goals through control of the "world financial system" and its mastery of "mind control" techniques. Its goal is "a world government to which every continent would be subordinate," a plan that, according to Icke, had been laid out in *The Protocols of the Elders of Zion*. Although Icke is careful to suggest, in the manner of Cooper, that the Illuminati rather than the Jews wrote *The Protocols,* this is the first of a number of instances in which Icke moves into the dangerous terrain of anti-Semitism.[17]

The ideas presented in *The Robots' Rebellion* reprise the early New World Order concepts described in chapter 3. They differ little from material found in such authors as Webster or Pat Robertson. There is little concerning UFOs, beyond a brief but sympathetic reference to Cooper's claim that earthly conspirators have entered into an alliance with extraterrestrials.[18]

Although . . . *And the Truth Shall Set You Free* was published only a year later, it significantly extends the ideas presented in *The Robots' Rebellion*. In addition to more anti-Semitic material (discussed further in chapter 9), it greatly elaborates the concept of the Brotherhood in two ways: first, by a much more detailed description of the secret societies that allegedly compose its membership; and second, by explicitly linking the Brotherhood to extraterrestrial masters.

The "Global Elite," Icke wrote, operates the Brotherhood and through the Brotherhood the world, by controlling a "pyramid of manipulation." This pyramid consists of a set of hierarchical structures, each of which dominates a sphere of human life: banking, business, military, politics, education, media, religion, intelligence agencies, medicine and drug companies, and illegal drugs and organized crime. The lower a functionary is in any hierarchy, the less he or she is aware of carrying out the policies of the Brotherhood. This segmented view of the conspiracy was not particularly original, but it allowed Icke to present separate descriptions of each sector. The originality in his thesis lay in his new conviction that there is a layer of control above the Global Elite itself.[19]

The topmost level of the conspiracy Icke calls "the Prison Warders." He makes clear his view that the Prison Warders are extraterrestrials without being specific about where they came from: "A pyramidal structure of human beings has been created under the influence and design of the extraterrestrial Prison Warders and their overall master, the Luciferic Consciousness. They control the human clique at the top of the pyramid, which I have dubbed the Global Elite." The means by which these nonearthly Prison Warders exercise their control is left somewhat vague. In his work, Icke began to speak in New Age terms of "negative energy" and "blocking vibration." By utilizing these forces, the aliens have imprisoned us in "a frequency 'net' thrown around this planet."[20]

One consequence of Icke's new conviction was a greatly heightened interest in UFOs and their occupants. He now spoke of "The UFO Coverup." Icke believed that only such a cover-up could keep human beings from breaking out of "the vibratory prison." Once the truth was known, Icke believed, the power of the Global Elite and its masters would be broken.[21]

There was little to prepare Icke's readers for his third work, *The Biggest Secret*. The cover proclaimed it "The book that will change the world. . . . The blockbuster of all blockbusters," for in addition to the usual material on the Rothschilds and the Trilateral Commission, Icke now claimed to identify the nonhumans he regarded as the cause of humanity's enslavement.

The essence of the book's central thesis is as follows. The extraterrestrials come from the constellation Draco. They are reptilians who walk erect and may appear "humanoid" on casual inspection. They live not only on the planets from which they came but under the earth itself, in a hidden world of caverns and tunnels. There may be, wrote Icke, both "native" reptilians and "outer space" reptilians on earth at the same time. They control the Global Elite and Brotherhood by a combination of methods. They have crossbred with human beings, creating creatures that look human but are inwardly reptilian. These "hybrids" are "possessed" by their "fullblood" reptilian masters. The hybrid "bloodlines" continually interbreed, moreover, so that the Brotherhood is not simply nonhuman but is also the product of intentionally manipulated unions.[22]

Children of the Matrix is essentially an elaboration of the reptilian thesis presented in *The Biggest Secret*. In it, Icke integrates the concept of a malevolent serpent race with the more conventional conspiracism contained in his earlier works such as . . . *And the Truth Shall Set You Free,* presenting the reptilians as the capstone of a conspiratorial structure replete with usual collaborators like the Illuminati, the Rothschilds, and the Trilateral Commission. Icke also increases his emphasis on the "other-dimensional" origin of the reptilians. They supposedly come from and return to another dimension, providing the ultimate concealment. The resemblance of these ideas to the ones Keith was developing late in his life is clear, though it is less clear whether Icke was aware of Keith's speculations.[23]

Icke's notions expressed in *The Biggest Secret* and *Children of the Matrix* are bizarre even when viewed in the larger context of contemporary conspiracy theories. As the next chapter illustrates, he certainly did not invent the concept of evil inner-earth reptilians, an idea that spread rapidly in the 1990s; but no one has done more to spread it. Within months of *The Biggest Secret*'s publication, he claimed thirty thousand copies in print. At the same time, Icke conceded that the idea of reptilians operating from the fourth and fifth dimensions was not one that had gained general acceptance even among fellow conspiracy theorists: "some of the most fierce abuse that I've had since the book came out has not been from the public, actually, it's been from some other conspiracy researchers who can't get their head around anything beyond the physical." Icke's increasing insistence that the evildoers come from other dimensions has a number of advantages. It allows him to skirt such embarrassing questions as what part of the universe they come from and how they got here, and it allows them to violate the laws of nature at will by suddenly changing shape or location. At the same time, Icke can castigate his critics as stodgy materialists unable to grasp a new paradigm.[24]

Icke has moved aggressively to increase the size of his audience, with an elaborate Web site and speaking tours in North America, Australia, New Zealand, and South Africa, as well as publishing books and videotapes. He speaks variously to New Age believers seeking spiritual enlightenment and growth, to conspiracists and conspiracy-minded ufologists, and to those on the antigovernment right. The promoters of a 2001 lecture in Fort Worth, Texas, advertised Icke as someone who "teaches that every person, regardless of religious upbringing, corporate entanglements, needs to search for truth" in an enterprise that "includes developing the spiritual side of every person seeking truth." In 1996, by contrast, he spoke at a Reno, Nevada, "Constitutional Justice Conference" dominated by opponents of the Brady handgun law, including Mullins and white nationalist attorney Kirk Lyons.[25]

Icke has an ongoing relationship with the editors of the Phoenix publications (whose convoluted story is told in chapter 9), which pub-

lish purported communications received from a Pleiadean extraterrestrial named Hatonn. These publications—based at various times in
Tehachapi, California, and Las Vegas—represent the most openly anti-
Semitic segments of ufology; they are marked by an obsessive fear of a
global Jewish conspiracy against which the extraterrestrial called Hatonn warns virtuous earthlings. Icke was interviewed at length in these
journals in 1997 and 1999. In 1997, he lectured in Yelm, Washington, at
Val Valerian's Leading Edge Research Group, whose elaborate fusion of
ufology and the New World Order was described earlier.[26]

Icke's relationship with militias and Christian patriots is complex.
The London *Evening Standard* reported (correctly) in 1995 that "un-
canny parallels are emerging between Icke's thoughts . . . and the writings of senior figures in the armed militia movement in America." While
Icke has clearly sought to cultivate the extreme right, however, the
effort has not been without tension, largely a product of the New Age
baggage attached to his political ideas. As a result, his attitude about
the American radical right seems to be a mixture of admiration and
frustration.[27]

The positive side of Icke's ambivalence lies in his belief that Christian
patriots are the only Americans who know the truth about the New
World Order: "I have great sympathy in the way that they are trying to
expose some levels of the conspiracy." He calls the radical right a movement that "has understood many elements of the global conspiracy"
and admires *The Spotlight* for its "excellent research and . . . long and
proven record of accuracy."[28]

On the other side, Icke sees Christian patriots as dogmatists who are
nearly as rigid as their adversaries. He claims to have told one of them,
"I don't know which I dislike more, the world controlled by the Brotherhood, or the one you want to replace it with"—presumably, a world
dominated by Christian fundamentalism. He is also put off by the right's
belief that "spirituality, as expressed metaphysically in the New-Age
stuff, is the bloody devil."[29]

Keith, Icke, and the Radical Right

It is clear that neither Keith nor Icke has been a direct participant in
the radical right. Neither is known to have belonged to any of the
subculture's core organizations, be they militias, klans, or Christian
Identity groups. Keith published through *Steamshovel Press* and pub-

lishing houses that cater to conspiracist readerships. Icke's early work was issued by British New Age publisher Gateway, which allegedly dropped him because of concerns about anti-Semitic material. His later work has appeared under the imprint of Bridge of Love Publications, which seems entirely devoted to publishing work he has written or supports.[30]

Thus from a purely organizational standpoint, each has kept his distance from the American radical right. Nevertheless, each has absorbed its world view virtually intact. Indeed, there is no more complete codification of New World Order ideas about mind control and black helicopters than Keith's, and no fuller explication of its beliefs about ruling elites than Icke's. At the same time, both Keith and Icke challenge the epistemology of the radical right, based as it is on the claim that physical evidence provides all of the information one needs to penetrate to the truth about the New World Order. Icke rejected that view with his assertion that the reptilians influence our world through the fourth and fifth dimensions. Keith was clearly moving in a similar direction before his death. Both tried to fuse UFOs and their passengers with the New World Order by somehow locating either flying saucers or aliens in supramundane dimensions that confer superhuman power. There is little indication that such approaches will convince many in militia circles. As the earlier discussion of conspiracies suggests, New World Order believers routinely claim the ability to verify the conspiracy's existence and machinations by means of conventional rules of evidence.

Keith's final speculations and Icke's recent work, however, fall clearly into the category of improvisational millennialism. Both lay out end-of-history scenarios in which good and evil must fight a final battle. They construct these end-time scripts from an eclectic combination of ingredients—Babylonian mystery religions and *The Protocols of the Elders of Zion,* Masonic magicians and UFOs, the Illuminati and the UN. As everything in the conspiracist's world is interconnected, so every source may be mined for something useful, no matter what taboos may attach to it. Indeed, as pointed out earlier, the greater the stigma, the more attractive the source becomes, for the intensity of rejection is taken to be a measure of its truthfulness. Doubtless, Icke has gravitated to the reptilian literature in part because he takes its very outrageousness as a warrant of its validity.

Icke's appropriation of reptilian themes—bizarre as they are—and his success in disseminating them through books, lectures, and his Web site, raise questions about where such ideas originated. They arose almost contemporaneously with the post–World War II UFO sightings but from two entirely different sources: occultism and esotericism, and pulp fantasy fiction. The next chapter examines how the two were synthesized in the mid and late 1940s and quickly associated with alien visitation.

CHAPTER 7

Armageddon Below

As we have seen, much of UFO conspiracism mimics the New World Order ideas prevalent in Christian patriot circles. Tales of UN troops, black helicopters, and implanted microchips appear in both. But conspiracy-minded ufologists have also developed their own, idiosyncratic variations. The most distinctive of these variants concerns so-called inner-earth motifs.

The inner-earth materials place the alien presence underground—in tunnels, installations, and caverns. In some cases, the aliens come from outer space and merely choose a subsurface realm because they feel more secure there. In other instances, they are said to be native to this netherworld. Indeed, in some versions the flying saucers themselves are said to come from within the earth. The underground denizens are always described as malevolent. They are never enlightened "space brothers"—perhaps a reflection of the long-standing identification of underground realms with the domain of the dead. Hell is always below, heaven above.

The earliest inner-earth conspiracy theory focused on an underground alien base allegedly located near Dulce, New Mexico. As the Dulce legend spread, the alien base was said to be merely one element in a worldwide subterranean network. Ever more detailed descriptions dealt not only with the caverns and tunnels themselves but with their inhabitants. In early versions it was the domain of the evil Greys, the short, large-headed aliens of popular imagery; but more recently the Greys have been joined by reptoids—reptilian creatures who walk erect and may take on the general appearance, though not the nature, of human beings.

As the stories grew and were embellished, they drew on other influences, many of which existed long before ufology. The strongest of these influences was occultism, particularly Theosophy and neo-Theosophical groups, as well as crank science and the pulp fiction of the 1930s and 1940s.

The Dulce Legend

As mentioned in earlier chapters, the Dulce legend asserts that a vast underground base exists outside the town of Dulce in northern New Mexico. Pursuant to a treaty supposedly brokered between the aliens and the U.S. government, the base was to be operated jointly by the aliens and the CIA; treaty violations by the aliens eventually led to open conflict between them and their human collaborators. Such is the aliens' power, however, that they cannot be dislodged.

The earliest descriptions of activities around Dulce appear to have come from Paul Bennewitz, an Albuquerque businessman. Beginning in 1979, Bennewitz became convinced that he was intercepting electronic communications from alien spacecraft and installations outside of Albuquerque. By the early 1980s, he also believed he had discovered the Dulce base. The association of aliens with Dulce was not fortuitous, because the area had already attracted the attention of people interested in the paranormal.[1]

The Colorado–New Mexico border region had emerged as one of the major sites for the cattle-mutilation stories then current in the West, and as discussed in chapter 5, when cattle-mutilation stories appeared, reports of UFO sightings were generally not far behind. At the center of the reports in the Dulce area was a New Mexico State Police officer, Gabriel Valdez, who had been reporting sensational mutilations since the mid 1970s. These stories eventually attracted the attention of a wide range of individuals interested not only in the mutilations but in the possibility of alien visitations. Among them was Paul Bennewitz.[2]

By 1982, Bennewitz had begun to spread his ideas about the Dulce base to others in the ufology community. The first public charges came in the statement made by John Lear at the end of 1987. In 1988, William F. Hamilton III and Jason Bishop III, both of whom were to write extensively about the base, visited Dulce. Bennewitz himself wrote a paper, titled "Project Beta," dated October 15, 1988, which was mostly concerned with how the base might be successfully attacked. In a second public statement, on May 15, 1990, Lear announced that he had had "four independent confirmations" of Dulce's existence. The underground base story thereafter spread rapidly.[3]

Dulce proved to be an attractive legend for two reasons. In the first place, the Cold War had stimulated substantial discussion about and extensive implementation of "hardened" sites that could withstand nuclear attack to maintain the U.S. government's command and control capabilities. Such underground installations tended to be secret for security reasons, which gave a superficial plausibility to stories of yet another such bunker in northern New Mexico or adjacent areas of southern Colorado. The Dulce stories of grotesque experiments on abductees and of firefights between aliens and Delta Force, of course, lay well outside even the most far-fetched reports of secret underground bases. But such bizarre goings-on did not exceed the limits of other beliefs that already lay within the domain of stigmatized knowledge. In particular, Dulce proved compatible with long-standing ideas about an inner-earth domain—ideas that derived from crank-science notions of a hollow earth as well as motifs in occultism.[4]

Lore of the Inner Earth

For the past five centuries, ever since the spherical shape of the earth came to be generally accepted, there have been speculations about the planet's interior. For a number of reasons, it was long possible for some to maintain that another world lay within, perhaps with its own creatures and civilizations. The range of speculation existed in part because direct access to the earth's core was impossible; as a result, those on the surface could speculate with little fear of being quickly disproved. Limited access through caves only made the ultimate question more mysterious, as well as giving new life to a wide range of legends and folklore about strange creatures who emerged from the openings. As long as the earth's surface had not been fully explored and surveyed, it was also possible for some to argue that there were yet-undiscovered openings through which an intrepid explorer might reach the world within. These hypothesized entrances were usually placed at one or the other of the polar regions, where their presence could have remained undetected. Even after the progress of geology and exploration had made such views increasingly difficult to maintain, there was a fall-back position: belief that while the planet might not actually be hollow, its interior might be honeycombed with chambers connected by tunnels.[5]

Today, the difficulty of defending a hollow-earth theory has not stopped some individuals from doing so. Indeed, as new forms of communication, such as the Internet, have become available, the frequency with which such ideas are expressed increases rather than decreases. This trend occurs because more extensive communication networks facilitate the spread of all forms of stigmatized knowledge, regardless of the quantity or quality of supporting evidence. As one scholar of pseudoscience, Henry H. Bauer, points out, individuals "resistant to orthodoxy are likely to be so in a range of fields and not just in one." He also points out that opponents of one kind of orthodoxy often seek allies from among those opposed to an unrelated orthodoxy. The more aware rebels are of others whose views are unorthodox, the easier it is to identify potential allies. The quest for allies is structured by the nature of pseudoscience, which avoids seeking the consensus of the scientific community. Instead, its partisans utilize popular media and similar venues to present their views. To the extent that they receive support from those with academic credentials, it comes from individuals whose scientific expertise lies in areas remote from the matters in question. In this respect, changes in modes of communication can be crucial. Mechanisms like the Internet acquaint people who believe in one form of stigmatized knowledge with other forms. This process favors the expansion of their stigmatized-knowledge belief systems. Because those who accept stigmatized knowledge claims often link stigmatization to conspiracies, they argue that powerful and immoral forces have plotted to suppress or delegitimize ideas that are true but work against the plotters' interests. For this reason, those who believe the earth is hollow, or that aliens visit the earth in flying saucers, also often believe the world is run by a secret cabal.[6]

In the case of the inner-earth beliefs considered here, the claims of crank science partially overlapped with other ideas rooted in occultism. The occult beliefs in question involve claims that human societies have either in the past or in the present inhabited underground caverns, and that these subterranean groups have exerted powerful influences on those who live above.[7]

The most important occult writer on this subject was Madame Helena Petrovna Blavatsky (1831–1891), under whose inspiration the Theosophical Society was founded in 1875. Mme Blavatsky claimed to have recovered ancient wisdom and mystical teachings, many of Asian origin, that illuminated the nature of the cosmos and would stimulate human spiritual development. Blavatsky claimed to have received her esoteric knowledge from "Himalyan masters" in Tibet, but there is no evidence that she ever reached that country, which was closed to outsiders at the time. Instead, she seems simply to have cobbled together material from the mass of Asian religious texts and Western esotericism widely available in Europe. Nonetheless, her personal magnetism and flair for the dramatic gave her teachings the requisite air of authenticity. Blavatsky, while not a hollow-earth believer, was profoundly interested in ideas about an underground world, as a result of the influence of her contemporary, writer and populist politician Ignatius Donnelly (1831–1901). Donnelly was largely responsible for the late-nineteenth-century revival of interest in the lost continent of Atlantis.[8]

In line with Donnelly, Blavatsky believed that a superior civilization had once existed on Atlantis, before the island disappeared in a prehistoric catastrophe. Even though the continent itself had vanished, Blavatsky concluded that some of its works remained, notably a worldwide "net-work [sic] of subterranean passages running in all directions."[9]

She was also intrigued by reports of a second lost continent, referred to by some as Mu and by others as Lemuria. Mu/Lemuria had been popularized by a British engineer and businessman, James Churchward (1850–1936). While Atlantis was supposedly sited in the Atlantic, Mu/Lemuria was located in the Pacific Ocean and, like its eastern counterpart, was said to have sunk as a result of a geological cataclysm.[10]

Blavatsky's fascination with lost continents and their underground remains continued into the twentieth century among the Theosophists and their associates. Lost-continent themes quickly spread, because Theosophy had a tendency to splinter and throw off independent "prophets" and organizations. Insofar as subsequent UFO conspiracism is concerned, the two most important neo-Theosophists were Guy Ballard and Maurice Doreal.

Guy W. Ballard (1878–1939) was the founder, with his wife Edna, of the "I AM" Religious Activity. In 1930, Ballard claimed, he was truth-seeking on the slopes of Mount Shasta in Northern California when he met Ascended Master Saint Germain, who whisked him to caverns beneath the Grand Teton Mountains. Ballard had a number of subsequent meetings with Saint Germain, whose teachings became the basis of I AM's belief system. The Ballards' chief critic, Gerald B. Bryan, was quick to point out that Guy Ballard's published accounts of this and other paranormal experiences were shot through with contradictions. Nevertheless, the I AM Activity achieved considerable success, especially in the years just before Guy Ballard's death. The better-known contemporary movement, Montana-based Church Universal and Trium-

phant—established in 1958 and led by Mark Prophet and later by Elizabeth Clare Prophet—is an I AM offshoot.[11]

Mount Shasta has had a long association with occultism, both before
and after Ballard's epiphany. It has been particularly associated with lost
continents, whose survivors were said to have taken refuge in its interior. The connection with Mu has been particularly strong, because Mu
was thought to have been located in the Pacific Ocean, adjacent to or
even overlapping the West Coast. Hence refugees from its sinking fled
to the only part of their continent that did not sink, namely, Mount
Shasta.[12]

An even more significant Mount Shasta seeker was Maurice Doreal,
also known as Claude Doggins (d. 1963). Dr. Doreal, as he preferred to
be called, founded the Brotherhood of the White Temple in Denver
about 1930. He claimed that as he was lecturing in Los Angeles in 1931,
the year after Ballard's experiences, he met two Atlanteans who trans-
ported him to a gigantic cavern twelve miles beneath Shasta. Unlike
Ballard, who concentrated more on teachings than on subterranean locations, Doreal subsequently developed an elaborate inner-earth cos-
mology, including descriptions of underground races gleaned from the
testimony of the Atlanteans. Fearful of nuclear attack, he relocated the
Brotherhood to a rockbound valley west of Sedalia, Colorado, in the
late 1940s and early 1950s. Doreal achieved local notoriety with a prediction that a nuclear war would occur in 1953, from which he expected
to be protected by the mountain walls that surrounded his community.
While Ballard died well before the epidemic of UFO sightings, Doreal
was active for more than fifteen years of the modern UFO period, during which he incorporated extraterrestrials into his occult vision.[13]

The Shaver Mystery

In 1945, a science-fiction pulp magazine, *Amazing Stories,* began to
publish the work of a hitherto unknown author, Richard S. Shaver
(1907–1975). Shaver grew up in Philadelphia and Detroit, studied art,
and had a brief flirtation with communism. He was hospitalized briefly
for psychiatric problems in 1934, but there does not appear to have been
a clear diagnosis. His life during the late 1930s and early 1940s cannot
be traced, but he clearly took up work in the auto industry, where he
was at the time his publicly documented life resumed. Shaver wrote to
Amazing Stories's editor, Raymond Palmer, claiming that he had heard

voices emanating from unknown subterranean civilizations. Shaver seems clearly to have been delusional. He had spent eight years in a mental hospital, and while his stories about the origin of the voices were inconsistent, in the most common version, he first heard them through his welding equipment while working at a Ford Motor Company plant. Initially, he heard the thoughts of fellow workers, but they were soon displaced by voices he believed originated in the inner earth. In time, he found that he could hear the voices without his welding equipment and also became convinced he could telepathically visit the underground world.[14]

Shaver's initial writing took the form of letters to Palmer. Palmer encouraged his correspondent, who eventually turned in a novella that Palmer published in March 1945 as "I Remember Lemuria!" Palmer rewrote Shaver's original manuscript to incorporate the conventions of pulp fiction, though the extent of Palmer's changes in this and subsequent stories has remained a source of disagreement. In 1957, Palmer wrote that he accepted Shaver's story "as the statement of a man who sincerely believes every word he has said is the truth. As an editor, I expanded the basic 10,000 word manuscript to the 31,000 words, and added the 'action' and 'plot flavor' that would make it read less like a dull recitation." Be that as it may, there are two points about which there is no disagreement. First, despite the presence of characters, dialogue, and plot, in the manner of *Amazing Stories*'s traditional fiction, the magazine presented the Shaver stories as true, albeit retouched to make them more entertaining. Second, this and subsequent stories were extraordinary circulation builders, pushing readership from 135,000 to 185,000. Palmer's doctoring must have been extensive, for between 1945 and 1948, fully three-fourths of the magazine's issues contained work attributed to Shaver. Palmer, no mean marketer, quickly dubbed the material the Shaver Mystery, a label that continues to be applied.[15]

At the core of the Shaver Mystery was a complex mythology built around two types of "robots"—in fact, not robots at all, but human beings enslaved to their passions. These he divided into two varieties, the good "teros" (i.e., "integrated robots") and the malevolent "deros" ("detrimental robots"). In Martin Gardner's summary,

Long ago the earth had been the home of the Atlans and the Titans, godlike creatures who flourished on the now sunken continents of Atlantis and Lemuria. To protect themselves from harmful solar radiation they constructed enormous caverns below the earth's surface. But the rays still damaged them, and they were forced to abandon the planet. An inferior race of humans discovered the caverns and the fantastic machines the superbeings had left behind. Alas, radiation from the machines turned the humans into midgetlike idiots whom Shaver called the "deros."

The deros' psychic power can wreak havoc on the surface of the earth. The sensation caused by Shaver's reports quickly drew in other occult material. Thus in August 1946, the *Amazing Stories* editors wrote a short piece recommending Doreal's pamphlets to "all students of the Shaver matter." Doreal himself responded with a letter the following month, confirming that evil was indeed afoot in the caverns, and that humanity might well be a target.[16]

It is worth bearing in mind that the Shaver Mystery was well under way before the first publicized UFO sighting in 1947. Nonetheless, there were ample opportunities for linkage. In the first place, although Shaver focused on Lemurian survivors, he believed that thousands of years ago, some beings from earth had mastered space travel and colonized other worlds, from which they were in a position to return. In addition, just as Palmer was quick to see the opportunities presented by Shaver, so he immediately grasped the potential of flying saucers. Shaver himself eventually formulated a variety of UFO scenarios, ranging from raids from other planets to saucers emanating from the underground world. The Shaver material peaked in 1947, the saucers' initial year, and in 1948 Palmer's boss, William Ziff, ordered an end to it. Palmer himself left *Amazing Stories* soon after, and devoted much of his subsequent career to spreading belief in UFOs, particularly the view that they came from within the earth.[17]

Others were also quick to connect UFOs to Shaver's obsession with the inner earth. An exchange took place in *Amazing Stories* in 1947, after the editors reported that a certain W. C. Hefferlin had written a letter asserting that flying saucers came from a place called Rainbow City, alleged to be beneath the South Pole. A letter from Hefferlin to that effect was published in January 1948, though it may not have been the one initially referred to. At the time, Hefferlin and his wife were privately circulating a manuscript about flying saucers and underground cities in Antarctica, which was extending the ongoing interest in polar matters on the part of inner-earth believers. The essence of the Hefferlin manuscript was eventually published in a 1960 pamphlet directed at New Age readers.[18]

The Search for Agharti

Mount Shasta and the South Pole were not the only points of interest for inner-earth believers. They were also attracted to the idea of an underground realm in the interior of Asia. Somewhere in the Asian hinterland lay a society ruled by figures of incomparable wisdom and insight, from whom teachings of great spiritual depth would eventually come. The terminology for this place was confusing, since it was sometimes referred to as Agharti and sometimes as Shambhala. The two are sometimes treated as the names of different places, and sometimes differentiated in terms of respective forces of good and evil. Nonetheless, the usage has become so inconsistent that no conclusive basis for distinguishing them can be maintained. The question of which is employed seems to vary with the whim of the author.[19]

Agharti is the more common name in the literature examined here and generally refers to an underground city beneath Tibet or some adjacent part of inner Asia. The legend describing such a place seems to have developed first among French writers around the turn of the twentieth century, but the principal conduit in English was a 1922 volume by prolific Polish scientist and adventurer Ferdinand Ossendowski.[20]

Ossendowski devoted the final four chapters of his book *Beasts, Men and Gods* to an account of stories he claimed to have heard from Mongolian and Tibetan guides, princes, and lamas. According to these tales, Agharti and subsidiary underground realms were ruled by a "King of the World," a spiritually advanced figure of messianic properties who at some time in the future would "lead all of the good people of the world against all the bad." At the end of history, this subterranean monarch would bring his people to the surface to effect the final millennial consummation.[21]

Ossendowski was certainly not the only person seeking this land. Artist and mystic Nicholas Roerich was simultaneously searching for Shambhala and in time secured U.S. government aid with the help of his disciple, Vice President Henry A. Wallace. But it was primarily Ossendowski's Agharti writing that made its way into the stigmatized knowledge domain that was ultimately tapped by conspiracists.[22]

Ossendowski's book apparently fell into the hands of Raymond Palmer, for in May 1946 the *Amazing Stories* editor wrote a short but prominently displayed piece called "The King of the World?" In Palmer's hands, Agharti's ruler became a Venusian who would "when Mankind is ready . . . emerge and establish a new civilization of peace and plenty." A month later, one of Palmer's authors, Heinrich Hauser, summarized Ossendowski's account, describing the King of the World as one of a long line of elevated souls who, despite their remote location, used telepathy to influence "men of destiny" on the surface. Thus even as Shaver's stories of underground evil were running, they appeared side by side with suggestions of a subterranean redeemer.[23]

The Serpent Race

There was yet one significant piece missing from what was to become the underground-alien scenario of the 1990s. That component was the claim that subsurface dwellers were both evil and nonhuman—an important characteristic in light of the monstrous aliens who ultimately populated the Dulce base.

Descriptions of the Dulce aliens differed somewhat, but there was considerable agreement about their general appearance: they were short, walked upright, and resembled reptiles. A shadowy figure named Thomas Edwin Costello, who claimed he had been a security guard at Dulce, called them "reptilian humanoids." Hamilton described them as "small humanoid beings [that] may belong to the class we know as *Reptilia* rather than *Mammalia*." Bishop called them "descendent [*sic*] from a Reptilian Humanoid Specie."[24]

As earlier sections of this chapter demonstrate, there was ample raw material for stories of an underground world. But how did it come to be populated by reptilians? There are hints in the writings of Doreal. In a pamphlet called "Mysteries of the Gobi," he had offered an exotic revisionist history of the world, one of whose key features was an ancient war between human beings and a "Serpent Race." The latter, he wrote, had "bodies like man, but . . . heads . . . like a great snake and . . . bodies faintly scaled." They also possessed hypnotic powers that allowed them to appear fully human when necessary. Doreal suggested that in this long-ago era of primeval warfare, the Serpent Race had been exterminated. But in another—and possibly later—pamphlet, "Flying Saucers: An Occult Viewpoint," Doreal significantly altered his position, arguing that the Serpent Race were extraterrestrials and that they had not been destroyed. Instead, their members existed in a state of suspended animation, to be revived in the twentieth century as allies of the Antichrist.[25]

Many of the same ideas also appeared in a long poem, "The Emerald Tablets," reputedly the work of "Thoth, an Atlantean Priest-King." Doreal claimed to have been given access to the tablets from the Great Pyramid of Egypt in 1925, when he translated them. According to the tablets,

> Yet, beware, the serpent still liveth
> in a place that is open at times to the world.
> Unseen they walk among thee
> in places where the rites have been said.
> Again as time passes onward
> shall they take the semblance of man.

In his accompanying commentary, Doreal repeats earlier assertions about their serpent heads and hypnotic powers, adding a disconcerting political warning: "gradually, they and the men who called them took over the control of the nations." Doreal's "translation" of the tablets was used extensively by David Icke in his book on the reptilians, *Children of the Matrix*. In Icke's account, the tablets had been found in a Mayan temple, where they had been deposited by Egyptian priests. Their supposed author, Thoth, had written them thirty-six thousand years ago in an Atlantean colony in Egypt.[26]

Pulp Fiction

Where did Doreal's ideas come from? The issue is made more complex by the fact that it is difficult to date his writings. He apparently began to publish about 1940 and continued to do so until his death in 1963. His work from the early 1940s consists of fairly traditional biblical exegesis. Most of the pamphlets, if they bear any date at all, bear that of their most recent reprinting. It seems likely, however, that the material on the Serpent Race first appeared sometime between the mid 1940s and the mistaken nuclear war prediction of 1953.[27]

Although Doreal and the others spoke of the serpent race as a confirmable historic reality, the idea almost certainly came from pulp fiction—indeed, from publications similar to those in which Shaver's work had appeared. Here again we encounter the fact-fiction reversals characteristic of stigmatized knowledge. Shaver's work read like fiction and had been rewritten by Palmer to simulate fiction, yet both Shaver and Palmer insisted it was true. The original serpent-race material was different, in that it was a case of intentional fiction that came to be appropriated as fact.

In all likelihood, the notion of a shape-changing serpent race first came from the imagination of an obscure pulp fiction author, Robert E. Howard (1906–1936). Howard was a fantasy writer of the sword-and-sorcery variety, best known for his character Conan the Barbarian. In August 1929, he published a story in *Weird Tales* magazine called "The Shadow Kingdom" in which the evil power was the snake-men whose adversary, Kull, came from Atlantis. These creatures had the bodies of men but the heads of serpents, just as Doreal was later to assert, and like his Serpent Race, they had the capacity to change shape, appearing human when they wished. In Howard's story they were thought to have been destroyed, but they returned insidiously, insinuating themselves into positions of power.[28]

While Howard was well known among devotees of fantasy fiction, he never received widespread recognition and committed suicide at an early age. He shared a common mythology, however, with two other *Weird Tales* authors, Clarke Ashton Smith and the much better known H. P. Lovecraft. Both Ashton Smith and Lovecraft consequently incorporated serpent men into their own work. Doreal's appearance in *Amazing Stories* provides grounds for believing he was familiar with pulp fiction and thus makes plausible his appropriation of one of Howard's motifs.[29]

It is clear that by the early 1950s, the pieces were being put together in a manner that would make them available to the Dulce writers nearly forty years later. This is strikingly evident in a 1951 publication by Robert Ernst Dickhoff, *Agharta*. Dickhoff styled himself the "Sungma Red Lama of the Dordjelutru Lamasery," though in fact the lamasery was apparently located in Dickhoff's New York City bookshop. Dickhoff cited "The Emerald Tablets," but did not mention Doreal by name. In addition, he wrote about humanoid serpent men who came from Venus, exploiting an antediluvian tunnel system in order to infiltrate and capture Atlantis and Lemuria. Survivors of the sunken continents escaped to underground hideouts in Agharta and in the Antarctic Rainbow City. Although the serpent men seem to have been defeated, they and their agents have infiltrated high policymaking circles through their powers of mind control. The remaining reptilians lie in polar suspended animation, awaiting the moment to strike.[30]

By the time reports of underground alien installations began to appear in the late 1980s, the fictional scenario of reptoids, presented as fact by occultists like Dickhoff, was available, fully formed.

The Reptilian Conspiracy

In the wake of the Dulce base stories, increasingly elaborate plots came to be floated based on the twin themes of reptilian aliens and an underground world. The most indefatigable advocate of a link between the two has been a writer identified by the pseudonym Branton. Though sometimes said to be "a collective-name for a group of individuals," Branton has more often been identified as a Utah-based writer named Bruce Alan Walton or Bruce Alan De Walton. Most Branton material has appeared in the form of long Internet postings, but in 1999 and 2000, three Branton volumes were published. These, as well as many of the Internet items, consist of long extracts from the writings of others, with Branton's commentaries and interpolations. In addition, closely related material has been published under the names Bruce Walton and Bruce A. Walton, some of which has been cited by Branton.[31]

By his own account, Branton is a former Mormon in his thirties, who grew up in "the Southeast corner of Salt Lake Valley." He claims to be an abductee who has had contact through "altered states" of consciousness with human beings living in the inner earth. He admits to "a jail record . . . a result of my own irresponsibility," as well as "emotional and psychological disabilities resulting from years of suppressed interactions with what I believe to be malevolent alien agendas and certain human agencies that are or were involved with them." He admits that he has no conscious memory of the nonhuman species, but claims " 'intuitive' memories in the form of dreams and so on of being involved in some sort of government-alien interaction scenario, since a child." The scenario contained elements developed in his writings, including treaties between the government and aliens, underground colonies of both humans and nonhumans, and, of course, reptilians. He claims to have met a number of individuals in the Salt Lake City area who have had direct experience with this subterranean domain.[32]

Branton's complex and convoluted conspiracism has led one reader to characterize it as "high-fantasy." His own attempts to summarize it provide the following schematic view. There has been a cosmic multi-species war under way for millennia in which aliens and their human allies are arrayed in massive coalitions. The major locus of this war is a gigantic series of underground caverns, tunnels, and installations beneath the western United States. This domain he refers to as Dreamland—a term that ufologists normally apply to the base known as Area 51 north of Las Vegas, but that is here applied to "an underground system of vast

proportions." According to Branton, the United States is "the last ob-
stacle standing in the way of the joint Reptilian-Bavarian Illuminati's
NEW WORLD ORDER, which is based after the Reptilian collective-
mind-control/annihilation-of-consciousness system as opposed to the
Christian idea of INDIVIDUAL liberty and free thought." The outcome
of this subterranean war will decide whether good or evil rules this part
of the universe.[33]

As others have taken up the reptilian theme, Branton's influence has
spread. By 2001, David Icke was including lengthy quotations from
Branton's Web sites in his own writings as the voice of authority on reptoid questions. Icke has applied all of his considerable marketing savvy
to legitimizing the reptilian hypothesis. His elaborate and sophisticated
Web site contains a large section called "The Reptilian Connection." A
similar site, maintained by John Rhodes, is called simply reptoids.com.[34]

The Serpent in the Garden

The interrelationship of inner-earth and reptilian themes is complex.
They are often intertwined but occasionally separate. The link stems
from their associations with death and evil. The underworld is the domain of the dead and dwelling place of those whose lives have not mer-
ited a heavenly reward. In the popular imagination, it is the location of
hell, where the devil supervises the punishments endured by the wicked.
And Satan, the Evil One, is also the serpent who deceived Eve in the
Garden of Eden, bringing humanity sin and mortality.

Identifying the reptilians with the serpent in the story of the Fall allows conspiracists to appropriate the Bible's authority and to claim biblical evidence for the reptoid-human confrontation. Just as they recycle
other forms of evidence such as myth, folklore, newspaper reports, science, and pseudoscience, so they use biblical stories to bolster their
claims. In the manner of improvisational millenarians, they see no difficulty in combining materials that employ radically different vocabular-
ies and arguments.

According to conspiracists, the serpent in Eden was, if not the first
reptoid, certainly the first to interact with human beings. For Branton, it
is enough that the serpent's cunning, described in Genesis, fits his contemporary counterparts. Costello—the alleged Dulce security guard,
whose interview Branton reprints—speculates that the reptoids, including the one who deceived Eve, are "the Fallen Angels." Rhodes sees

the rebellion at Eden's Tree of Knowledge repeated today and asks, "Could the DULCE BASE be the modern TREE OF KNOWLEDGE [cunning] where the seed of the SERPENT and the seed of EVE have once again met in an unholy alliance, yet in a much more sophisticated form?"[35]

This allusion to the seed of the serpent and the seed of Eve echoes the two-seedline theme common in the white-supremacist Christian Identity movement. There, it takes the form of an anti-Semitic theology in which the serpent sexually seduces Eve, thereby fathering Cain, who for Christian Identity theorists is the putative ancestor of Jews (Eve goes on to bear two other sons by Adam, Abel and Seth). The two seedlines are then destined to struggle until one destroys the other at the end of history.[36]

Reptoid conspiracists retain elements of two-seedline theology without giving it Christian Identity's anti-Semitic twist. But like Christian Identity exegetes, they fasten on the Hebrew word for the serpent (*nachash*), which they too allege implies an intelligent creature who walks upright: "The original 'Nachash' was not actually a 'snake,' . . . but actually an extremely intelligent . . . creature possessed with the ability to speak and reason." The two species are involved in nothing less than a war of apocalyptic dimensions, "a Species War, between the Eveadamic Seed and the 'Serpent' (draconian) Seed."[37]

In some cases, however, the conspiracists' belief in a primordial conflict between the seed of the Serpent and the seed of Eve moves perilously close to Christian Identity's anti-Semitic theology. Thus the pseudonymous Commander X, supposedly a "Retired Military Intelligence Operative," resists the idea that any single people constitutes the serpent seedline: "The Serpent's seed is today sown among all nations, races and peoples." Nevertheless, he links the seedline with high finance, a common coded designation for Jews: "Today, as always, they occupy positions of authority and financial power." Describing them as a "counterfeit race," he implies the same duplicity and misrepresentation evident in Christian Identity theology when it asserts that Jews merely masquerade as descendants of the Israelites.[38]

The ultimate origin of the reptilians is immaterial. They may be native to the earth, as some conspiracists maintain; or visitors from other worlds; or an earth species that left and has now returned. What matters to devotees of the reptilian thesis is that reptilians are the embodiment of cosmic evil, Satan's representatives on earth. With their minions and allies—hybrid reptoid-humans and humans manipulated into their service—they seek nothing less than the destruction of the human race.

In the hands of the reptoid conspiracists, therefore, legends like the Dulce stories take on a millennial significance, for Dulce and underground warrens like it have become the locus for the final conflict. The battles, said to be already in progress, are thus the prelude to a subterranean Armageddon.

CHAPTER 8

UFOs and the Search for Scapegoats I

Anti-Catholicism and Anti-Masonry

The more widely New World Order conspiracy theory has diffused, the harder it is to generalize about its racist propensities. In at least some of the venues where it appears (e.g., in John Birch Society material), it is devoid of anti-Semitism and racism. In other cases (e.g., Pat Robertson's book *The New World Order*), there is no overt anti-Semitism, but anti-Semitic motifs are clearly evident. Much New World Order material pays little attention to nonwhites, as its focus is on an all-powerful elite that allegedly manipulates nations. Because New World Order adherents can either ignore or adopt racist and anti-Semitic ideas, their constructs have spread rapidly; they may be "sanitized" or not, according to the preference of the believer. Hence they can be presented to new audiences in ways that make them less offensive. As New World Order materials passed into the UFO subculture, however, matters took an odd turn.

Some New World Order ideas in ufology have been free of any overt racial or religious bias, but a surprising amount has not. UFO conspiracists often reproduce the biases of nineteenth-century American nativism, concentrating on the malevolence of the three groups that obsessed nativists in that century: Catholics, Freemasons, and Jews. There is no immediately evident reason for these groups to gain so prominent a place in the literature of space aliens. Before that question can be addressed, it is necessary to discuss the place Catholics, Freemasons, and Jews occupied in nativist thought, and the role they play in contemporary ufology.

Nativism

Nativism's most influential chronicler, John Higham, suggests that the term was coined about 1840 by opponents of the antiforeign parties that had begun to appear in eastern seaboard cities. In search of a more precise definition, he suggests that "Nativism . . . should be defined as intense opposition to an internal minority on the ground of its foreign (i.e., 'un-American') connections." More concretely, as David Bennett points out, it came to stand for "fear of 'foreign' religions and 'foreign' peoples." [1]

Although the breadth of these definitions suggests that a wide range of groups might attract the attention of nativists, in fact nineteenth-century nativists had a short list of enemies. Higham identifies three pervasive themes: anti-Catholicism, fear of foreign radicals, and fear of non-Anglo-Saxon "races." The roots of all, and especially of the first two, could be found prior to 1800. Anti-Catholicism entered with the Puritan settlers of New England, while antiradicalism was evident by the late 1700s. Regardless, each of the themes reached peak intensity in the nineteenth century.[2]

Among the groups most often targeted by nativists, three in particular stand out. First, as already indicated, the animus toward Catholics began early in the colonization process and grew explosively after the mid nineteenth century. Not only were Catholics present in increasing numbers, but they tended to be immigrants from southern and eastern Europe, and therefore despised not only for their religion but for their non-Anglo-Saxon ethnicities. Fear of the second group, Masons, arose from the more general apprehension about "alien" ideologies that grew out of the insecurities of a newly independent state. This fear increased in proportion to an ideology's allegedly hidden and duplicitous modes of operation. Thus secret societies, of which the Masonic ones were preeminent, fell under particular suspicion. Finally, by the late nineteenth century, the immigration of large numbers of Jews from eastern Europe led to hostility based both on religious prejudice and on fear of non-Anglo-Saxon peoples, in a manner not unlike that which had faced Catholics.

Richard Hofstadter observed in the 1960s that "Anti-Catholicism has always been the pornography of the Puritan," by which he meant that anti-Catholic propaganda mixed fear of the church with lurid tales of "libertine priests, . . . licentious convents and monasteries, and the like." Opposition to the Catholic Church was a function not only of its allegedly foreign character—believers and clergy were said to owe fealty to a distant pontiff—but of its rituals and institutions as well.[3]

In time, these motifs came to be linked to themes of American nationalism. By the 1870s, with American nationalism in the ascendant, Catholics were suspect as the pawns of a foreign power whose interests were thought to diverge from those of the United States. Through the efforts of such nativist organizations as the American Protective Association, these fears peaked in the 1890s, a time of both rampant nationalism and (at least in the early part of the decade) severe economic dislocations.[4]

The line between anti-Masonry and other forms of nativism proved difficult to draw. In theory, the anti-Masons of the 1820s and 1830s feared the order because they identified it with such subversive organizations as the Bavarian Illuminati, discussed in chapter 3. Masonry was an alien secret society boring at American institutions from within. But its very secrecy allowed its enemies to link it to a variety of other groups and organizations, including Jews and Jesuits, prefiguring the more complex conspiratorial linkages of later periods. All were deemed to be inimical to republicanism by virtue of both their foreign origins and their secret rites and teachings: as Bennett points out, "Like Catholic conspiracy, Masonic secrecy represented an unpardonable sin in an age of egalitarianism."[5]

Because Freemasonry is a secret fraternal order, it has been particularly vulnerable to the projected fears and fantasies of others. In point of fact, however, its origins were far less dramatic than either its representatives or its opponents claim. Freemasonry, far from having a continuous existence since ancient times, originated in the early modern period as an outgrowth of some artisan guilds, beginning in the late 1600s.[6]

The original Masonic lodges—guild organizations for stonemasons—began to go into decline in the late seventeenth century. Along with other craft organizations, they suffered from the expansion of market economies, which more and more effectively challenged the hold guilds maintained over skilled crafts. The Masonic organizations, faced with this crisis, sometimes opted for an unusual solution: the admission to their lodges of gentlemen unconnected to the craft. From the lodges' standpoint, this brought in needed revenue. From the standpoint of the new members, there was a cachet associated with the Masons' symbolism, ritual, and reputed antiquity. By the early 1700s, few of the genuine traditional Masons remained in English lodges, so thoroughly did the new Masons supersede the old.

This transformed membership brought a range of new ideas into Masonic lodges, which contributed to their later reputation as hotbeds of radicalism: opposition to absolute monarchy, support for social mobility, religious tolerance, and, in some circles, pantheism and republicanism. Given the presence of such ideas, it was inevitable that some Masons would participate in the American and French revolutions, a phenomenon that gave a gloss of plausibility to the conspiracy theories of early anti-Illuminatists such as John Robison and Abbé Barruel.

Like the Catholics, Masons were believed to have hidden lives, enforced in this case by oaths and initiations about which their enemies evinced an obsessive interest. Notwithstanding the doctrinal chasm separating Masonry and Catholicism, anti-Masons often assumed that secret organizations necessarily cooperated with one another. This presumption introduced a theme that was to be more highly developed in the twentieth century—namely, the belief that nothing is as it seems, and that apparent enemies were in reality covert allies.[7]

Compared with anti-Catholicism and anti-Masonry, large-scale anti-Semitism was a latecomer to America, ignited only by the mass immigration that began in the late 1800s. Once introduced, however, it was not inhibited by the fact that Judaism was neither a secret society nor a centrally organized religious community. Seymour Lipset and Earl Raab, in their study of right-wing extremism, remark that "They had no Pope and no Vatican, but a special aura of secrecy and intrigue deeply imbedded in the folklore of Christian civilization." This perception, developed over centuries of ghettoization, helps explain why, by the turn of the twentieth century, Jews were scapegoats for other immigrant groups as well as the objects of scorn on the part of native-born elites. Although earlier Sephardic and German Jews had suffered occasional discrimination, the rapidity with which they assimilated and their relatively small numbers blunted the force of anti-Semitism. Their Eastern European coreligionists, who came in the last decades of the nineteenth and the first decades of the twentieth centuries, lacked these advantages. Their numbers were much larger, and their impoverished lives in the shtetls of the Russian Empire left them far less able to adapt quickly to America.[8]

Finally, the folk image of the Jew as moneylender and economic manipulator fitted uncomfortably well with the biases of late-nineteenth-century politics, particularly those of populism. Then, as later, American radicals demonstrated a peculiar fascination with the role of money in human history, demonizing bankers, hypothesizing outlandish monetary schemes, and imagining bizarre financial conspiracies. In such a milieu, Jews attracted unwanted attention out of proportion to their numbers.

These themes of hatred for Catholics, Masons, and Jews—however important they might be in historical terms—might be thought largely irrelevant to the present. Indeed, Bennett argues persuasively that by the post–World War II years, nativism was, for all practical purposes, dead: "By the end of World War II, the demise of nativism—that assault on alien people—had eliminated one part of [the] ancient right-wing tradition. Robbed of its intellectual underpinning, weakened by the political, economic, demographic, and social changes of the interwar years, nativism was no longer viable by 1950." Anti-Semitism declined rapidly, a Catholic was elected president, and little negative was heard about the Masons.[9]

Yet in one strange byway, the old hatreds are not merely preserved, they prosper. That byway is the world of political conspiracy theories, and particularly those linked to concerns about UFOs. In that literature—cheek by jowl with speculation about alien beings and interstellar spaceships—are diatribes against the Masons and the Illuminati, the pope and the Jesuits, the Anti-Defamation League and the Jewish banker. It is a milieu in which *The Protocols of the Elders of Zion* is approvingly cited and obscene rituals in the Vatican are taken for granted.

This nativist renascence is peculiar for a number of reasons. First, it contradicts the broader tendencies to which Bennett refers. Second, it occurs among people ostensibly concerned about cosmic matters, not the mundane details of national policy; they inhabit a science-fiction realm of alien beings and distant worlds. Third, many of its purveyors disclaim any animus toward individual Jews, Catholics, or Masons. They hasten to assure their audiences that they do not countenance prejudice. Finally, despite their fascination with the advanced technology that the aliens allegedly deploy, ufologists' nativism is steeped in earlier eras. They draw freely on such figures as Abbé Barruel in the eighteenth century, Alexander Hislop in the nineteenth, and Nesta Webster in the early twentieth. It is as if for them no idea has ever been lost or forgotten, no matter how much it has been overtaken by changing attitudes or more reliable knowledge.

Contemporary conspiracy theories cannot be easily divided into those that concentrate on Catholics, those that concentrate on Masons, and those that concentrate on Jews. As conspiracy theories have become increasingly broad and multilayered, they have identified an ever-wider array of conspiratorial agents. I concentrate here only on the groups whose targeters draw on traditional nativist concerns, and for convenience I discuss them individually, bearing in mind that more often than not, the same conspiracist writer may refer to all three. I examine conspiracy ideas focusing on the Catholics and Freemasons in this chapter, and those focusing on the Jews in chapter 9.

Catholics, Jesuits, and the Vatican

The Roman Catholic Church has become an attractive target for conspiracy theorists in the past half-century not because of doctrinal disputes but because of the church's perceived organizational structure. Unlike nineteenth-century Protestant nativists, who had doctrinal disputes with the church or regarded it as inimical to democratic institutions, contemporary anti-Catholic conspiracy theorists have little interest in theology and even less in democratic politics. Instead, their anti-Catholicism springs from their conviction that all significant power is wielded in secret. Hence, to their mind, the Catholic Church, with its hierarchical structure and international reach, is the model secret society. Not surprisingly, both the Vatican and the Jesuit order occupy prominent places in contemporary conspiracism.

Three strands of anti-Catholicism have emerged as particularly important in UFO variations on New World Order conspiracy theory. First, many conspiracists trace the Catholic Church back to an obscene pre-Christian religion allegedly practiced in Babylonia by Nimrod and his descendants. Second, anti-Catholic conspiracists often assign an important role to Jesuits, who allegedly work in concert with other secret centers of evil, such as the Illuminati. Third, the pope supposedly possesses secret knowledge too explosive to reveal to the world at large and often associated with the messages transmitted by Marian apparitions. In addition, the Vatican is sometimes believed to be infiltrated by conspirators and impostors who have taken control of the church's administrative machinery.

Numerous believers in UFOs and alien visitors subscribe to a common myth of origin concerning the Catholic Church. This myth links the church to an alleged "Babylonian 'Mystery Religion,'" originating in "the unholy . . . incestuous relation of Semiramis and Nimrod the King of Babylon." This Babylonian religion of sexual perversion and human sacrifice allegedly metamorphosed into a Christian ecclesiastical structure. David Icke notes, "The Roman Church and the Babylonian Brotherhood are one and the same." According to the pseudonymous writer Branton, the Catholic "Mary Queen of Heaven" is "no doubt the same pagan goddess worshipped by the ancient Babylonians—none other than the ancient Queen Semiramis." [10]

This notion of church origins can be traced to an anti-Catholic tract by a Scottish divine, Alexander Hislop, first published in Edinburgh in 1853. *The Two Babylons; or, The Papal Worship Proved to Be the Worship of Nimrod and His Wife* erected a complex structure of argument around the obscure biblical figures of Nimrod and his father, Cush. Cush allegedly built the city of Babylon, later governed by his son Nimrod and Nimrod's consort, Semiramis, who created an obscene and bloody cult. Their religion subsequently went underground, only to emerge in disguised form as the Catholic Church, which Hislop took to be the "Mystery Babylon" of the Book of Revelation. [11]

In addition to an insistence on the church's fundamentally evil character, conspiracists seek to expose what they regard as its innermost centers of power. In this respect, the Jesuits, with their history of discipline and their direct relationship with the pope, are a favorite target. Jesuits figure prominently in contemporary UFO conspiracy theories because, as a tightly structured order, they can be accommodated among the secret societies that obsess conspiracists. Milton William Cooper, in his widely read book *Behold a Pale Horse*, follows a lengthy discussion of the Illuminati and the Trilateral Commission with what purports to be the oath of some Catholic organization (he suggests the Jesuits, Knights of Columbus, and Knights of Malta as possibilities). The blood-curdling oath commits the taker to renounce all allegiance to Protestant or liberal rulers; to obey unquestioningly the commands of the pope, his representatives, or any "superior of the Brotherhood of the Holy Father of the Society of Jesus"; and, finally, to deal with Protestants and Masons by "rip[ping] up the stomachs and wombs of their women, and crush-[ing] their infants' heads against the walls in order to annihilate their execrable race." While Cooper considers it "highly unlikely that it is a forgery," it has all the earmarks of a nineteenth-century nativist fabrication, with its emphasis on the genocidal extermination of Protestants. [12]

Although the oath published by Cooper groups Protestants and Masons together as mortal enemies of the church, the conspiracy literature often asserts that Jesuits and Masons work together for common, diabolical ends. Their opposition is supposedly manufactured in order to mask the scope and cohesiveness of the conspiracy. This motif—that

enmity has been deliberately created in order to camouflage cooperation—is, in fact, common in conspiracist literature. Along with links
between Jesuits and Masons, we find charges of cooperation between
communists and capitalists, Jews and Nazis, the United States and the
Soviet Union. Branton claims that the Jesuits not only cooperate with
Masons but actually created Scottish Rite Masonry, and Commander X
blames the Jesuits for creating Nazism. Conspiracists take it for granted
that the Illuminati are linked to the Jesuits through some Masonic
network; Branton does not provide the text of an alleged Jesuit oath
but paraphrases it as part of a discussion of the Illuminati as "a Jesuit
invention." [13]

At times the network of relations becomes so complex that the conspiracists themselves are confused. An Internet posting of uncertain authorship claims that there are multiple Masonic conspiracies, some tied
to Jesuits, some tied to Jews, some to Wiccans, and some to Bilderbergers. But wait, the author tells us, there may be yet another level of plots,
in which the various Masonic cabals are tied to different extraterrestrial
civilizations. Indeed, the writer cannot quite determine whether the
Masonic-alien alliances are fighting with each other or are merely arms
of a single plot to take over the earth.[14]

A thread that links contemporary conspiracy literature with the ful-
minations of nineteenth-century nativists is the theme of sexual violation and perversion. The so-called convent literature of the nineteenth
century, epitomized by the supposed autobiography *The Awful Disclo-
sures of Maria Monk* (1836), painted a picture of priests and members of
Catholic religious orders as sexual predators. That motif has resurfaced
in the contemporary work *Trance Formation of America,* allegedly the
memoirs of a Michigan woman, Cathy O'Brien. O'Brien claims to have
been trained since childhood as a government "sex slave," and then to
have been ravished by a succession of high government officials, including presidents Gerald Ford and George H. W. Bush, and Vice President
Dick Cheney. She claims that her recovered memories also include
sexual violation by priests. The church allegedly worked together with
government mind-control projects such as Project Monarch and MK-
ULTRA, discussed in chapter 4.[15]

O'Brien's book, coauthored with her "deprogrammer," Mark Phillips, purports to expose a CIA program to produce "mind-controlled
slaves" for the sexual whims of "New World Order leaders." Her narrative simultaneously implicates religious institutions and well-known
politicians in a macabre quasipornography that is eerily reminiscent

of nativist convent tracts, but for the contemporary apparatus of alleged scientific mind-control technology. O'Brien's claim that President George H. W. Bush turned into a "lizard-like 'alien'" in her presence has given her book a special cachet among devotees of reptilian theories, such as Icke.[16]

Trance Formation of America and related confessional materials have had a wide circulation, appearing in the New World Order literature as well as UFO conspiracy writing. Their attraction lies in their message that the lack of popular acceptance of conspiracy beliefs results from the alleged power the conspirators have to control the minds and memories of those who "know too much." Hence believers can think of themselves as heroic souls who have had the strength to break free of mind-control bonds. The subsidiary theme of sexual violation connects the contemporary narratives with the earlier tradition that linked perverted sexuality with secret religious rites. Icke smugly remarks that "The Roman Catholic Church is the epitome of hypocrisy and deeply, deeply, sick."[17]

A related strain of conspiracism with antireligious overtones is the pseudonymous Branton's anti-Mormon UFO material. Branton was raised in the Church of Jesus Christ of Latter-Day Saints and apparently still resides in Utah. For Branton's purposes, the Mormon Church is an appealing target because, like Roman Catholicism, it is hierarchically organized, with the appearance of secretive decision making at the summit. In addition, its underground repository for the safekeeping of genealogical records, together with the computerized storage of the records, fits well into existing New World Order scenarios. Despite the nineteenth-century tradition of sexually charged anti-Mormon materials, with their obsessive concern about plural marriage, Branton makes no charges of Mormon sexual misconduct. The reason appears to be his desire to target the official church leadership rather than Mormon schismatics, some of whom still practice plural marriage. Indeed, Branton evinces some sympathy for Latter-Day Saints sectarians, whom he calls "Patriots" trying to warn the church about the dangers of the New World Order.[18]

In an environment in which such charges are leveled at church leaders, it is hardly surprising that the intersection of UFO and New World Order conspiracies should find a place for the Vatican and the papacy. The Vatican and the pope enter principally through speculations about the so-called secrets of Fatima, as well as through allegations that a recent pope was murdered and replaced by an impostor. The secrets of Fatima were a series of revelations supposedly communicated by the Virgin to a group of Portuguese children in 1917. While the first two secrets were made public in 1941, the third was transmitted to the Vatican in 1959 and read by the pope, but not made public until spring 2000. The third secret has been at the center of a quasisectarian subculture within Catholicism since the 1970s. Some elements of this subculture have been preoccupied with a struggle against a communist conspiracy, and others have been principally concerned to reverse the reforms instituted by the Second Vatican Council. When the text of the third secret was released, Cardinal Karl Ratzinger observed, "A careful reading of the text of the so-called third 'secret' of Fatima . . . will probably prove disappointing or surprising after all the speculation it has stirred. No great mystery is revealed; nor is the future unveiled." Given the mindset of conspiracism, however, the likely consequence will be a new charge of a cover-up through which the true text of the secret has been suppressed.[19]

Before the third secret's release, however, its contents had become a concern for UFO conspiracists. Thus, in *Behold a Pale Horse,* Cooper claimed that the secret had been investigated by inner circles of the U.S. government, who found, through "Vatican moles," that it concerned the Antichrist and the end-times. This inquiry also revealed that the Fatima apparition was engineered by the aliens—an explanation the aliens allegedly confirmed. Although Cooper later had second thoughts about whether aliens are really out there, Fatima material continued to appear on his Web site.[20]

The other point at which Catholic conspiracism overlaps UFO plot literature concerns the brief papacy of John Paul I, who died in 1978 after a reign of only a month. Not surprisingly, this too generated conspiracy literature among fringe Catholics, who claimed he had been murdered. By 1986, this claim had appeared in the UFO literature; George C. Andrews speculates in *Extra-Terrestrials among Us* that it was no accident that UFOs appeared over Rome two weeks before the pontiff's death. He also suggests that John Paul I was poisoned because he was about to reveal the third secret of Fatima. Commander X goes several steps further in suggesting that the murderers were either Jesuits or Masons. The Las Vegas–based publication *Contact: The Phoenix Project,* which reports transmissions from extraterrestrials, carried all-too-earthly speculations in 1997 that "Luciferians," perhaps in league with Marxist and secular-humanist Jesuits, had done the deed. The murder-in-the-Vatican scenario, like the speculations about Fatima, are insured against charges of anti-Catholicism because both originated in Catholic circles, albeit very much at the church's margins.[21]

Freemasons

Masonic conspiracies cannot easily be separated from other plots in contemporary literature. In the first place, they were already linked with others, notably with those about Jesuits, in nineteenth-century material, and that connection is still maintained. Second, the Illuminati have had a place of special prominence in conspiracy literature since the late eighteenth century, often appearing as the masters of plots with many other participants. Given the real Illuminati's Masonic origins, Masonry can easily be characterized as an associate of other conspiratorial players. As a result, conspiracists frequently portray Masons as part of a conspiracy directed not merely at personal or organizational advancement but at control of the world.

The myth of a Masonic plot to control the world has its roots in early anti-Masonic literature that blamed the Illuminati for the French Revolution. Because the French revolutionary troops conquered Europe all the way to the gates of Moscow, it did not seem too great a leap to infer a Masonic plan for global domination. That conception continued to develop long after the French defeat in 1815, appearing even in the teachings of the shadowy conspiracist-evangelist John Todd in the 1970s. Todd, like other anti-Masons, envisioned a hierarchy of Masonic evil, with Masonic lodges at the bottom, Scottish Rite Masons above them, and the Illuminati near the conspiratorial summit. Des Griffin proposes a different hierarchy by suggesting that the nineteenth-century Scottish Rite official Albert Pike controlled the Illuminati.[22]

In view of the long association of conspiracy theories and anti-Masonry, it is not surprising that schemes of Masonic world domination have penetrated the UFO-alien species literature as well. According to Cooper, "Freemasonry is one of the most wicked and terrible organizations upon this earth." He tells us that a segment of thirty-third-degree Masons form the "core of the Luciferian Illuminati," whose "goal is to rule the world." Icke also places Masons at the center of a diabolical web of interlocking secret societies, "a sort of central meeting place" for the conspirators.[23]

Whenever conspiracy writers deal with organizations that have a public face, be it the Masons or the Council on Foreign Relations, they need to explain how it is that such groups can act simultaneously openly and conspiratorially. In the case of the Masons, the principal reason alleged is that there are two Masonries, one open and one hidden. This conception was already well developed in the secret-society literature published between the two world wars. Nesta Webster concluded in 1924 that British Masonry was a force for religion, stability, and patriotism, but she warned that the danger of subversion was ever-present. If Masonic societies should ever fall under the control of evildoers, "this great stabilizing force might become a gigantic engine of destruction." Lady Queenborough, writing in 1933, was considerably more pessimistic, concluding that "*Luciferian Occultism controls Freemasonry.*"[24]

Just as the anti-Catholic material claims that most Catholics know nothing of the hierarchy's nefarious activities, so anti-Masonry distinguishes between the innocuous Masonry known to the vast majority of members and a sinister version revealed only to a select few. For Icke, the unknowing constitute fully 90 percent of the membership: "They are the fodder and the front." Branton places the dividing point at Masons of the thirty-third degree, above whom the diabolical activities allegedly take place: "This is the work of the Scottish Rite which infiltrated Masonic Lodges for the purposes of using them as a framework for the establishment of their Godless New World Order."[25]

In keeping with their supposed central position in the conspirators' world, the Masons are said to maintain contacts with other evil organizations. Conspiracy theorist John Coleman, for instance, believes that a "Jesuit Freemason ring" exists inside the CIA, and such views have been easily absorbed into accounts of a secret government that makes deals with alien invaders. In the interlinked hypothesis of secret societies, a place can be found for every player, and new components can easily be added. Masons can be connected to Jesuits, and the combined group can be joined by extraterrestrials.[26]

Although the Jesuit-Mason connection is the more prominent, some foes of Masonry also manage to incorporate anti-Semitism. Griffin claims that in an 1871 letter, Pike predicted that Illuminati agents would cause World War II "through manipulation of the differences that existed between the German Nationalists and the Political Zionists." Griffin adds that the same Illuminati agents then created the state of Israel in order to plant the seeds of World War III. For the most part, however, notions of Jewish-Masonic machinations have been both less numerous and less apt to penetrate the UFO subculture. In part this reflects patterns in older anti-Masonic literature, in which the Jesuit connection was always more prominent. It is also attributable to special characteristics of anti-Semitism as it has developed among UFO conspiracists—a subject discussed in detail in the next chapter.[27]

RECENT ANTI-MASONIC THEMES

While much of the currently circulating material on Masonry reproduces motifs from earlier nativist writing, a number of themes are distinctly contemporary. Some involve subject matter specifically drawn from UFO speculation, but even ideas not clearly linked to aliens have moved rapidly into UFO writing. Four areas in particular require special consideration: the assassination of John F. Kennedy; the street plan of Washington, D.C.; the Denver airport; and Alternative 3.

At one time or another, almost every group, ideology, or power center has figured in speculation about the Kennedy assassination. It is not more surprising that Masons should be implicated than corporations, the CIA, or organized crime. Curiously, however, alleged connections between Masonry and the assassination appear particularly prominent in UFO sources. Branton implicates the Masonic movement in an assassination cover-up, claiming that the Secret Service prevented an autopsy that might have identified the true assassins and adding that "the Secret Service . . . is patched directly into the highest levels of Scottish Rite Masonry, or the Bavarian Illuminati." The UFO periodical *Contact*, which contains material from both named human authors and alleged extraterrestrial sources, also associates the Masons with a cover-up. In this case, the innuendo comes in the form of a claim that many members of the Warren Commission were thirty-third-degree Masons, and therefore a cover-up must have taken place.[28]

The matter of the Washington, D.C., street plan is considerably stranger. Indeed, it is one of the odder byways of contemporary conspiracy literature. Some conspiracists believe city planners, architects, and authorities with Masonic connections contrived the city's street plan and the siting of its buildings and monuments in accordance with occult Masonic teachings. The result of these decisions has been to focus invisible forces in ways that increase the power of the conspirators.

It is unclear when or how such teachings developed. To the extent that exponents attribute their ideas to others, they cite undated anti-Masonic literature. A self-published religious tract from the early 1990s asserts, "L'Enfant, the original designer and planner of Washington, D.C., was an artistic and talented Luciferic worshiping Mason from

France. Every detail he incorporated into the overall design of streets, circles, and 'squares' contains numerous Babylonian, Assyrian, and Egyptian symbols and images of Satan." Ideas like these were quickly picked up by authors claiming to unmask alien conspiracies.[29]

Diverse speculations by believers have sought to explain how the occult structure of Washington might be associated with aliens or spaceships. Branton has a wide range of choices, because he believes that the earth is being visited not only by inhabitants of distant star systems, but also by the reptilians who live in subterranean caverns on this planet. In any case, he believes that the Washington Scottish Rite Temple has been placed at the apex of a pentagram defined by downtown streets, providing a point of entry into a Luciferian realm. In addition, "it sits directly over an antediluvian system of 'Atlantean' tunnels and ancient underground chambers called the 'NOD' complex, which serves as a major NSA-Sirian-Grey center of collaboration." [30]

Commander X offers a similar picture, adding the Washington Monument as yet another pagan intrusion, an "EXACT DUPLICATE" of the "alters [sic] of Baal which stood in ancient Babylon and Egypt." [31]

One of the most recent, and most elaborate, analyses comes from the prolific pen of Icke. He sees no end to the sinister occult symbols—satanic, astrological, and Masonic. He finds no fewer than three satanic pentagrams in the Washington street plan and carefully notes that the Pentagon can be viewed as the inside of a pentagram. As to the Scottish Rite Temple, even its street number, 1733, is filled with significance, for is not the thirty-third-degree Mason at the threshold of dangerous secrets? [32]

If the obsessive interest in the Washington street plan seems eccentric, the Denver airport literature is even more bizarre. According to it, the terminal building that opened in 1995 is filled with Masonic, satanic, apocalyptic, and pagan symbols, although the airport's innards are known to the general public mainly for having lost or mangled passengers' baggage in the early months. Conspiracists insist that beneath the terminal lies a frightening subterranean realm. What this portends for aliens is laid out in two different scenarios.[33]

Conspiracist Alex Christopher claims that the terminal has Masonic symbols and was designed with a "homing beacon" to allow alien spaceships to fly directly into the terminal's Great Hall. Branton produces an even more sweeping theory involving the world's secret government, which has been divided between reptilian aliens and the human New World Order. A system of caverns below Mount Archuleta, near Dulce,

New Mexico, houses the reptilian capital, while their human counter-parts operate from beneath the Denver airport.[34]

Branton also links Masons with *Alternative 3*–style plans to survive terrestrial catastrophe by fleeing to secret lunar and Martian bases (an idea described in chapter 5). Alternative 3 writers spend much of their time trying to determine who will make the escape. Branton concludes that Masons above the thirty-third degree will make the cut.[35]

As was the case in the appropriation of anti-Catholic themes, the use of anti-Masonic motifs allows purveyors of alien plots to incorporate ideas that may already be familiar to their audience. Even though these traditional nativist themes have been largely banned from public dis-course, they remain alive through subculture modes of transmission — tracts, fringe publications, oral communication, and Web sites. This un-derground tradition continues to portray the Catholic Church and the Masonic movement as institutions whose public faces conceal mysteri-ous, evil activities known only to initiates. Just as government is alleged to have two faces — a deceptive public face and a secret government be-hind it — so the church and Masonry are said to function on two levels.

This fascination with secrecy and duplicity would seem to make the alien-conspiracy literature a perfect site for anti-Semitism. In fact, the connection in this case is considerably more complex. Despite the fact that overt anti-Semitism may be found mixed with allegations about aliens, it is often accompanied by strong assertions that the authors are neither anti-Semites nor racists. Rather, they claim to reject racism and to seek only to protect the interests of Jews. The result is occasion-ally overt anti-Semitism, but more often a refracted racism and anti-Semitism that allow those who use them simultaneously to repudi-ate them.

CHAPTER 9

UFOs and the Search
for Scapegoats II

Anti-Semitism among the Aliens

Negative references to Catholics and Freemasons are numerous in the alien and conspiracy literatures, but the attitudes expressed about Jews range from sympathy to anti-Semitism; and that anti-Semitism is sometimes cloaked in euphemisms and sometimes undisguised. This broad range of attitudes is possible because of the very open-endedness of New World Order ideas.

Although belief in a New World Order conspiracy assumes the existence of a master plot responsible for many aspects of the world's evil, conspiracists differ in the arrangement of the conspiratorial hierarchy. As described in chapter 1, such superconspiracies tend to be structured in the form of plots nested within plots, each layer more evil, powerful, and inclusive than those beneath. Hence the architects of conspiracy scenarios are free to place Jews at any of a number of points in the hierarchy—at the pinnacle, in a subordinate position, or as victims completely outside the domain of evil.

This chapter deals with all three variants. Conspiracy theories that reject anti-Semitism and portray Jews entirely as victims are a relatively minor area of the literature. A larger and more influential body of materials claims to reject anti-Semitism while linking some Jews to the conspiracy. And the most significant case of unalloyed anti-Semitism—the Phoenix publications—will be dealt with later in the chapter.

Anti-Semitism appears in several forms. Sometimes traditional anti-Jewish stereotypes are projected onto a world of alien races, so that some extraterrestrials function as surrogate Jews; that is, they receive the physical and behavioral characteristics imputed to Jews in traditional anti-

Semitism. This refracted racism can occur even in writers who view Jews themselves as innocent victims. Anti-Semitism also appears via the overt use of traditional anti-Semitic materials, particularly *The Protocols of the Elders of Zion,* the most important anti-Semitic text of modern times. Finally, anti-Semitism is sometimes filtered through an occult sensibility whose condemnation of Jews is said to derive from transhuman, spirit sources. The most famous exponent of this approach, William Dudley Pelley, lived well into the UFO period and appears to have left his mark on some important UFO conspiracists.

Jews as Victims

One of the byways of UFO speculation has associated UFOs and aliens with Nazi Germany. In the hands of neo-Nazis, such as Canadian Holocaust denier Ernst Zundel, this has taken the form of claims that Hitler and the Nazi elite escaped to an Antarctic sanctuary, and from there to the inner earth, where they developed UFO technology. In others hands, however, it has led to an identification of evil aliens with Nazi coconspirators.[1]

The pseudonymous Branton is particularly uncompromising in his hostility to Nazism and, by extension, his repudiation of anti-Semitism. In Branton's ever more baroque plots, Nazis are one element, albeit a strategically important one, in a larger cabal seeking world dominion: "German-Bavarian FASCISTS who are behind the New World Order agenda" seek to complete a genocidal mission begun in the two world wars—namely, "the massive 'de-population' of Blacks, Asians, Jews, Slavs, and many others—excepting, of course, the 'Aryan elite' class." Members of this elite found that even Hitler was too moderate for their tastes; hence he was "drugged . . . into oblivion" so that effective power passed into the hands of his more reliable henchmen. After the war, Branton continues, sympathizers within the Allied powers saw to it that a core Nazi group survived to finish the job.[2]

As to the aliens, Branton—like many conspiracy theorists—imagines a Faustian bargain between evil extraterrestrials and their equally malignant earthly confederates. Branton appears to believe that after the requisite depopulation occurs, "the planet will be officially turned over to alien invaders," in return for which the Nazi-Illuminati conspirators "expect . . . to get 25% of the Earth for themselves." Why they would settle for 25 percent when they appear sufficiently powerful to have it all is an awkward question. The willingness of the shadowy human elites to enter such a bargain, however, seems predicated on their belief that the alternative is an outright alien invasion in which all humans would be either killed or enslaved.[3]

However Branton's scenario is modified, it leaves Jews among the victims and Nazis among the planetary enemies. The same sharp division between good and evil appears in the writings of Stan Deyo, an American expatriate conspiracist living in Australia. But Deyo inserts his conspiracy theories into the traditional Christian millenarian context associated with dispensational premillennialism (described in chapter 3). According to the dispensationalist scenario, Jews in the last days will face the final onslaught of Satan until the surviving remnant converts at the time of the Second Coming. Deyo incorporates this ambivalent philo-Semitism into an alien scenario. Large numbers of Jews will be killed by Satan "in the greatest anti-Semitic purge the world has ever known." Jews and their Christian allies should do all they can to seek safety, Deyo advises, but the bloody outcome is foreordained. The aliens are necessary to God's plan, bringing about the fulfillment of biblical prophecies that are essential preconditions for the Second Coming.[4]

Ufology as Refracted Racism and Anti-Semitism

The hostility to Nazis and anti-Semitism found in some UFO literature reflects a racism peculiar to students of extraterrestrial visitation. Most literature on race deals with alleged differences between different human societies. The UFO literature, by analogy, is replete with racial typologies of the aliens that supposedly visit the earth. Although some UFO writers think in terms of a single alien race, others claim that several such races are active here, with different agendas, dispositions, and temperaments.

Milton William Cooper, whose conspiracy theories were discussed earlier, told Jacques Vallee that "There are four types of aliens . . . There are two kinds of Grays, including one race, not commonly seen, that has a large nose. Then there are the Nordic types, tall blond Aryans, and finally the Orange ones." George C. Andrews draws a similar distinction, between short "Grays" from the star Rigel and tall "Blonds" from Procyon. The Grays, he says, worked closely with both Hitler and the CIA. Branton divides aliens into "Benevolents" and "Malevolents." The former "are Blond-Nordic and/or Aryan-like people."[5]

This type of speculation projects terrestrial racial categories onto creatures from outer space. The extraterrestrial races are not so much distinguishable in terms of intelligence or ability as in terms of outward appearance and their propensity for good or evil behavior. Even among authors clearly hostile to Nazis and anti-Semitism, Nordics and Aryans are well-meaning and benign, while gnomelike, dwarfish Grays are a mortal threat. Such racial classificatory schemata are common among those who argue for multiple types of alien visitors. Even among writers who most unambiguously reject anti-Semitism, the alien racial types disquietingly appear to reproduce old stereotypes. The evil Grays are dwarfish with grotesque features—not unlike stereotypes of the short, swarthy, hook-nosed Jew of European anti-Semitic folklore. They are contrasted to the tall, virtuous Nordics or Aryans. Although there is little to suggest that those who employ such terms do so to make direct parallels to earthbound categories, the images seem clearly to be refracted versions of older racial anti-Semitism.

A similar ambivalence surrounds many conspiracists' references to Jews, at once claiming that they are not the villains yet implying that they are associated with evil. Thus Cooper instructs his readers,

I hope you caught on to the fact that the secret power structure is toward a totalitarian socialist state (fascism) [*sic*]. It is not the Nazis, as they were a product of this power structure. It is not the Jews, although some very wealthy Jews are involved. It is not the Communists, as they fit the same category as the Nazis. It is not the bankers, but they do play an important role.

Such an approach, in which Jews are implicated but seemingly not central to the conspiracy, reappears in other writers. A particularly complex form can be found in the work of Valdamar Valerian, also known as John Grace. According to him, the interconnected elements of the conspiracy range from the Hell-Fire Club and the Fabians to the Mafia and the Theosophical Society. Among the most prominent components, however, are the house of Rothschild and the world Zionist movement.[6]

David Icke also seeks to have it both ways, simultaneously claiming to be offended at the thought that anyone might find him anti-Semitic and hinting at the dark activities of Jewish elites. He protests that the charge of anti-Semitism is merely a ruse to silence truth seekers, a tactic of the shadowy "Global Elite," who "denounce anyone who gets closer to the truth as an 'anti-Semite.'" According to Icke, the Anti-Defamation League is the conspiracy's tool for silencing "researchers who are getting too close to the truth about the global conspiracy." Indeed, he claims to find the ADL's attacks "very comforting," since they serve as "confirmation that I am going in the correct direction." The more strongly Icke is condemned for anti-Semitism, the stranger are his protestations of innocence. He attacks alleged exploiters of the Jewish people, including the B'nai B'rith, which he identifies as the Roth-schilds' "intelligence arm," used "to defame and destroy legitimate re-searchers with the label 'anti-Semitic.'" It was supposedly the Roth-schilds who brought Hitler to power, created Zionism, and "control the State of Israel." Among Icke's other Jewish villains are Henry Kissinger and "the Canadian gangster family, the Bronfmans."[7]

Icke claims that he is actually acting in the interests of the Jewish masses. Those masses have allegedly been sold out by the shadowy "Jew-ish clique" that does the bidding of the conspiracy's leaders. "[T]he Jewish people," by contrast, "are used as mere propaganda fodder by the upper reaches of their own hierarchy." This hierarchy, Icke claims, was behind not only the Russian Revolution but also the rise of the Nazis. While Icke is not a Holocaust denier, his ultimate inversion is to lay blame for the Holocaust at the feet of mysterious Jewish elites who used the Nazis to accomplish their own nefarious purposes.[8]

Like the earlier nativists discussed in the preceding chapter, Icke and other UFO anti-Semites obsess about "Jewish bankers." They are al-leged to be the international wire-pullers behind countless episodes of national collapse and international turmoil. The old names, such as Rothschild and the firm of Kuhn, Loeb, continually recur. Given this penchant for recycling old themes, it is scarcely surprising that that hoary forgery, *The Protocols of the Elders of Zion*, exerts an abiding fascination.

The Return of *The Protocols*

Purporting to come from the first Zionist Congress, which was held in Basel in 1897, *The Protocols* is without question the most influential piece of anti-Semitic literature of modern times. As discussed in chap-ter 3, it was concocted in Paris at the end of the nineteenth century by agents of the czar's secret police from two sources: Maurice Joly's *A Dialogue in Hell: Conversations between Machiavelli and Montesquieu about Power and Right,* published in 1864 as an attack on the autocratic tendencies of Napoleon III; and passages from an 1868 novel by "Sir John Retcliffe" (a.k.a. Hermann Goedsche) called *Biarritz,* which was familiar in both Russian and French anti-Semitic circles. The freshly minted *Protocols* appeared in book form in Russia in 1905 and in Britain in 1920. By 1921, the *Times* of London had exposed it as a forgery.[9]

The Protocols' heyday was in the 1920s and 1930s. It was popularized in the United States by Henry Ford's weekly newspaper, *The Dearborn Independent*, whose *Protocols*-based articles were later republished as *The International Jew*. In time, however, the irrefutable evidence of forgery overtook *The Protocols*. By the end of World War II, the work had disappeared from mainstream discourse in the West, maintaining credibility only in the most tenaciously anti-Semitic circles.[10]

One might wonder, therefore, how so discredited a document could make a reappearance in the last quarter of the twentieth century. As the central text of twentieth-century anti-Semitism and a forgery, it would seem too dangerous to utilize. Nonetheless, it is widely referred to in contemporary conspiracist literature—even (or, perhaps, especially) by those who claim not to be anti-Semitic. Thus, Deyo insists not only that "The Protocols are real; they do exist," but that they have nothing to do with Jews, who have been made their "scapegoat."[11]

Cooper takes the argument for authenticity one step further, by validating the work not through textual analysis or an inquiry into origins but on the basis that "[e]very aspect of this plan to subjugate the world has since become reality." Indeed, he reprints *The Protocols* in their entirety as an appendix to *Behold a Pale Horse*. By way of separating himself from charges of anti-Semitism, he attaches to the text a somewhat disingenuous prefatory note, claiming that "This has been written intentionally to deceive people" and offering a series of word substitutions aimed at purging its Jewishness: "'Zion' should be 'Sion'; any reference to 'Jews' should be replaced with the word 'Illuminati'; and the word 'goyim' should be replaced with the word 'cattle.'" The pseudonymous Commander X also tries to detach *The Protocols* from anti-Semitism by suggesting that they are really about a "Jesuit-Masonic" or "Vatican-Buckingham [Palace]" conspiracy.[12]

Icke also appropriates *The Protocols* while disclaiming anti-Semitism. In 1995, he called them "the Illuminati Protocols" and insisted that he wanted "to get away from the Jewish emphasis." As far as forgery was concerned, he refused to address the issue directly, but merely characterized them as "a quite stunning prophecy of what has happened in the twentieth century." By 1999, his views on their origin had crystallized: "These documents were very much the creation of the Rothschilds and the reptile-Aryans," placed in Hitler's hands by Nazi ideologist Alfred Rosenberg, who now becomes "a Rothschild agent of Khazar descent."

Jews, in other words, are still behind *The Protocols,* in the form of the ubiquitous Jewish bankers and an Asiatic Khazar, behind whom are the reptilians introduced in chapter 7.[13]

The Khazars were a people who once lived on the shores of the Black Sea and whose rulers converted to Judaism in the seventh century. A prominent strain in modern anti-Semitism has asserted that most European Jews were descended from these Khazarian converts. This thesis, for which no compelling evidence exists, has two advantages for anti-Semites: it deprived most Jews of any direct links to the biblical Israelites, while simultaneously branding them as uncivilized "Asiatics."[14]

The Protocols has recently been reinsinuated into more mainstream discourse. An example is Jim Marrs's *Rule by Secrecy,* published in 2000 by a major commercial press (HarperCollins). Marrs is the author of earlier conspiracy works dealing with the Kennedy assassination and with UFOs. *Rule by Secrecy* is a digest of contemporary conspiracy theories ranging from the Trilateral Commission to Icke's reptilian thesis. As far as *The Protocols* is concerned, Marrs begins by summarizing the circumstances of its creation by the czarist secret police. Yet he concludes that even if forged, they must in some fundamental sense be true: "*The Protocols* may indeed reflect a deeper conspiracy beyond its intended use to encourage anti-Semitism, one hidden within the secret upper ranks of the Illuminati and Freemasonry."[15]

The idea that *The Protocols of the Elders of Zion* was written by the Illuminati has circulated for decades. It appears in Des Griffin's 1976 anti-Semitic tract, *The Fourth Reich of the Rich.* Long before that, in 1924—only three years after the forgery was exposed—Nesta Webster speculated that authorship lay with "An International circle of world revolutionaries working on the lines of the Illuminati." Although she was unwilling to surrender the idea of Jewish authorship, the idea of an Illuminati connection has obviously been around for a long time. Its reappearance in the contemporary alien literature is evidence of the resilience of this older tradition.[16]

The Phoenix Publications

The most intense and sustained anti-Semitism in UFO-related material appears in a series of interrelated publications issued in the far West since about 1989. As a result of complex internal disputes, business decisions, and litigation, the name of the publication has changed several times.

It was initially known as the *Phoenix Journal Express,* and successor publications have appeared under such titles as *Phoenix Liberator, Contact,* and *The Spectrum.* The first editorial offices were in Tehachapi, California, but they were transferred to Las Vegas, Nevada, in 1992. Although there have been bitter disputes among those involved, there are sufficient continuities in personnel and editorial policies that the publications can be analyzed together. To avoid confusing shifts in nomenclature, they are collectively referred to here as the Phoenix publications.[17]

The Phoenix publications purport to print radio transmissions received from extraterrestrials. The publications have principally served as the mouthpiece for pronouncements from Commander Gyeorgos Ceres Hatonn, more familiarly known simply as Hatonn. Hatonn claims to be "Commander in Chief, Earth Project Transition, Pleiades Sector Flight command, Intergalactic Federation Fleet—Ashtar Command; Earth Representative to the Cosmic Council and Intergalactic Federation Council on Earth Transition." His spaceship is named *Phoenix*— hence the titles of the periodicals. In what was claimed to be a radio interview with Hatonn in Phoenix, Arizona, in 1992, he said that he had "well over a million ships" under his command, and that "My mission is to remove God's people from the planet when that becomes necessary . . . if that becomes necessary."[18]

Up to this point, there is nothing particularly unusual, much less sinister, about Hatonn. Indeed, as we shall see, many others since the 1950s have claimed contact with him, though the messages often differ. Hatonn falls in the category of so-called space brothers: benevolent, spiritually enlightened alien entities who desire to help humanity. In this, they closely resemble the ascended masters who appear in such neo-Theosophical movements as I AM and the Church Universal and Triumphant.

The concept of ascended masters had its origin in the Theosophical movement founded by Mme Blavatsky in the late nineteenth century. Blavatsky, her followers, and the neo-Theosophical groups that sprang from her activities posit the existence of certain spiritually evolved individuals who can serve as guides for the spiritual development of humanity as a whole. Even when these masters suffer the deaths of their physical bodies, they remain accessible to seekers, who can contact them through paranormal means.[19]

The Phoenix publications' distinctiveness lies in their content, which closely tracks stridently anti-Semitic non-UFO conspiracy materials. Hatonn, through his earthly contacts, seeks to protect humanity from the "Satanic Elite" and "the Elite anti-Christ controllers" whose plans for a New World Order will, if left unchecked, reduce America "to a slave-state level of existence." While the satanic elite includes such traditional villains as the Rockefellers and the Trilateral Commission, significant roles are occupied by Jews.[20]

The Contactee Material

The Hatonn material in the Phoenix journals places it in that stream of UFO literature known as contactee material. Contactee material is distinct from abductee accounts. Abductees claim to have been taken, usually against their will, by an alien craft for purposes of macabre and invasive medical procedures during which little if any communication with the aliens occurs. Indeed, many abductees claim to have no conscious awareness of their abduction, relying for validation on time periods they cannot account for or on repressed memories they have recovered. By contrast, contactees claim to have received direct messages from aliens. These experiences are viewed as overwhelmingly positive, because the communications are said to be for the purpose of warning humans of danger or guiding them to a higher spiritual level. The means by which the messages are transmitted may involve face-to-face contact, paranormal communication such as telepathy or mediumistic channeling, or radio transmissions. In the broadest sense, channeling involves access to and transmission of information "from a source other than ordinary consciousness and memory." The individual who serves as the channel can receive these communications in a variety of ways, including trance states, automatic writing, and situations in which the voice of the entity being channeled speaks through the mouth of the channeler, who is fully conscious. There is, therefore, considerable truth to Brenda Denzler's contention that "the contactee movement was, in effect, a conduit through which established spiritualist and Theosophical ideas and practices moved into the UFO community." In a manner not unlike its nineteenth-century predecessors, the contactee movement claims to receive spiritual communication as a result of extraordinary, often paranormal, experiences. Unlike spiritualists, however, contactees do not employ the sorts of rapping noises, voices, and glowing figures associated with séances, nor do they contact the spirits of the dead. They see themselves, rather, as the links through which spiritually significant teachings are brought to humanity from advanced entities who normally dwell in other star systems.[21]

In historical terms, contactee narratives preceded abductee narratives. Thomas Bullard's exhaustive study of abduction stories found no reports before 1957, though a few individuals claimed that such occurrences took place earlier. By contrast, contactee stories emerged shortly after the first modern UFO sightings in 1947. The first major contactee narrative came from George Adamski (1891–1965), who claimed that on November 20, 1952, he had an encounter with a Venusian in the California desert. Adamski had a history of Theosophical speculation that extended back to the mid 1930s, when he founded something called the Royal Order of Tibet. He was also reportedly an anti-Semite, but unlike his fellow contactee, George Hunt Williamson (see below), he kept those views to himself. His messages from the Venusian sounded suspiciously like his own earlier occult teachings. He was accompanied that November day by several friends, including Williamson, who later emerged as a major link between contactees and anti-Semite William Dudley Pelley (discussed later in the chapter). After Adamski met with the Venusian, Williamson took a plaster cast of what purported to be the extraterrestrial's footprint. It was through Adamski's associate Williamson that the name *Hatonn* first appeared.[22]

George Hunt Williamson (1926–1986), a prolific writer on occult matters, claimed to have witnessed Adamski's 1952 encounter. Subsequently, in 1952 and 1953, he and associates supposedly established radiotelegraphic contact with extraterrestrials, in which they received Morse code messages. Hatonn appears in these messages—not as the name of an extraterrestrial being, as it is in the Phoenix publications, but as the name of a place: "the Planet Hatonn in Andromeda," the alleged site of the universal "Temple of Records." Evidently, Williamson's extragalactic informant held the planet Hatonn in high regard, for, referring to its role as custodian of records, he remarked that "only a world of great spiritual advancement could be so honored." By the time of the Phoenix journals more than thirty-five years later, Hatonn is an entity, not a place, and he hails from the Pleiades, not Andromeda. The shift in location is likely the result of the context in which Williamson's Hatonn references were embedded. He was at pains to contrast the dark and negative worlds of Orion with the positive worlds of the Pleiades, which "send . . . forth vibrations of peace and love." In fact, the motif of Pleiadean virtue and enlightenment is commonplace in New Age literature.[23]

Long before Phoenix, however, Hatonn had metamorphosed into a being, largely as a result of the experiences of Richard T. Miller, a Detroit television repairman who heard a lecture by Williamson in 1954. Inspired by Williamson's account, Miller and some friends sought to establish radio contact with extraterrestrials and, Miller reported, quickly succeeded in doing so. So successful were these communications that on October 30, 1954, Miller and his associates were able to meet with an extraterrestrial and enter his spacecraft, the *Phoenix*. The principal individual with whom they spoke, however, was not Hatonn but someone named Soltec, who subsequently appeared in a subsidiary role in Phoenix publications. Miller and Williamson jointly founded an organization called the Telonic Research Center in Williamson's Prescott, Arizona, home, but parted company about a year later. Miller's own published space messages contain numerous dispatches from the creature known as Hatonn, the first dated September 1, 1974. In a 1992 Internet posting, Miller called the Phoenix journals "thoroughly disgusting" and their use of Hatonn's name "fraudulent." He claimed that he had once had authentic contact with Hatonn but had "not been active in such activities for many years."[24]

Hatonn and his associates have communicated through others as well. One such channel has been the Ashtar Command. In 1952, an early contactee, George Van Tassel, began to channel an extraterrestrial entity named Ashtar, whose messages became the basis for Van Tassel's Ministry of Universal Wisdom. In addition to Van Tassel's activities as a channeler, he hosted the annual Interplanetary Spacecraft Convention at Giant Rock in the Mojave Desert. The Giant Rock gatherings began in 1954, with Williamson prominent on the roster of speakers. After Van Tassel's death in 1970, other channelers claimed access to Ashtar's messages. The most prominent among them has been Tuella (Thelma B. Terrell), who emphasizes the role of extraterrestrials in evacuating "purified" souls from the earth in order to escape coming natural calamities. While Tuella's messages come from many of Ashtar's associates, Hatonn seems to have a special place among the subordinates. He is not simply a "Great Commander" but also "the Record Keeper of the Galaxy and the records are kept on the planet bearing his name"—thus resolving the contradiction between Hatonn the place and Hatonn the personage.[25]

HATONN AND THE PHOENIX PUBLICATIONS

Another of Hatonn's contactees, George Green, was central to the development of the Phoenix publications. Green claimed to have seen an alien craft at Edwards Air Force Base in 1958. According to him, he was contacted by "space beings" in October 1989, entering into an agreement with them to "publish the material transmitted from the spacecraft called 'THE PHOENIX.'" Sometime thereafter he was also approached by a husband and wife, E. J. and Doris Ekker, who claimed to be in touch with the same group of extraterrestrials. Doris Ekker, under the name Dharma, was the principal receiver, though not apparently in a mediumistic capacity.[26]

At this point, an already complex series of linkages became even murkier. On the one hand, Green claimed that he financed the publication of the Ekkers' messages through the Phoenix journals. At an early point, however, a separate set of Phoenix materials was produced by Miller, so that two different publishers were simultaneously issuing material under the rubric of The Phoenix Project.

In 1979, Miller began issuing a series of Phoenix Project Reports through his Advent Publishing Company. He continues to issue this material, along with a newsletter, *Insights*. *Insights* contains a substantial amount of material alleging various conspiracies in which both humans and malevolent extraterrestrials are participating; but his material does not contain any of the anti-Semitic themes that figure so prominently in the Phoenix journals.[27]

Green is another matter. His publishing company, America West, specializes in conspiracy works, the best known of which is John Coleman's *Conspirators' Hierarchy: The Story of the Committee of 300*. According to Coleman, the megaconspiracy that rules the world includes "Universal Zionism" and something called "The Order of the Elders of Zion." Green's own writings and activities make no secret of his anti-Semitism. A 1999 Internet posting of Green's refers to "the so called [*sic*] Jews" and invokes Arthur Koestler's book about the Khazars, *The Thirteenth Tribe*. When an appearance by Green and his wife, Desiree, in Victoria, British Columbia, led to charges of anti-Semitism, he explained that it was only the "Zionist Jews" who were in league with Satan. "The Zionist philosophy is to take over the world. That's where the anti-Christ comes in."[28]

By 1992 or 1993, the relationship between the Greens and the Phoenix journals was fraying. Initially, ties were amicably loosened to relieve the Greens of some of the publication responsibilities, but by mid 1993, the relationship had broken down in mutual recriminations. Such bitter struggles seem endemic to these publications: six years later, in March 1999, the Ekkers locked out the editorial staff, who then started a separate publication, *The Spectrum*. Again, there were charges of fraudulent extraterrestrial communications. Internet supporters of *The Spectrum* observe darkly that "Doris Ekker is NOT receiving from Lighted Source at this time!"[29]

These conflicts only slightly muted the intensity of the Phoenix publications' anti-Semitism. A 1992 message from Hatonn concluded that "Most ones who call themselves 'Jewish' actually *are from the Russian Khazarian line.*" At the end of 1998, Phoenix was still selling essays by Father Charles Coughlin, the "radio priest" whose anti-Semitic broadcasts in the 1930s made him a national figure, as well as articles reprinted from Henry Ford's *The International Jew,* together with a statement from Hatonn suggesting that the only reason the "Jewish controllers" do not shut down *Contact* is that it would draw unwanted attention to their secret plots. When *The Spectrum* began publication in 1999, it featured a lengthy interview with Icke. The interview, focused on his book *The Biggest Secret* (discussed in chapter 6), contained Icke's charge that Hitler had been "funded and bankrolled" by the Rothschilds.[30]

Notwithstanding the gloss of aliens and spacecraft, the Phoenix materials owe less to science fiction than to late-nineteenth- and early-twentieth-century anti-Semitism. The predatory behavior of international bankers, usually Jewish, and the insistence that Jews are really Asiatic Khazars in disguise, have roots that go back more than a century. By associating these ideas with Hatonn and his associates, the Phoenix publications seek to validate familiar anti-Semitic motifs by providing a galactic imprimatur.

Occult Anti-Semitism

Although the precise origins of this otherworldly anti-Semitism are difficult to trace, they may ultimately lie with William Dudley Pelley (1890–1965), a well-known figure in American anti-Semitism. Founder and head of the Depression-era Silver Legion, Pelley is often classified as a homegrown fascist; and indeed, his Silver Shirts resembled the Nazi brownshirts not only in their uniformity of dress but in their ideology. Pelley, however, was also an occultist and mystic whose taste for metaphysics and the supernatural went back to the late 1920s.[31]

Pelley's mysticism was obscured by his fascist proclivities, particularly after the entry of the United States into World War II. Convicted of sedition during the war, he was finally paroled in 1950 on condition that he not engage in political activity. He appears to have complied for the most part during his remaining fifteen years, but he ran a significant publishing operation in Indiana, in connection with which he crossed paths with Williamson.[32]

About 1950, Williamson—then in his mid twenties—moved to Noblesville, Indiana, where Pelley lived, and began writing for Pelley's periodical, *Valor*. Williamson worked for Pelley for a year or two before moving on to California, where he witnessed the alleged Venusian contact with Adamski. Vallee suggests that Adamski may have known Pelley before World War II, during Pelley's fascist period, and that "Pelley may have put Williamson in touch with Adamski." Pelley and Adamski also appear to have had a common interest in the Ballards' I AM movement. Whatever the exact sequence, Williamson seems to have had brief but intense involvement with Pelley prior to his contactee phase. Although Pelley's postwar publications were a fuzzy mix of mysticism, there is no reason to believe that he had abandoned his earlier anti-Semitism.[33]

Pelley's influence on Williamson seems to have been extensive. Although Pelley did not directly refer to flying saucers until 1952—after Williamson had left his employ—he published a major work on extraterrestrial life during Williamson's time in Noblesville. The book, *Star Guests*, consists largely of channeled communications that Pelley claimed to have been receiving from spirit entities since the late 1920s, interlarded with his own reflections and interpretations.[34]

Star Guests is nothing less than a revisionist account of the origin of human life. According to Pelley, sentient life came to earth from planets near Sirius, at the behest of the divine principle he called "Thought Incarnate." The development of humanity, however, turned out to be a complex and conflicted enterprise. Unfortunately, the "semi-intelligent spirits" who arrived here seventeen million years ago, Pelley explained, interbred with indigenous apelike life forms. This miscegenation caused the Fall, which he clearly viewed as a sin of interracial breeding. Like many racists, he linked this sexual dalliance with the obscure account in Genesis of liaisons between the "sons of God" and "daughters of men" that preceded the Deluge. Restoring virtue required yet another extraterrestrial migration, this time of "Christ People" from outer space. As Pelley put it, "Of thirty persons in a given street-crowd, ten may be the beast-progeny of the ape-mothers of long ago, ten may be reincarnated spirits from the original Sirian migration, and ten may be members of the Goodly Company of the Avatar trying to repair the moral damage done long ago when the members of the Migration ran riot in sodomy."[35]

Star Guests contains a few unmistakable hints of Pelley's fascist past. He pondered, "Why did I go off upon a political departure that seemed for a time to delay in ignominy?" He answered that he needed to confront Soviet communism, "the Beast at its strongest." There is no overt anti-Semitism, yet *Star Guests* characterizes the ancient Hebrews as "one little tribe of Semitic menials." Pelley also made clear that despite the salvationist mission of the Christ People, evil remained powerful. Evil spirits have invaded the earth from elsewhere in the universe, first incarnated in Napoleon and later in the leaders of the Soviet Union. If they are not stopped, he wrote, "a coalition of oriental nations—of which Russia is leader— . . . [will] subjugate the globe, reducing its white and Christian peoples to bondage." [36]

Pelley's book clearly had a strong influence on the young Williamson. In 1953, Williamson published *Other Tongues—Other Flesh,* with an entire chapter devoted to a summary of Pelley's ideas. According to James W. Moseley and Karl T. Pflock, Williamson—by then living in Prescott, Arizona—was planning to go on a lecture tour with Pelley, though it is not clear whether he ever did so. Where Pelley tended to be vague about the relations between the Sirians and entities from other star systems such as the Pleiades and Orion, though, Williamson believed he could clearly distinguish the loci of good and evil. He became increasingly convinced that there was a division of the cosmos between virtuous Pleiadeans and evil aliens from Orion. The Orion forces were being aided by people on earth, whom he described in terms close to traditional anti-Semitic stereotypes:

These people are sometimes small in stature with strange, oriental type eyes. Their faces are thin and they possess weak bodies. . . . They prey on the unsuspecting; they are talkative; they astound intellects with their words of magnificence. While their wisdom may have merit, it is materialistic, and not of pure aspiration toward the Father. . . . We try to help them and suggest work to aid them, but they are a stubborn race. [37]

Williamson soon became much more explicit about the identities of these evildoers. In the 1958 work *UFOs Confidential!* he discussed the evils of "International Bankers." Although the book was coauthored with John McCoy, each wrote a separate section, and virtually all of the anti-Semitic material appears in Williamson's chapters. According to Williamson, "*all governments . . .* are under the *complete control* of the 'International Bankers.'" Among them, he named Bernard Baruch, Herbert Lehman, Supreme Court Associate Justice Felix Frankfurter, and the Warburgs. In addition to their political and financial manipulations, they allegedly "removed vital books and sections of the Holy Bible." They operate in part through the UN, which seeks to "destroy our sovereignty and nullify our Constitution." This was fairly standard right-wing rhetoric in the 1950s. In fact, Williamson relied heavily on a pamphlet issued by the California-based Cinema Educational Guild, an organization cofounded and largely funded by Gerald L. K. Smith, the most prominent anti-Semite in America at the time.[38]

Williamson's extremist politics incorporated not only the beliefs of Pelley and Smith but Pelley's occult sensibilities as well. These interests inspired a strange expedition to Peru in December 1956. Convinced that he could best contact the ascended masters from the Andes, he and a small group of fellow occultists spent most of 1957 near Lake Titicaca, where they established a retreat called the Abbey of the Seven Rays. An eventual product of the Peruvian trip was a thin volume of channeled ascended-master communications, written under Williamson's nom de plume, Brother Philip. *Secret of the Andes* (1961) was for the most part couched in the impenetrable language of neo-Theosophy. But it also contained passages similar to those in *UFOs Confidential!*

The United Nations must collapse because that which you read from the Nostradamus forces is true. The war lords, the "International Bankers" will use the United Nations to form their super-government. This will not be.

We can tread upon serpents and scorpions. He [the Father] gives us that power. And His further promise of power over the enemy—the enemy which is the anti-Christ, which we recognize in the International Bankers and the others who would enslave man upon the Earth.[39]

Brother Philip almost certainly cribbed large parts of the book from his companions in Peru. One of them was Dorothy Martin (1900 – 1992), who went by the name Sister Thedra. In 1949, Martin was at the center of an extraordinary apocalyptic sect that was to make her the best known of recent channelers. She learned from extraterrestrial informants that vast natural disasters were to occur on December 21 of that year, but that spaceships would rescue her and her followers. Her group was exceedingly small, and the episode would not have gained attention but for the fact that behavioral scientists had been allowed to observe its members. This study became a classic of social psychology— *When Prophecy Fails,* by Leon Festinger, Henry W. Riecken, and Stanley Schachter, in which Martin appears under the pseudonym Marian Keech.[40]

As the authors of *When Prophecy Fails* point out, Martin never seriously questioned the validity of her messages, even after the disconfirmation of her prediction had become stunningly evident. By an odd coincidence, the book appeared at the same time that she and Williamson left for South America, though it was not until some time later that the real identity of Marian Keech became widely known.[41]

Martin as Sister Thedra brought to the Peruvian enterprise many of the same influences as Williamson. She, too, was a devotee of flying saucer literature. She may also have had some indirect acquaintance with Pelley's ideas. Her followers certainly knew Pelley's mystical writings, and she herself was familiar with the teachings of Guy and Edna Ballard's I AM movement, which had close ties with some of the Silver Shirts. She returned to the United States in 1961, apparently well after Williamson did, and in 1965 established the Association of Sananda and Sanat Kumara in Mount Shasta, California. Her posthumous Web site, in addition to containing transcripts of her channelings, is interlarded with excerpts from Pelley's mystical writings. Of course, one cannot be sure whether the Pelley material was selected by Sister Thedra or by a follower.[42]

There were, then, multiple ties among channelers, occultists, UFO buffs, and followers of Pelley. Although it cannot be demonstrated with certainty that these links account for the strident anti-Semitism in the Phoenix publications, they do suggest that the domain of stigmatized knowledge in the 1950s was one in which mystic and anti-Semitic teachings mingled freely.

A signal characteristic of the domain of stigmatized knowledge has always been its laissez-faire character. The devotee is free to choose whichever ideas appeal and ignore the rest. Millenarian expressions of stigmatized knowledge are no different in this regard. Improvisational millennialists select and combine elements in idiosyncratic ways. Some, therefore, have chosen previously dormant anti-Semitic elements, while others have passed them by. As free of regulation as this milieu is, however, the obsessive concern with secret machinations has drawn improvisationalists to motifs long associated with allegations of covert evil, whether those charges have centered on Catholics, Masons, or Jews.

CHAPTER 10

September 11

The Aftermath

After the September 11, 2001, attacks on the World Trade Center and the Pentagon, it was said that nothing would be the same again. This profound sense of dislocation was not shared, however, by conspiracists, who believed they already held the master key to events. They were aided by the ambiguity of the initial media reports, which facilitated the rise of a host of urban legends. These legends multiplied far more rapidly than they could be checked; and despite the fact that they eventually turned out to be false, they nevertheless developed lives of their own, independent of disconfirming evidence, in a manner not unlike the *Alternative 3* broadcast discussed earlier.[1]

In addition, the sheer scope of the attacks and the dramatic, real-time television coverage created potent apocalyptic imagery. The collapse of the towers, from whose bases crowds fled in panic, was violence on a world-destroying scale. The September 12, 2001, issue of the London *Daily Mail* carried a one-word headline: "Apocalypse."

The Millenarian Response

Within weeks of September 11, millennialists began issuing their end-time analyses. They were in no doubt that the attacks were of eschatological importance. This conviction was in part a function of the attacks' intensity and in part a result of the hijackers' Middle Eastern connections. The Middle East has always been central to Christian premillennial expectations, as the region where the Battle of Armageddon will be fought at the end of history. The dissolution of the Soviet Union and the 1991 defeat of Iraq had made the area politically marginal, but now it had suddenly reemerged at the center of public attention.

The key issue for millenarians was what the attacks meant in terms of history's final trajectory. Where did the attacks place the world on the path between the Creation and the Final Judgment? Recounting his reactions to the events of September 11, evangelist John Hagee observed, "Without question, I recognized that the Third World War had begun and that it would escalate from this day until the Battle of Armageddon." Another evangelist, Arno Froese, put it somewhat differently: "The message is clear to those who are believers in the Lord: we are entering the final stages of the endtimes which will climax in the Rapture of the Church, followed by the beginning of the Great Tribulation."[2]

Canadian evangelist Grant R. Jeffrey concentrated less on the attack itself than on the events that would transpire as a result. In particular, Jeffrey saw coming prophetic fulfillment in a war with "Babylon"—that is to say, Iraq. He betrayed the disappointment many millenarians felt when the Gulf War ended without Iraq's total defeat. Jeffrey also noted the role surveillance technology was likely to play in counterterrorism, which he saw leading to the reign of the Antichrist: "It is impossible to contemplate the growing capabilities of governments throughout the world without being reminded of the ancient biblical prophecy from the book of Revelation about an unprecedented totalitarian police system arising in the final dictatorship of the Antichrist in the last days."[3]

Such characterizations simultaneously assured believers that the endtimes were closer without being very precise about timing. The same combination of assurance and uncertainty appeared in a poll conducted by a book service catering to millenarians that surveyed its customers. The results are suggestive, if unscientific. Only 8 percent believed the world was at the beginning of or already in the Tribulation period, but fully 65 percent agreed with the statement that "It's setting the stage for the end-times." Asked whether the attacks meant that New York City was the Babylon of Revelation, opinions were divided: 18 percent agreed; 11 percent thought it "very likely"; 11 percent felt it was "not likely"; 50 percent disagreed; and 9 percent were unsure, with 1 percent not responding to the question.[4]

The Esotericist Response

Christian evangelicals were not the only ones seeking the hidden significance of September 11; the same was true of devotees of esoteric knowledge derived from occult and metaphysical sources. Their concern accounts for an extraordinary increase in interest in Nostradamus. When the operators of the Google Internet search engine tabulated results for 2001, they found an extraordinary shift in the frequency with which certain search terms were used. *Nostradamus* was the query that gained most, followed by *CNN, World Trade Center, Harry Potter,* and *anthrax.* Nostradamus was also the male name most often sought out by users, followed by that of Osama bin Laden. Nostradamus inquiries rose steeply on the morning of September 11 and peaked at about noon. They remained above one hundred searches a minute throughout the rest of the day.[5]

A number of different prophetic verses said to be composed by Nostradamus were disseminated by Web sites, listservs, and individual e-mails. Although Nostradamus's quatrains are notoriously obscure and hence subject to multiple interpretations, the many post–September 11 verses in circulation were either alterations of existing texts or fabrications. The idea that the attacks had been foretold centuries ago seemed briefly to convert chaos into order. It also suggested that just as evangelicals could draw comfort from the Bible, so those of a New Age persuasion could seek recourse in their own texts.[6]

In typical esotericist fashion, Richard Hoagland claimed to uncover numerological meanings in the date September 11, 2001. Each World Trade Center tower had 110 floors, a multiple of 11. One of them was struck by Flight 11, which had 11 crew members, and so on. And that was only the beginning. The order of the Knights Templar was recognized by the Vatican in the year 1118, whose integers add up to 11. There are 883 years between that date and 2001, and the sum of those numbers, 19, is the same as the number of hijackers. The number 19 allowed Hoagland to introduce the Koranic numerology of Rashad Khalifa, in which it is central. By the time Hoagland had finished, the events of September 11 were revealed to be an attack by none other than the Islamic Order of Assassins on the Knights Templar and the Masons![7]

The UFO Legend

The malleability of Nostradamus's language and numerical manipulations made them obvious candidates for speculation in stressful and uncertain times. UFO motifs might seem a more difficult fit, especially inasmuch as the proximate causes of the New York City and Arlington,

Virginia, disasters were known from the outset. Nonetheless, a UFO did figure prominently in the initial urban legends.

The UFO legend resulted from a video taken of the second plane's impact in New York. The video, circulated by the Gamma Press USA Agency, was picked up by the widely read Web site run by Matt Drudge, the Drudge Report. Immediately after impact, a long, thin object tilted at a forty-five-degree angle appeared to the right of the towers. To some, it resembled a UFO approaching edge-on. It was in fact either debris or some object that momentarily passed in front of the lens; but the credulous found it to be unassailable evidence of UFO involvement. Kenn Thomas, publisher of the periodical *Steamshovel Press,* asked rhetorically, "Does the average American really understand the impor-tance of UFO watching now?" Sister Tynetta Muhammad, a theologian long associated with the Nation of Islam, saw the object as "the Angelic Watchmen hovering over men's souls." As we shall see, however, most conspiracists—even those with a long history of interest in UFOs and extraterrestrials—were able to accommodate the September 11 events without recourse to questionable imagery.[8]

The Conspiracist Response

Conspiracists quickly responded to the attacks. They rejected the con-ventional explanation that Al Qaeda was responsible, because they al-ready had an ample reservoir of evildoers on whom to pin blame. They also already believed that the conspiracy had an accelerated timetable for the New World Order takeover, so the magnitude of the attacks ap-peared to constitute confirmation of preexisting fears.

None were willing to attribute the attacks to Osama bin Laden and his organization. Indeed, for believers in secret knowledge, the breadth of support for the Al Qaeda explanation made it prima facie suspect. Duncan M. Roads, the editor of *Nexus* magazine, characterized accounts in the mainstream media as "manufactured reality." Texe Marrs blamed the Illuminati, concluding that "Orwellian Illusion [*sic*] is rampant as the Illuminist, global psychodrama continues unabated." The right-wing magazine *Free American* was willing to concede that Bin Laden played a role but saw in subsequent counterterrorism measures a means to control opponents of the New World Order. "Homeland defense" was merely a cover for a "military police state" run by FEMA.[9]

The Phoenix publications, in their current incarnation as *The Spec-*

trum, advanced the now-familiar theme that the airplane hijackings were part of a plan to manipulate the public into accepting new levels of control; or, as the editors put it, "New World Order Thru 'Terrorism.'" The anthrax scare, too, was part of the plan. Leonard G. Horowitz, a dentist who is now the right's most visible authority figure on medical matters, wrote that the anthrax mailings were intended to benefit pharmaceutical companies and to provide a push for "forced 'emergency' legislation effecting stringent population controls." In a later elaboration, Horowitz expanded the anthrax outbreak into "a military-industrial conspiracy involving chief biological weapons 'preparedness' firms and the CIA." He wondered whether "America . . . [is] under attack from within our own national security system." [10]

An even more strident voice was that of the probably pseudonymous Patrick H. Bellringer. His Web site claims complete independence from any Phoenix-related publications, individuals, or organizations, but he reissues large bodies of Phoenix material and provides links to related sites. His own essay on the September 11 events was couched in the anti-Semitic rhetoric reminiscent of earlier Phoenix writers, including Hatonn. The attacks, he said, were the work of "the Khazarian Zionist Bolshevik (KZB) world controllers." Unlike some who saw the attacks as a sign of the conspirators' power, however, Bellringer regarded them as an indication that the plotters were lagging behind "in their plans for world domination and have become desperate." In their desperation, they sought to use the attacks as a catalyst to ignite a world war. They would stoop to so bloodthirsty an act, he continued, because they are not really human. Rather, they are "robotoids [who] have given their free-will over to the darkside." They are, in fact, none other than "The Serpent People [who] originally came to Earth Shan [*sic*] with Satan, as evil aliens, and have fourth dimensional shape-shifting capabilities." This account provides the full panoply of conspiracist motifs: aliens, Satan, reptilians, Jews, and Bolsheviks. [11]

Some familiar conspiracist voices, meanwhile, had fallen silent. Jim Keith had died in 1999. Branton was alive on September 11 but unable to respond to the events, even though he had written prolifically through the first months of 2001. In early spring of that year, he was struck by a car while riding his bicycle. After a week in a coma and two months in an intensive care unit, he was transferred to what he described as a "care center." He was still there more than a year after the accident and claims to have little memory of events after 1999. But another Internet author, who identifies himself only as TCA and writes in an idiom similar to

Branton's, posted views with which Branton might well agree. According to TCA, the September 11 attack was planned by the "gray aliens," operating through the Illuminati. The CIA, as an arm of the Illuminati, had trained Osama bin Laden. The aim of the attack was to ignite a world war in whose chaotic aftermath the aliens would be able "to abduct great amount of bodies [*sic*] to the hybrid project"—presumably a reference to legends about the creation of a human-alien hybrid species.[12]

DAVID ICKE'S RESPONSE

David Icke has always been the most fluent of conspiracist authors, which gives his writings a clarity rarely found in the genre. His initial response to September 11 was an essay that appeared in *The Spectrum* a month after the attacks. Though presented in his customarily breezy style, it was substantively indistinguishable from the views expressed by others: the Illuminati were behind the attacks, Bin Laden had been "set up," and the aim was to trigger a nuclear war that would end in an Illuminati-controlled world government. To the extent that he brought anything new to the speculations, it was an especially strong emphasis on mind control. In his view, "One of the biggest potential obstacles to the 'New World Order' . . . is the psyche of most American people." He saw that psyche weakened in two phases, first by the traumatic impact of the attacks, and then by mind-control technology masquerading as counterterrorism.[13]

As the months went by, however, Icke developed a more distinctive position. He attributed this shift to an unidentified "channeled dimensional source," by which he presumably meant communication from some nonmaterial entity by paranormal means. Icke's Web site reproduced dialogue between him and his source, so he was himself the channeler. As is common in such communications, the source combined detailed statements with delphic ambiguity.[14]

The revelations fell into two categories. The first consisted of a variety of political and financial accusations and predictions: that gold would be removed from Fort Knox; that wealthy families like the Rockefellers would suddenly "undertake great acts of world charity"; and that President George W. Bush and British prime minister Tony Blair had advance knowledge of the September attacks. The source's other observations were considerably stranger and concerned the claim that an unusual number of celebrities would undergo mind-control operations under the pretext of having cosmetic surgery. As a result, they would be turned into "genetically manipulated . . . zombies" by the conspirators in order to influence the masses to accept domination. Icke placed these messages in the context he had established in such works as *The Biggest Secret* and *Children of the Matrix*. The "world leaders and controllers in politics, finance and media are possessed beings, possessed in thought and emotion by entities from this frequency range of existence between this physical dimension and the non-physical." These are the "other-dimensional" creatures who take physical form as the reptilians, operating through their robotic human slaves.[15]

However bizarre Icke's observations might seem, they are entirely consistent with the position he had developed prior to the attacks. His views also strongly resemble the "interdimensional" ideas about UFOs circulated by Keith just before his death. In comparison, the position of Milton William Cooper on the September 11 attacks seems altogether mundane. Nevertheless, Cooper's view commands special attention, not only because of his influence in the conspiracist milieu, but also because of his violent death shortly afterward.

MILTON WILLIAM COOPER: DEATH OF A CONSPIRACIST

Cooper moved immediately to address the attacks on his Web site. Like his book, *Behold a Pale Horse,* the Web site is a pastiche of documents, essays by others, and Cooper's own, often disconnected thoughts, added through the middle and end of September 2001. His most sustained response was an article titled "Who Benefits? The Question No One Dares to Ask!" It consisted largely of rhetorical questions and insinuations suggesting that those identified as the hijackers either had not committed the crimes or had done so with the cooperation of the U.S. government. In the end, Cooper identified those whom he believed benefited from the attacks—not Muslims or an Arab state, but rather the Bush family, the oil industry, "the defense industrial complex," the UN, and Israel, along with "tyranny in the name of security."[16]

Cooper would no doubt have elaborated on these ideas had he lived. But less than two months after the attacks he was dead, at age fifty-eight. He was killed outside his home in eastern Arizona during a gunfight with sheriff's deputies. At the time, Cooper was a federal fugitive, having been charged in 1998 with tax evasion and bank fraud, and declared a fugitive when he failed to appear at a court hearing. Even though his whereabouts were well known, federal authorities made no attempt to apprehend him. He was known to go about armed and claimed he would never be taken alive. Unwilling to risk bloodshed, authorities decided to wait him out. The November 2001 gunfight in fact had nothing to do with the federal warrants; Cooper ran afoul of the Apache County sheriff over a purely local matter.[17]

The preceding July, Cooper had ordered a local man off of land near Cooper's home, though it was not land he owned. He followed the man back to his house and threatened him with the gun he always kept in his car. The threat with a weapon made a local law-enforcement response inevitable, but because of Cooper's reputation for belligerence, the sheriff decided to effect arrest by a ruse. Seventeen undercover officers approached Cooper's home at night, seeking to lure him from the house. When he left by car rather than on foot, the plan began to unravel. In the ensuing gun battle, Cooper shot and seriously wounded a deputy before he himself was fatally shot, early on the morning of November 6, 2001.[18]

No one who knew Cooper, including friends, was surprised by his violent death. He had a history of making threats and intimating that he would come to a violent end. According to a Phoenix, Arizona, spokesperson for the U.S. Marshals Service, "He had vowed that he would not be taken alive." The sheriff's report of the gunfight noted that "Cooper has a history of harassing and threatening local residents with deadly force." Even his admirers found it difficult to paint a flattering picture of his personality. Michele Marie Moore, a close collaborator, conceded that he had "a dark and uncontrollable side." Norio Hayakawa noted that "to many he was an arrogant, obnoxious, cholic, self-aggrandizing, rude, vitriolic and vengeful person."[19]

Even though Cooper's death was consistent with his life and personality, conspiracism shaped some of the reactions. His prominence as a "crossover" conspiracist influential among both ufologists and Christian patriots, together with the proximity of his death to September 11, made conspiracist interpretations inevitable. The Hal Turner radio show asked whether "Bill Cooper was set-up to be gunned down or [was] a victim of his own big mouth and prudent police planning." The publisher of *Free American* acknowledged the justifications given by the sheriff's men, but persisted in calling them Cooper's "executioners."[20]

It is somewhat ironic that Thomas of *Steamshovel Press* blamed the federal government for its failure to arrest Cooper on the tax charges. "He died from federal neglect," wrote Thomas, which allowed "bullets-before-brains local police" to kill him. Like all conspiracists, however,

Thomas was loath to acknowledge the role of accident. He hinted darkly that those who saw only the hand of local authorities "ignore the close cooperation that exists between local police and federal authorities." Even the mysterious Commander X weighed in, not only by editing a book about Cooper's death but also by implying that the shooting was merely one in a string of "unusual deaths" and accidents, including those of Phillip Schneider, Jim Keith, and Branton. Commander X asked whether Cooper's death might not be part of "a conspiracy to silence those who strive to make a complacent world aware of the evil that lies just underneath the veneer of our society." [21]

Ufologists approached the Cooper shooting with ambivalence, for Cooper, after elaborating his baroque thesis about government-extraterrestrial collaboration, recanted his own ET stories as just another instance of disinformation engineered by the conspiracy. James Moseley, in his gadfly newsletter about the ufology community, *Saucer Smear*, called Cooper a "tortured soul," while William F. Hamilton III hoped he would rest more easily in the afterlife than he had in this one. By contrast, prominent ufologist Don Ecker spared little sympathy for someone he called "simply a thuggish, armed felon resisting arrest." [22]

The War in Afghanistan

The armed conflict against Al Qaeda and the Taliban that began in October 2001 was not at the forefront of conspiracists' attention, not so much because of a lack of potential connections to conspiracies as because of conspiracists' obsession with domestic developments—in particular, their fear that the September 11 attacks would be the pretext for the imposition of the New World Order. Nonetheless, Afghanistan provides a rich locus for future conspiracist speculation, as a result of a long history of esoteric preoccupation with central Asia. The extreme right, for example, had long sought the Asian homeland of the "Aryans." Heinrich Himmler believed they were descended from survivors of Atlantis who had escaped to an Asian sanctuary, and used the resources of the Nazi SS to try to substantiate that claim. Although such beliefs often centered on Tibet rather than Afghanistan, the very vagueness of the ideas made any mountainous area of the Asian heartland a potential location for momentous developments. These occult byways also intersected with the legends of Shambhala and Agharti, discussed earlier, as well as with assertions that the area might have been the site of the biblical Eden. [23]

Some of these motifs were brought to the fore after Osama bin Laden's disappearance late in 2001. The attempts during military operations in December by Afghan, American, and British forces to flush him from his hiding place failed. While the hunt was going on, much media attention was paid to Al Qaeda's underground redoubts, developed by tunneling from mountain caves such as those in the vicinity of Tora Bora. It was therefore not surprising that Bin Laden's disappearance was linked to esoteric beliefs about a subterranean realm in central Asia. A UFO newsletter asked rhetorically, "Did Osama and his son-in-law [the Taliban leader Mullah Mohammed Omar] take refuge in Shambhala after fleeing Kandahar?" This source in no way supported Bin Laden's cause, but its suggestion of underground escape resonates with a large body of partisan legends.[24]

Esoteric publications, eager to comment on the war in Afghanistan, quickly sought out material on the region. The widely distributed periodical *Atlantis Rising* asked on its cover: "In the Ancient Past Was This War Torn Region Something Else?" The article to which the question referred provided a digest of occult materials concerned with central Asia. Much of it dealt with Shambhala, but the author, David Hatcher Childress, also noted other themes: namely, that the Pamir Plateau was supposedly the site of the Garden of Eden, and that the adjacent Tarim Basin had been the locale of the biblical Deluge. By implication, then, the conflict in Afghanistan and adjoining areas might tap powerful spiritual energies.[25]

Childress derived this connection from two early-twentieth-century authors, E. Raymond Capt and Frederick Haberman. Both were American exponents of British-Israelism. British- or Anglo-Israelism was a movement in segments of anglophone Protestantism that argued for the direct Israelite ancestry of certain European peoples. In some versions, the Israelites were ancestors only of the British; in others, of the "Anglo-Saxon–Celtic peoples"; and occasionally, of all northern Europeans. They reached this conclusion by reconstructing the purported wanderings of the Ten Lost Tribes. They also drew in other ideas, including esoteric meanings of the Great Pyramid (about which Capt wrote at length) and revisionist histories of the ancient Near East.[26]

Theories about the Asiatic location of Eden and the Flood received particular emphasis in an American offshoot of British-Israelism, Christian Identity. Christian Identity emphasized the Israelite origins of the white race, or, in its followers' terminology, Aryans. Its virulently racist and anti-Semitic theology was most forcefully expressed in the 1940s and 1950s by a California preacher, Wesley Swift, who had been deeply influenced by the ideas of Capt and Haberman. Childress appears to have drawn from the same reservoir of stigmatized knowledge, unaware of the political uses to which others, such as Swift, had put it.[27]

Unintended Consequences of the September 11 Crisis

Precisely because crises are by definition unexpected, they can produce effects unanticipated by those who provoke them. This is true of September 11, 2001, even though the World Trade Center and Pentagon attacks were apparently the result of meticulous planning. In addition to the consequences anticipated by Osama bin Laden, therefore, there were results that lay completely outside the terrorists' calculations.

Insofar as the unintended consequences involve conspiracists, they fall into two categories: those that result directly from the attacks themselves, and those that derive from the government's response to the attacks. The attacks inflicted a collective trauma on Americans not seen since the assassination of John F. Kennedy nearly forty years earlier. There was, however, an important difference: the Kennedy assassination created a conspiracist subculture where little previously existed, while September 11 occurred in the presence of an already flourishing atmosphere of conspiracism. In 2001, conspiracists needed only to insert the attacks into any of a number of preexisting plots. In doing so, as seen here, they freely added all sorts of legends, rumors, and false reports. Their fundamental conclusion did not depend on the confirmation of such legends and reports. Rather, they argued that they already knew who was responsible for the world's evil; therefore, the attacks were seen as merely an additional demonstration of what was already established truth. To the extent that September 11 required any revision of conspiracy theories, it suggested that the plotters were even more brazen and desperate than previously thought.

Bin Laden and his minions, in addition to the damage they inflicted, thus reinforced a conspiracy culture of whose existence they were likely unaware. The fact that the perpetrators of the attacks were quickly identified made little difference, because as far as conspiracists are concerned, the visible world is deception, while reality is always hidden. The conspiracists' task, which they performed immediately, was to identify the forces behind the hijackers.

The more significant unintended consequences, however, came later, after the federal government began to propose and implement new counterterrorism measures. Both the proposals and the rhetoric used to describe them inadvertently evoked parallels with the New World Order ideas that undergird contemporary American conspiracism. For example, conspiracists took *homeland defense* to mean that the imposition of martial law was imminent. Proposals to make FEMA part of a new, cabinet-level homeland-security agency raised even greater conspiracist anxieties. As already described in chapter 4, the demonization of FEMA had become a virtual article of faith in conspiracist circles, whether among militia members, fundamentalists, or ufologists. They therefore viewed anything that empowered FEMA as particularly sinister.[28]

In the atmosphere of fear that followed September 11, such concerns were, of course, the furthest thing from the minds of either policymakers or the general public. There is no reason to think that any of the measures proposed or taken had any connection with conspiracist fantasies. Nonetheless, for those who already believed that history is a plot, the post–September 11 developments were read as validation. Given the closed, self-perpetuating character of conspiracy ideas, there was little anyone could have done to eradicate such beliefs.

The danger lies less in such beliefs themselves, however, than in the behavior they might stimulate or justify. As long as the New World Order appeared to be almost but not quite a reality, devotees of conspiracy theories could be expected to confine their activities to propagandizing. On the other hand, should they believe that the prophesied evil day had in fact arrived, their behavior would become far more difficult to predict.

As students of apocalyptic beliefs have learned, predictions of violence made on the basis of beliefs alone are notoriously unreliable. Inflammatory rhetoric can come from otherwise peaceable individuals. It does appear, however, that apocalypticists are more likely to engage in violence if they believe themselves to be trapped or under attack. Both conditions are as much the product of their own perception as of outside forces. Measures that appear innocuous to some may seem threatening to others if the information is filtered through the appropriate belief system. It remains to be seen whether that volatile conjunction of perception, belief, and action will emerge out of the post–September 11 environment.

CHAPTER 11

Conclusion

Millennialists from Outer Space

Millennialism and New World Order conspiracy theories have been closely intertwined. As discussed earlier, many of the religious New World Order writers were attracted to conspiracy theories precisely because they seemed to provide a way of predicting the emergence of the Antichrist. Improvisational millenarians, operating outside of any single religious or secular tradition, have had a wider palette available with which to paint a picture of end-time events.

Insofar as UFO authors are concerned, some have seen the ships' inhabitants as the catalysts for the millennial consummation. This has been particularly true of those who characterize extraterrestrials as spiritually elevated saviors whose arrival will herald a new age for humanity. While believers in "space brothers" have sometimes been conspiracists, they have more often simply awaited the ETs' arrival without positing an evil cabal in opposition. The most famous group in this category, the Canada-based Raelian Movement, is now intent on cloning human beings as a way of achieving perfection.[1]

Among the conspiracy-minded, millennialism has included a generalized belief in the end of history, attempts to fuse alien arrival with Christian millennialism, the addition of non-Western millenarian ideas, and even the belief that millennialism itself is part of the conspirators' plot.

UFOs as an End-Time Sign

Conspiracy-charged UFO material lends itself to apocalyptic imagery. It combines an unprecedented event—the arrival of intelligent, nonhuman species—with groups that are demonically evil, made up either of human beings alone, or aliens, or some pernicious alliance between the two. Once these elements are in place, one need not engage in much elaboration to envision an end to ordinary history.

That is essentially the posture Milton William Cooper took in *Behold a Pale Horse,* whose very title is drawn from the Book of Revelation. Despite the millennialism implicit in this scenario, Cooper never developed a conventionally Christian millenarian position. Indeed, he appeared to be simultaneously convinced that epochal events were coming and agnostic about the form they would take.

Cooper speculated about both apocalyptic destruction and world salvation. On the one hand, he suggested that economic, environmental, and military instabilities might cause a series of calamities that would result in human beings becoming extinct. On the other, he offered the possibility that biblical end-time events are imminent. In this vein, he reported that at a meeting between the aliens and government officials, the visitors showed the officials a hologram of the crucifixion, which prompted Cooper to pose a series of rhetorical questions: "Were they using our GENUINE religions to manipulate us? Or were they indeed the source of our religions with which they had been manipulating us all along? Or was this the beginning scenario of the genuine END-TIMES and the RETURN OF CHRIST which had been predicted in the Bible?" Despite Cooper's own fervent belief in Christianity, he could only reply: "I DO NOT KNOW THE ANSWER."[2]

Aliens and Christian Millennialism

Others do not share Cooper's uncertainty and are far more willing to integrate aliens into the Book of Revelation's eschatological script. By absorbing New World Order conspiracy beliefs, UFO writers have been able to link ideas about extraterrestrials with more traditional apocalyptic expectations. Because conceptions of the New World Order had already been made signposts of the Antichrist, there was now a natural point of contact between dispensational premillennialism and alien visitation.

Commander X summarizes the entire dispensationalist scenario, while Branton liberally quotes Revelation, including much of the twelfth chapter's description of the war in heaven between the archangel Michael and the dragon. In similar fashion, the thirteenth chapter, which contains the famous passage about the mark of the beast, merges effortlessly with conspiracists' stories about devices allegedly implanted in abductees.[3]

UFO conspiracists have also co-opted the Rapture. Those who are worthy will be lifted off the earth, not by Christ but by alien spaceships. According to Timothy Green Beckley, the Tribulation and the Rapture are nothing less than predictions of the calamities that will soon befall the earth and of the arrival of aliens to effect what he and others refer to as "the Evacuation." The Phoenix publications provide an even more overtly Christological version. It comes not from Hatonn but from one Jesus Sananda, who tells the faithful, "Until it is finished I will leave My messengers upon your place and then, they shall be lifted up into the security of My places of safety and Light and you who choose to listen not and continue to abandon My Truth shall remain outside My city with the sorcerers and the immoral and murderers and idolators."[4]

Sananda's transmission goes on to describe, among other things, a "United States . . . rent in twain in the area of the Mississippi River and the region of Canada, the Great Lakes as you call them, and that river shall be split to the Gulf of Mexico, into Central America and all that environ shall be changed." In addition, much of the rest of the country, with the exception of the highest mountains, will be under water; there will be a vast new mountain range in the East, even as the seaboard is flooded; and England, France, and Russia will disappear. Then, for three thousand years, there will be "A RESTING PLACE OF PLANET EARTH" until she is repeopled from other solar systems. But of course, those who hear the message "SHALL BE LIFTED UP INTO THOSE CRAFT WHICH RIDE THE WAVES OF THE ENERGIES OF THE UNIVERSE" and will escape the destruction.[5]

Expectations of turmoil requiring the virtuous to leave the planet— the calamities also associated with Alternative 3—blend Christian conceptions of the Tribulation with "earth changes." *Earth changes* refers to imminent cataclysmic events affecting all or most of the planet, involving dramatic alterations such as massive earthquakes, the melting of the polar ice cap, and the shifting of the planet's axis. These predictions occur frequently in New Age literature, often without any explicit association with either Christian millennialism or UFOs. In the infinitely permeable realm of improvisational millennialism, however, they have established connections with both.

Although some earth changes exponents posit physical causes susceptible to scientific investigation, most claim knowledge derived from paranormal sources. Among the earliest was Kentucky psychic Edgar

Cayce (1877–1945), who, beginning in the 1920s, produced predictions of earth changes while in trance states. More recently, Gordon-Michael Scallion claims to receive such forecasts in dreams, while J. Z. Knight does so as a channeler for a Lemurian named Ramtha. Since the 1970s, these and similar claims have spread widely in New Age circles. As a conspicuous element in the domain of stigmatized knowledge, they would inevitably come to the attention of UFO believers. For many, earth changes have consequently become the functional equivalent of the dispensationalist Tribulation—the time of chaos and calamity that will help bring mundane history to an end. They also serve as the justification for the secular equivalent of the Rapture—the partial evacuation of the planet by benign extraterrestrials. In the more secular scenario, however, the calamities require the knowing and powerful few to exit the earth on their own, leaving the majority to an unkind fate. This is the Alternative 3 script. It sometimes includes alien allies, but sometimes expects that there will be a manufactured alien invasion in order to justify the dictatorship required to organize space colonization.[6]

An Alternative Millennium

Not all improvisational millennialists considered here rely on Christian motifs. Just as improvisationalists can combine dispensationalism with earth changes, so too they can appropriate non-Christian end-time ideas. This has increasingly been the case for David Icke, who claims to have little use for conventional religion.

Icke believes the momentous time of change lies ahead—more specifically, on December 12, 2012. For him, the year 2000 was only a "manufactured Millennium," manipulated by the hidden conspirators to mislead the masses. The date 12/12/12, by contrast, is "the real focal point of transformation," the "gateway . . . which open[s] for those who are ready to move through into a much higher state of consciousness." He derives the date from the ancient Mayan calendar and sees it as the culmination of a 26,000-year "transformative cycle." If humanity can grasp this concept, Icke claims, it can throw off the conspiracy's yoke.[7]

The immediate advantages of the date are clear. First, it offered insurance against disappointments in the year 2000, since the latter was not the "real" millennial date. Second, it pushed the actual date forward. As the Millerites found in the 1840s, date setting has its pitfalls. But the greater the emphasis on imminent changes, the greater the internal pressure for specificity. In addition, the more specific the prediction, the more temporarily authoritative is the claim to privileged knowledge.

Icke almost certainly got the date from the writings of José Arguelles, who more than anyone else has popularized Mayan calendrical speculation in New Age circles. Arguelles became briefly famous in August 1987 for having predicted the "harmonic convergence," a moment when, according to him, "if 144,000 persons could respond to the call of meditating at dawn, on August 16 and 17, 1987, the world would be renewed and humanity would enter a 'new age.'" Arguelles's fusion of the Mayan calendar (or at least his representation of it) with the 144,000 saved of Revelation epitomizes the hybridizing tendencies of improvisational millennialism.[8]

In the years after the harmonic convergence phenomenon, Arguelles has emphasized the greater importance of 2012. The millennial consummation on that date will expose the true nature of UFOs "as interdimensional, Earth-generated, galactically programmed electromagnetic cells, available to us for our own educational purposes, . . . [and as] the meeting grounds of intelligence from different sectors of the galaxy." In the meantime, he fears that the New World Order has at least temporarily "sealed the fate of the planet in an evil dumb-show in which the only option is enforced enslavement to an out-of-control machine."[9]

Icke's absorption of Arguelles's neo-Mayan millennialism again suggests the omnivorous character of the improvisational style. Truth is deemed to be everywhere, particularly in those niches of rejected knowledge marked with the stigma applied by mainstream institutions.

The Fraudulent Millennium

UFO conspiracists are sometimes surprisingly hostile to prevalent millenarian ideas, which they see as part of the apparatus of deception constructed by their adversaries. As the year 2000 approached, Icke came to regard commemorative activities as worse than irrelevant. Not only did the year 2000 signify nothing of genuine importance; the efforts to mark it, especially in Britain, were part of a larger plan to keep humanity in servitude to the secret ruling elite. The specific object of Icke's scorn was the Millennium Dome, the massive exhibition facility constructed in Greenwich. Long before it became evident that the dome would be a colossal popular and financial failure, Icke was convinced that it represented a diabolical attempt to "scramble human consciousness." [10]

Even though "the Millennium is a manufactured point in time," according to Icke, the placement of the dome near the Greenwich meridian ("the zero point of so-called Greenwich Mean Time") held the potential for altering human consciousness. This peculiar thesis was an outgrowth of Icke's belief in the magical properties of symbols and their spatial arrangement. We have already seen an example of this type of magical thinking in speculation about the occult purposes of the Washington, D.C., street plan (discussed in chapter 8). Conspiracy writers—Icke above all—increasingly assert that what matters is not merely the content of a symbol but its spatial location relative to other symbols. Strategic placement allegedly releases invisible forces that have profound effects on human behavior. In a manner not unlike that of feng shui believers, they see danger in seemingly innocuous locational decisions, except that of course they do not consider such arrangements to be innocent. Rather, these arrangements represent conscious decisions on the part of conspirators to deprive humanity of the powers of free choice.[11]

An even more radical antimillennialism appears in the work of Valdamar Valerian. Valerian, it will be recalled, is a former air force enlisted man who moved from relatively traditional UFO studies to sweeping conspiracy theories about wholesale attempts to alter human consciousness. Valerian's massive *Matrix* volumes consist largely of texts reprinted from other sources, many of which emphasize the malevolent and deceptive nature of alien races.

Among these texts is one asserting that the aliens whose messages have been received by channelers or those in purported radio contact are in fact malevolent. These include such figures as Hatonn and those associated with the Ashtar Command, along with their earthbound receivers, Dharma (Doris Ekker), Sister Thedra (Dorothy Martin), and Tuella (Thelma B. Terrell). All have allegedly been deceived. The promise of a Rapture-like evacuation and an alien Jesus figure (Sananda), through whom the end-time Book of Revelation script will be fulfilled, are elements of a carefully crafted plan for domination.[12]

This does not mean that Icke and Valerian themselves are antimillenarian, only that they have distanced themselves from more conventional millenarian ideas. Icke has elaborated a New Age millennialism that pushes the final date forward to 2012. In somewhat similar fashion, Valerian promises that those who can break the bonds of illusion will achieve a millenniumlike "higher consciousness." [13]

Millennium versus Apocalypse

Millennium and *apocalypse* tend to be used interchangeably, but in fact they possess different associations. *Millennium* connotes a time of maximal fulfillment—whether of prophecy, human potentiality, or divine promise. *Apocalypse,* according to Chip Berlet, suggests "an approaching confrontation, cataclysmic event, or transformation of epochal proportion, about which a select few have forewarning." Much of the time, the two are tightly interwoven: the confrontational events associated with the apocalypse, such as the Battle of Armageddon, are deemed to be essential preconditions for the attainment of the millennium. Catherine Wessinger has this in mind when she speaks of "catastrophic millennialism," in which an era of bliss requires prior turmoil.[14]

Apocalypse and millennialism are not always seamlessly joined. For example, in what Wessinger calls "progressive millennialism," the millennium is incrementally achieved through a gradualism that makes apocalyptic disasters unnecessary. In its diluted form, this concept is not unlike the prevalent belief in inevitable progress, according to which cumulative knowledge and ingenuity will remedy most human ills.[15]

There is another possibility, however—one in which apocalypse stands alone, severed from any connection with the millennium. This notion might form part of a vision of the future in which history ends in cataclysmic upheavals, with no compensatory millennium to follow. Such gloomy finality is likely to have few takers, because most people desire a benign future. Nevertheless, the logic of their arguments often pushes conspiracists in precisely this direction.

The problem for conspiracists lies in the extraordinary power they impute to the conspiracy. Speaking of what he called the "paranoid political style," Richard Hofstadter wrote, "The apocalypticism of the paranoid style runs dangerously near to hopeless pessimism, but usually stops short of it." If the conspirators possess as much power and cunning as conspiracists believe, what assurance is there that the forces of good really will triumph in the end?[16]

A definitive apocalypse—a final calamity from which there is no escape—can be more easily sustained as a fictional conceit than as an authentic future expectation. Even in fiction, however, it appears difficult to believe in an apocalypse from which there is no exit. W. Warren Wagar, in his study of end-of-the-world literature, found that two-thirds of the examples posit a future different from the destroyed present. Many of the rest predict a cyclical return to a lost past. Only one fiction in six is genuinely a "dead end," which leads Wagar to conclude that "[t]he bulk of eschatological fictions . . . can be read as indicators of a growing consciousness within modern Western culture that its end is in view and that a new, higher, or radically different civilization . . . will replace it." [17]

Conspiracists find themselves in much the same dilemma as the apocalyptic authors. The logic of their narrative carries them to the edge of despair even as they yearn for a millennial outcome. Their problem is exacerbated by the fact that they often become so intent on elaborating descriptions of the conspiracy that they end up with an adversary who cannot be defeated.

This process may account for the dramatic reversals of position occasionally encountered in the genre. Cooper, after having long insisted on the veracity of his account of the aliens, suddenly concluded that he had been mistaken, duped by all-too-human conspirators who had concocted an alien threat to cloak their designs. Similarly, the fascination with *Alternative 3* (described in chapter 5) offers a welcome escape from all-powerful space beings. Even diabolical human conspirators can in principle be defeated—not necessarily true of extraterrestrials.

A Worldview without a Movement?

One of the most perplexing aspects of the material examined here is that it has spread with little in the way of an organized support structure. In this respect, it differs from positive, UFO-centered religious groups such as Unarius and the Raelians. Although the individuals considered here often have widely distributed publications and well-designed Web sites, none has become the leader of a group. Their ideas have diffused widely, but there are no clear structures through which believers might be mobilized on their behalf.

It is fashionable, of course, to speak of "virtual communities" created by the Internet, and certainly practices such as Web site links, multiple postings, and cross-citation reinforce the idea that Web authors and their readers share membership in a Net-mediated community. Nonetheless, the absence of formal organizations is striking. It raises a question of significance that cannot be evaded with such metaphors as *virtual community*.

If the conspiracy theories described here are relatively unconnected to means of mobilization, of what significance are the ideas? Put another way, what are the mechanisms through which these ideas might influence others? Influence can occur, despite the absence of an organizational framework, through three interrelated processes: repositioning, mainstreaming, and bridging.

REPOSITIONING CONSPIRACISM

Conspiracism is, first and foremost, an explanation of politics. It purports to locate and identify the true loci of power and thereby illuminate previously hidden decision making. The conspirators, often referred to as a shadow or hidden government, operate a concealed political system behind the visible one, whose functionaries are either ciphers or puppets.

The political content of conspiracy theories has been reinforced by their longtime identification with primarily political organizations. These have included groups at the outer reaches of normal politics, such as the John Birch Society, as well as pariah groups that operate entirely outside of conventional political discourse. The latter include militias, Posse Comitatus, Ku Klux Klan groups, and neo-Nazi organizations. Despite doctrinal differences, extreme right-wing political groups have historically attributed decisive power to conspirators—Jewish bankers, the Council on Foreign Relations, the Trilateral Commission, and similar dark forces of the sort discussed in chapter 4.

This preference for conspiracist explanations has been both a cause and an effect of group marginalization. By violating the norms of American democratic pluralism in their search for scapegoats, these groups guaranteed their exile to the political wilderness. At the same time, their exclusion, lack of sympathetic media coverage, and absence of large followings could be explained not by their own shortcomings but by the conspiracy's alleged machinations.

As long as conspiracy theories, such as those that posit a New World Order plot, were strongly linked to antigovernment militants, anti-Semites, and neo-Nazis, the audience for conspiracism was limited. This was true even though conspiracism has also found a niche among religious fundamentalists as part of Antichrist theology. This political exile, however, now seems to be over, thanks to the incorporation of New World Order conspiracy into UFO beliefs.

The result of that incorporation has been a repositioning of conspiracism. Instead of being primarily associated with anti-Semites, racists, and antigovernment protesters, it now cohabits with Atlantis believers, alien channelers, and others who have no obvious political identity.

More explicitly, conspiracism has now been placed squarely within the domain of stigmatized knowledge, where it shares attention with alternative cancer cures, free energy panaceas, and lore about the Great Pyramid.

These associations are not entirely new, of course. The cultic-milieu sympathies of those on the extreme right have long been evident in their support of alternative healing, natural foods, and revisionist history. Nonetheless, to the extent that conspiracism had its primary home among white racists and other outré political groups, the secondary associations with apolitical stigmatized knowledge offered little protective coloration. Conspiracism was doubly tainted, first as part of the stigmatized knowledge domain, and then through its links with particularly stigmatized political organizations.[18]

Because of the expansion into ufology, the politics of conspiracism now constitutes merely a segment of a large and diverse array of subjects, and not always the most important one. As one constituent among many, it benefits from the apparently nonpartisan character of the rest. The others may be stigmatized knowledge, and they may give rise to ridicule, but they are not necessarily viewed as irreparably tainted or politically suspect.

An example of this repositioning may be found in the Australian magazine *Nexus,* which circulates widely in conspiracist circles in the United States. The American edition professes no link "to any religious, philosophical or political ideology or organization." A banner across the top of the cover identifies its subjects as "Behind the News * Health * UFOs * Future Science." A typical issue included an article about President George W. Bush's and Vice President Dick Cheney's alleged links to a "global drug pipeline," but this exercise in conspiracism was nestled among articles on UFOs, the inner earth, and food irradiation.[19]

Recontextualizing conspiracism significantly reduces its association with tainted politics. At the same time, repositioning affords the opportunity for reaching large new audiences through mainstreaming.

MAINSTREAMING CONSPIRACISM

Prior to the early 1990s, New World Order conspiracism was limited to two subcultures, primarily the militantly antigovernment right, and secondarily Christian fundamentalists concerned with the end-time emergence of the Antichrist. Their beliefs did not spread readily to outsiders. The extreme right constituted a pariah group whose viewpoints were systematically excluded from channels of mass communication and distribution. Fundamentalists were in a different position, having at their disposal cable television and mass-market paperback books, but their audience consisted largely of those either already affiliated with evangelical churches or predisposed to seek out the messages of televangelists. Indeed, as noted earlier, Pat Robertson's book *The New World Order,* almost certainly the most widely available conspiracist tract, did not become a subject of broad discussion until four years after publication—suggesting that despite its appearance in such venues as airport paperback racks, its message was directed at a niche audience, and therefore ignored by others. In addition, when it was published, the Internet was not yet a mass medium of communication.

Diffusion of New World Order ideas into ufology still left it in a fringe cultural location, associated with yet another set of deviant beliefs, albeit a less tainted one. Nevertheless, this association proved to be a highly beneficial one for conspiracism. In the first place, ufology constituted a vast new potential audience. As pointed out in chapter 5, survey data over more than half a century has demonstrated consistently high levels of public awareness and acceptance of UFO and alien-visitation beliefs. So New World Order ideas now were linked to motifs regarded sympathetically by tens of millions of Americans. Second, the repositioning process just described resulted in a sanitized conspiracism, less clearly associated with anti-Semitism and racism and benefiting from its new proximity to such subjects as ancient civilizations and alternative healing. Finally, the migration of conspiracism into ufology just preceded the rise of the Internet, so that when Web-based communication began to surge in the early and middle 1990s, UFO conspiracism was in a position to take full advantage of the new medium. Strictly speaking, these developments did not amount to full mainstreaming; even so, they brought New World Order beliefs to a vastly larger audience.

A more overt form of mainstreaming, however, was also about to take place. This involved the recycling of core conspiracist themes into popular culture, particularly television and motion pictures. Such arcane conspiracist concepts as mind control, polar bases, and FEMA dictatorship reached immense audiences through *The X-Files* and similar television programs, and films including *The X-Files* and *Conspiracy Theory.* Although these shows did not include systematic expositions of New World Order ideas (the phrase was often not actually mentioned), ideas once limited to fringe audiences became commonplace in mass media.

This overt mainstreaming had two consequences. First, it advanced the process by which conspiracism was becoming culturally sanitized, because the association of conspiracism with major television networks and motion picture studios gave the material an implied stamp of legitimacy. If major organs of popular entertainment presented such ideas, they must be, at the least, respectable, regardless of whether one chose to believe them. Second, at the same time that a quasilegitimacy was conferred, the opportunity for huge new audiences opened up. Linked now to such nonstigmatized genres as science fiction, elements of conspiracism reached millions who would not otherwise have been exposed to it. In the past, access to such material required purposeful acts by the seeker: purchasing publications, searching for Web sites, and so on. Now conspiracism was integrated into cultural products widely regarded as innocuous forms of entertainment.

BRIDGING MECHANISMS

At the same time that repositioning and mainstreaming were making conspiracism palatable and accessible, the likelihood that these new audiences might be drawn more deeply into the domain of stigmatized knowledge was facilitated by bridging mechanisms. Bridging mechanisms are organizational devices that link the domain of stigmatized knowledge to accepted forms of political expression. Thus they constitute transmission belts that can take an individual from mainstream associations to fringe ones. This process has been significantly facilitated by the repositioning and mainstreaming just described, as the latter reduce the negative associations of conspiracism while making it more accessible. Three bridging mechanisms are of particular significance here: the cultivation of crossover audiences, the development of alternative communications systems, and the indivisibility of the stigmatized knowledge domain.[20]

To the extent that one can distinguish separate audiences, each made up of individuals drawn to a particular set of issues, they might be thought of in terms of such segments as New Age, ufology, alternative science and medicine, antigovernment, and so on. An increasing number of writers cultivate more than one such audience, explicitly reaching out to groups whose memberships may only slightly overlap. Thus, Cooper spoke to both antigovernment militants and ufologists, and Jim Marrs to ufologists and conspiracists.

Icke is the most significant crossover author, addressing both New

Age audiences and the antigovernment right. As described in chapter 6, Icke systematically speaks to both of these groups in his books and lecture tours. In the latter, he speaks at times under New Age sponsorship and at times at the "preparedness expos" whose clientele includes gun owners, survivalists, and militia members.

By openly addressing two or more audiences simultaneously, the writer or speaker signifies to each that it is a member of a larger, more inclusive community, made up of all those who are addressed, regardless of whether they usually associate with each other. The message is that otherwise dissimilar individuals—for example, UFO believers and right-wing antigovernment conspiracists—in fact share a fundamental worldview, notwithstanding their apparent differences. The message of inclusiveness is also reinforced by the unsegmented character of the domain of stigmatized knowledge.

That domain, as we have seen, is made up of rejected, outdated, and ignored knowledge claims, regardless of subject matter. It contains material drawn from revisionist history, pseudoscience, alternative medicine, occultism, new and alternative religions, and political sectarianism. Despite these differences of focus, all share certain overarching similarities: the disdain or disinterest of mainstream institutions, along with the common outsider status conferred by that disdain or disinterest, and a consequent suspicion of the institutions that have excluded them.

These fringe beliefs, and the resulting pariah status of the believers, have stimulated the growth of an alternative communications system by which stigmatized ideas can be spread. This alternative system is necessary even though mainstreaming has opened popular culture to some traditionally stigmatized beliefs. Although this access has promoted both recruitment and enhanced legitimacy, it has significant limits. First, it almost always occurs within the context of fictional representations of the world, such as films and television programs. It does not purport to offer an accurate picture of reality, even though the fact-fiction reversals discussed earlier lead believers to regard it as truthful. Second, it is fragmentary and episodic rather than systematic. That is, the stigmatized material usually takes the form of an individual motif incorporated into the story, as in the reference to the power of FEMA in the film *The X-Files*. It does not take the form of a comprehensive and logically developed presentation of an alternative view of reality.

Consequently, while conspiracists can draw the curious from those exposed to newly mainstreamed ideas, the mainstreaming itself does not fill the communications needs of the conspiracist subculture. Those needs are met by an alternative communications system cobbled together from a variety of both old and new media. The former include magazines for niche audiences, specialized publishers, and, in larger cities, bookshops that cater to conspiracist readers. The latter include videotapes, Web sites, and Internet chat rooms.

One of the striking characteristics of the messages diffused through this system is that they do not respect the distinctions among segments of the stigmatized knowledge domain. Such subject-specific areas as crank science, conspiracist politics, and occultism are not isolated from one another; rather, they are interconnected. Someone seeking information on UFOs, for example, can quickly find material on antigravity, free energy, Atlantis studies, alternative cancer cures, and conspiracy.

The consequence of such mingling is that an individual who enters the communications system pursuing one interest soon becomes aware of stigmatized material on a broad range of subjects. As a result, those who come across one form of stigmatized knowledge will learn of others, in connections that imply that stigmatized knowledge is a unified domain, an alternative worldview, rather than a collection of unrelated ideas.

From Conspiracism to Millennialism

As pointed out earlier, one can believe in conspiracies without expecting the millennium. To separate the two, however, leaves the conspiracist in a distinctly awkward position. Either the conspiracies one believes in must be limited in scope, so that the rest of one's worldview remains intact, or one's worldview comes to be dominated by the battles with evil. If the latter, the choice is between the despair of the virtuous weak, condemned to fighting rearguard actions that can do little more than delay the conspiracy's victory, and the hope of the millennialist who may appear weak at the moment but is confident of ultimate triumph. Little wonder, then, that those whose conspiracy beliefs are the most elaborate are likely to fit them into a vision of end-time conflict.

The conspiracism described in the preceding chapters developed over the last decade of the twentieth century into the connective tissue binding together a heterogeneous assortment of beliefs and ideas. They concern an alleged shadow government, the secret circles of religious and fraternal organizations, a hidden world beneath our feet, and the machinations of alien intelligences. The elements can be arranged in innumerable permutations. Because all that is visible is deception, one permutation may seem as likely as any other. All claim empirical truth, but none trusts conventional canons of evidence. Thus the empirical claims coexist with nonfalsifiability.

This combination of eclectic materials, hidden knowledge, and distrust of authority is the essence of improvisational millennialism. Because the disparate elements can be endlessly recombined, and because traditional religious authority is deemed to have been co-opted by the forces of evil, every practitioner of improvisational millennialism becomes his or her own millenarian entrepreneur. The bricolage required by the improvisational style permits anyone to try his or her hand at rearranging the blocks, so that, like Legos, they may be combined into new structures.

The millenarian entrepreneur is the individual who brings these components together to form a new end-time belief system. Like other entrepreneurs, the venturesome millenarian must merchandise the new ideological product in a marketplace filled with competitors. The latter, advancing their own idiosyncratic creeds, vie with one another for the allegiance of the seeker/consumers, in search of a satisfying transcendent vision. Because the improvisationalist works outside the confines of any single belief system, he or she now has an unprecedentedly large potential audience.

It might be supposed that such improvisation would produce only chaos, but oddly enough, the result tends to be the opposite of incoherence. The components keep reappearing from one structure to another, albeit in different roles—Vatican inner circles, malevolent aliens, secret councils of plutocrats, subterranean installations, and so on. In effect, as New World Order ideas have spread and have attached themselves to ufology, the result has been the development of a common millenarian vocabulary—a set of ideas held jointly by a large if ill-defined subculture. The individual combinations may be idiosyncratic, but the components are shared and understood. Ideas about the New World Order have consequently become the ideological glue binding together an ever more disparate array of elements, some political, some spiritual, some pseudoscientific.

As a result, this seemingly anarchic realm of stigmatized knowledge acquires an unexpected unity. Virtually no one of significance within the domain rejects New World Order beliefs, though there are different degrees of emphasis as well as disagreements about the control and timetable of New World Order operations. These are, however, disputes within belief systems that have a family resemblance and share a common, politically charged vocabulary.

How Permeable Are the Boundaries?

The concept of stigmatized knowledge implies boundaries separating a culturally and socially defined mainstream from beliefs and ideas outside it. The boundary is maintained in a variety of ways: by withholding access to the most powerful and prestigious channels of communication; by withholding institutional rewards and sponsorship from certain ideas; and by subjecting fringe ideas and those who hold them to scorn. Virtually everything discussed in the preceding chapters has at one time or another stood on the far side of this boundary. Like most boundaries, however, this one has not been an absolute barrier to interaction. There has been traffic in both directions. Sometimes ideas once held in repute have been rejected, as has been the case with scientific racism, which was an orthodoxy until World War II but is now regarded as without foundation. So, too, fringe ideas can sometimes leave the domain of stigmatized knowledge, as has now happened with some alternative therapies, such as acupuncture.

Ideas can also jump cultural boundaries. The presence of Asian motifs in some strains of Western millennialism has been noted since the late nineteenth century. Indeed, they figured at least indirectly in the earlier discussion of Theosophy. While less remarked upon, there is also movement in the opposite direction, from Western millennialism to non-Western cultures. David Cook has pointed out, for example, that elements of both Christian apocalyptic and anti-Semitic conspiracy theories have found their way into contemporary Islamic millennialism.[21]

But even though the boundary separating cultural orthodoxy from stigmatized knowledge claims has been permeable, it has largely held. At the turn of the twenty-first century, however, questions are now being raised about the continued strength—indeed, the very existence—of the boundary, and those questions are particularly significant for the conspiracism and improvisational millennialism I have been concerned with here.

The most extreme such position within recent scholarly explorations of this issue is that of Jodi Dean. Dean argues that there is no longer a "consensus reality" according to which contested questions of fact can be resolved. She suggests that on subjects such as alien abduction and political conspiracies, there are multiple contending realities, which keep contested issues from being decided. Further, the ease with which individuals who hold such views can communicate with one another allows them to form at least "virtual" communities and provide the requisite social support to one another.[22]

Dean's position, while extreme in its suggestion of epistemological anarchy, is sufficiently reflective of the material considered here that it must be taken seriously. One implication of her view is that with the dissolution of the boundary between fringe and mainstream, there is no longer a domain of stigmatized knowledge. Factors to which Dean points, such as the Internet and a widespread suspicion of authority, support such a position. Nevertheless, so radical a view strikes me as excessive. Although important changes have occurred, not every belief stands on an equal level.

Two other factors need to be borne in mind. First, there have always been individuals and subcultures wedded to alternative conceptions of reality, including artists, mystics, bohemians, and others, who voluntarily secede from the prevailing consensus reality. What happened to them in the past, and how they related to the majority, is a subject too complex to deal with here. Their outcomes depended on, among other things, the general level of social tolerance, the availability of social roles for deviants (e.g., the "eccentric artist," such as William Blake), and whether such persons sought to impose their view of reality on others. Second, at least some of those who espouse alternative conceptions of reality construct closed systems of belief, so that they enter any epistemological conversation already equipped to ignore, exclude, or reject any evidence that calls their beliefs into question.

A large part of my task has been to describe conspiracists who think in terms of such closed systems and to suggest that their ranks are increasing. To make such a claim, however, is not to say definitively that there is no longer a consensus reality. Rather, it is to say merely that the boundary has become more permeable. Ideas once relegated to the ghetto of stigmatized knowledge now more easily reach mainstream audiences. But that does not mean that the stories about Nostradamus, Bigfoot, and space aliens that spice the covers of supermarket tabloids and circulate on the Internet will also appear in *Time, Newsweek,* and *The New York Times,* or that the two segments of the mass media will be regarded as equally authoritative.

We have not yet entered a world of complete epistemological pluralism, and it is unclear how such a world would or could function in everyday life, where mundane social, economic, and governmental business is transacted. But conspiracists, particularly those who believe in superconspiracies, do seem to inhabit a different epistemic universe, where the usual rules for determining truth and falsity do not apply. To the extent that their ranks are growing, they pose a problem that is at once cultural and political.

Improvisational Millennialists Armed?

Popular stereotypes to the contrary, millennialists rarely employ violence, and those few who do rarely initiate it against outsiders. Among recent improvisational millennialists, only one group has done so, Aum Shinrikyo in Japan. Aum's belief system was typically eclectic, with a mixture of esoteric Buddhism, Nostradamus, Christian millennialism, and anti-Semitic conspiracism. Yet it was scarcely typical in its development of biological and chemical weapons. Indeed, its affinity for the latter is so atypical that it is best regarded as an aberration rather than a template.[23]

When millennialists do use violence, it is almost always in response to a perceived threat. There is no reason to suppose that the characteristic ideological complexion of the improvisational style will alter this tendency. On the other hand, might there be some attributes of the millennialism under consideration that would be conducive to an association with violence?

Let me begin by paraphrasing earlier conclusions. A growing number of people believe that a superconspiracy commonly referred to as the New World Order is on the verge of consolidating world domination, possibly in collaboration with malevolent aliens. The conspirators allegedly operate through so wide-ranging a network of confederates that they have co-opted authority figures in every sector of life. Through this control, in turn, they shape the information available to the general public and thus conceal the conspiracy's existence and activities.

Conspiracists who hold such views will, as a matter of course, reject any information from conventionally authoritative sources. In that sense, they lie outside some of the tacit understandings that constitute reality as most Americans understand it. At the moment, those understandings still appear to prevail. We are not yet in a situation of radical epistemological pluralism in which different groups espouse completely different ideas of what is real. Even those involved in bitterly contested "culture wars" over issues such as abortion still inhabit the same mental universe where other matters are concerned.

As indicated earlier, there have always been some genuine outsiders who contest everyday notions of reality. They have been effectively marginalized as eccentrics or tolerated in small groups, either in rural areas in which they might live in physical isolation, or in large cities where they benefit from the anonymity of urban life. In any case, their numbers have normally been small enough that terms like *fringe* appeared appropriate.

They may not be appropriate much longer. The nonfalsifiable conspiracism described here has made surprising inroads into the broader culture. That, after all, is what the mainstreaming process is all about. To be sure, the farther it has reached, the more diluted the ideas have become. In its complete and systematic form, belief in superconspiracies is still held by a relatively small segment of the population. Outreach to mass audiences takes the form of fragmentary references or suggestions rather than sustained exposition—a mention of FEMA here, an allusion to implanted microchips there. Nonetheless, these seemingly offhand references suggest a degree of boundary permeability unlike any that has existed in the recent past. When such intrusions stimulate curiosity, the Internet permits instant access to a mass of systematic conspiracist material.

The further spread of such material is not a foregone conclusion: it must, after all, compete with a vast array of other ideas for the attention of audiences. But such expansion is in principle possible, more so than at any other time. The terrorist attacks of September 11, 2001, reaffirmed conspiracists' belief that the world is pervaded by an invisible evil force. At the same time, the general public sought explanations for what seemed inexplicable. As we saw in the preceding chapter, the Internet provided the link between those with questions and those who claimed to have answers. The implications of such expansion are disquieting, for they involve the creation of a larger community of belief whose view of the world is at variance with the prevailing norm. And the variance goes beyond mere eccentricity, because it involves a deviant view of authority.

As we have seen, the domain of stigmatized knowledge has not disappeared, though its separateness has diminished. Stigmatized knowledge claims, however diverse in subject matter, share a common disdain for received ideas and for the institutions that formulate and transmit them. Hence intellectual, political, and spiritual authorities are all deemed to be equally complicit in the plot to suppress true knowledge. The common thread running through such areas as esotericism, pseudoscience, and revisionist history was once incidental, but these areas have now achieved a much greater degree of coherence. That coherence is attributable to the influence of New World Order conspiracism, which is ubiquitous among those who regard mainstream institutions as suspect.

As New World Order ideas and attendant elements of the improvisational milieu break out of their traditional confinement, a new and disconcerting array of possibilities opens up, because those who espouse such ideas represent dissent of a particularly radical sort, rooted in divergent ideas about reality and knowing. While *The X-Files* motto, "Trust no one," may appear innocuous in an escapist drama, its literal application implies a culture war far more extreme than anything seen previously.

If no one can be trusted (except, presumably, others in the truth-seeking cadre), a society becomes divided between believers in received ideas about what counts as knowledge and a no-longer-hidden minority of challengers. The likely outcome of such a polarization is not pleasant to contemplate, for the challengers do not believe their opponents are merely misguided. Rather, the supporters of the status quo are thought to be at best the conspirators' dupes and at worst their accomplices. Hence the alternative reality sees itself as a fighting faith that must obliterate its adversaries.

This is, to be sure, a worst-case scenario, and most worst-case scenarios melt away with time. One hopes that will be the case here. But the fact that the beliefs described in the preceding chapters are bizarre ought not to imply that they are necessarily innocuous or unworthy of careful scrutiny. Bizarre beliefs have broken into the open before. Indeed, new orthodoxies can emerge out of just such ideological undergrowth, sometimes with devastating effects.

Notes

Preface

1. Lou Michel and Dan Herbeck, *American Terrorist: Timothy McVeigh and the Oklahoma City Bombing* (New York: Regan Books, 2001), pp. 155–156. The authors erroneously place Area 51 near Roswell, New Mexico, instead of Las Vegas, Nevada. Mark Shaffer, "McVeigh Listened to Militia-Inspired Arizona Broadcaster," *Arizona Republic*, May 6, 2001; http://www.rickross.com/reference/militia/militia41.html (March 19, 2002).

2. Michael Barkun, *Religion and the Racist Right: The Origins of the Christian Identity Movement*, rev. ed. (Chapel Hill, N.C.: University of North Carolina Press, 1997), pp. xii–xiii.

1. The Nature of Conspiracy Belief

1. The account of the Bohemian Grove incident is based on Randi Rossmann and Lori A. Carter, "Bohemian Grove Intruder Says He Feared Human Sacrifices," *Sonoma Press Democrat*, January 22, 2002, republished on http://www.rense.com/general19/bo.htm (April 15, 2002). For accounts of the Bohemian Grove stories spread by Alex Jones and others, see David Icke, *The Children of the Matrix: How an Interdimensional Race Has Controlled the World for Thousands of Years—and Still Does* (Wildwood, Mo.: Bridge of Love, 2001), pp. 136–137, and idem, *The Biggest Secret* (Scottsdale, Ariz.: Bridge of Love, 1999), pp. 327–329.

2. Daniel Wojcik, *The End of the World as We Know It: Faith, Fatalism, and Apocalypse in America* (New York: New York University Press, 1997), p. 141. Stephen D. O'Leary, *Arguing the Apocalypse: A Theory of Millennial Rhetoric* (New York: Oxford University Press, 1994), p. 6.

3. Robert S. Robins and Jerrold M. Post, *Political Paranoia: The Psychopolitics of Hatred* (New Haven, Conn.: Yale University Press, 1997), pp. 39–40.

4. *The Protocols of the Meetings of the Learned Elders of Zion, with Preface and Explanatory Notes,* ed. and trans. Victor E. Marsden (1934), p. 139. As is often the case with *The Protocols,* the publisher and place of publication are not identified. In addition, the title often changes from edition to edition. For the sake of consistency, in the text I employ the title most frequently given. Stephen Eric Bronner, *A Rumor about the Jews: Reflections on Antisemitism and the Protocols of the Elders of Zion* (New York: St. Martin's Press, 2000), chap. 4.

5. Richard Hofstadter, *The Paranoid Style in American Politics and Other Essays* (New York: Knopf, 1965), pp. 38–39.

6. Hofstadter, *The Paranoid Style in American Politics,* p. 4.

7. Robins and Post, *Political Paranoia,* pp. 19, 53–54.

8. Hofstadter, *The Paranoid Style in American Politics,* pp. 38–39.

9. Ruth Alden Doan, *The Miller Heresy, Millennialism, and American Culture* (Philadelphia: Temple University Press, 1987), pp. 121–125.

10. O'Leary, *Arguing the Apocalypse,* p. 6.

11. Ibid.

12. Wojcik, *The End of the World,* p. 2.

13. Jan Harold Brunvand, *The Vanishing Hitchhiker: American Urban Legends and Their Meanings* (New York: W. W. Norton, 1981), p. 3 ("demigods"). Idem, *Curses! Boiled Again! The Hottest Urban Legends Going* (New York: W. W. Norton, 1989), p. 12 ("told as true"). Patricia A. Turner, *I Heard It through the Grapevine: Rumor in African-American Culture* (Berkeley: University of California Press, 1993), pp. 3–5. Brunvand, *The Vanishing Hitchhiker,* p. 194.

14. Brunvand, *The Vanishing Hitchhiker,* pp. 198–199.

15. Ibid., p. 5. Wojcik, *The End of the World,* p. 219.

2. Millennialism and Stigmatized Knowledge

1. William G. McLoughlin, *Revivals, Awakenings, and Reform: An Essay on Religion and Social Change in America, 1607–1977* (Chicago: University of Chicago Press, 1978), pp. 179–216.

2. Martin E. Marty and R. Scott Appleby, eds., *Fundamentalisms Comprehended* (Chicago: University of Chicago Press, 1995).

3. Daniel Bell, *The End of Ideology: On the Exhaustion of Political Ideas in the Fifties,* rev. ed. (New York: Collier, 1961), pp. 393–402. Francis Fukuyama, *The End of History and the Last Man* (New York: Avon, 1992). Samuel P. Huntington, *The Clash of Civilizations and the Remaking of World Order* (New York: Simon and Schuster, 1996), pp. 95–101.

4. The concept of bricolage employed here is derived from Claude Lévi-Strauss, *The Savage Mind* (Chicago: University of Chicago Press, 1966), pp. 17–22. Michael Barkun, "Politics and Apocalypticism," in *The Encyclopedia of Apocalypticism,* ed. Stephen J. Stein (New York: Continuum, 1998), vol. 3,

pp. 442–460. J. Gordon Melton, *Encyclopedic Handbook of Cults in America*, rev. ed. (New York: Garland, 1992), p. 172. A similar concept of the New Age appears in Michael York, "New Age Commodification and Appropriation of Spirituality," *Journal of Contemporary Religion* 16 (2001): 361–372.

5. The Left Behind volumes' positions on best-seller lists appear on the Web site for the series: http://www.leftbehind.com (March 27, 2002).

6. Each of these radio personalities also operates a Web site: Art Bell, www .artbell.com; Hal Turner, www.halturnershow.com; Alex Jones, www.infoware .com.

7. *The New York Times,* June 29, 2000, section G, 1.

8. James Webb, *The Occult Underground* (La Salle, Ill.: Open Court, 1974). Idem, *The Occult Establishment* (La Salle, Ill.: Open Court, 1976). Colin Campbell, "The Cult, the Cultic Milieu and Secularization," *Sociological Yearbook of Religion in Britain* 5 (London: SCM Press, 1972): 119–136. Michael Barkun, "Conspiracy Theories as Stigmatized Knowledge: The Basis for a New Age Racism?" in *Nation and Race: The Developing Euro-American Racist Subculture,* ed. Jeffrey Kaplan and Tore Bjorgo (Boston: Northeastern University Press, 1998), pp. 58–72.

9. Webb, *The Occult Underground*, pp. 191–192. Idem, *The Occult Establishment,* p. 15.

10. Webb, *The Occult Underground,* p. 192. J. Gordon Melton, *The Encyclopedia of American Religions,* 3d ed., repr. (Tarrytown, N.Y.: Triumph, 1991), vol. 3, p. 1.

11. Robert Galbreath, "Explaining Modern Occultism," in *The Occult in America: New Historical Perspectives,* ed. Howard Kerr and Charles L.Crow (Urbana: University of Illinois Press, 1986), p. 15.

12. Campbell, "The Cult, the Cultic Milieu."

13. Ibid., p. 122.

14. Ibid.

15. Ibid., p. 123.

16. Barkun, "Conspiracy Theories as Stigmatized Knowledge," pp. 61–62.

17. Richard Hofstadter, *The Paranoid Style in American Politics and Other Essays* (New York: Knopf, 1965), p. 36.

18. "Statement Released By: John Lear, December 29, 1987," in William F. Hamilton III, *Alien Magic* (Glendale, Calif.: Uforces, 1989), p. 4. "William Cooper Exhibit," http://www.teleport.com/ndkossy/cooper.html (December 4, 1997). The two fullest statements of the view that Hollywood films encode messages about aliens are Michael Mannion, *Project Mindshift: The Reeducation of the American Public Concerning Extraterrestrial Life 1947–Present* (New York: M. Evans, 1998); and Bruce Rux, *Hollywood vs. the Aliens: The Motion Picture Industry's Participation in UFO Disinformation* (Berkeley: Frog, 1997).

19. Chris Hayward, "Trick or Treat?" *Sightings,* pp. 37–38 (undated UFO magazine published in Great Britain). Jon King, "Deep Underground: Part I," *UFO Reality* 4 (1996): 44.

20. Kerry Noble, *Tabernacle of Hate: Why They Bombed Oklahoma City* (Prescott, Ont.: Voyageur, 1998), p. 71. Darryl E. Hicks and David A. Lewis, *The Todd Phenomenon: Ex-Grand Druid vs. the Illuminati, Fact or Fantasy?* (Harrison, Ark.: New Leaf, 1979), pp. 23, 25.

21. "Witchcraft and the Illuminati" (pamphlet; Zarephath-Horeb, Mo.: Covenant, Sword and Arm of the Lord, 1981). Although this pamphlet was published anonymously, Kerry Noble claims authorship; see Noble, *Tabernacle of Hate*, pp. 67–73.

22. Walter Kafton-Minkel, *Subterranean Worlds: 100,000 Years of Dragons, Dwarfs, the Dead, Lost Races & UFOs from Inside the Earth* (Port Townsend, Wash.: Loompanics Unlimited, 1989), pp. 258–261. Edward Bulwer-Lytton, *The Coming Race* (Edinburgh: W. Blackwood, 1871).

23. Alec Maclellan, *The Lost World of Agharti: The Mystery of Vril Power* (London: Souvenir, 1996), pp. 172, 183. Robert S. Elwood, "Theosophy," in *America's Alternative Religions,* ed. Timothy Miller (Albany: State University of New York Press, 1995), pp. 316–318. Kafton-Minkel, *Subterranean Worlds,* p. 262.

24. Timothy Green Beckley, *The Shaver Mystery and the Inner Earth* (Clarksburg, W. Va.: Saucerian Publications, 1967), pp. 115, 118. "Richard Shaver's Last Interview," in Gene Steinberg, "Ray Palmer's Son: Remembrances of a UFO Pioneer," *UFO Universe* 5 (1998): 27.

25. Maclellan, *The Lost World of Agharti*, pp. 167–168. Jason Bishop III, "The Dulce Base," in Hamilton, *Alien Magic*, p. 3, constitutes one of the earliest descriptions of an underground base, partially citing Milton William Cooper. Material of Bishop's was eventually recycled by the pseudonymous "Branton" in *The Dulce Wars: Underground Alien Bases & the Battle for Planet Earth* (New Brunswick, N.J.: Inner Light/Global Communications, 1999), pp. 17–21. On Shaver's own view of his material, see Kafton-Minkel, *Subterranean Worlds,* pp. 151–152.

26. Michael A. Hoffman II, "His Pursuers Are Not Theoretical," http:// www.hoffman-info.com/occult.html (December 8, 1998).

27. Alanna Nash, "Confused or Not, X-Philes Keep Coming," *The New York Times,* January 11, 1998, Arts & Leisure section, 41.

28. Jodi Dean, *Aliens in America: Conspiracy Cultures from Outerspace to Cyberspace* (Ithaca, N.Y.: Cornell University Press, 1998), pp. 9, 60.

29. Milton William Cooper, *Behold a Pale Horse* (Sedona, Ariz.: Light Technology, 1991). [Milton] William Cooper, "Majestytwelve," http://www .harvest-trust.org/majestyt.htm (February 27, 1998). Cooper's Internet site was subsequently changed to http://www.williamcooper.com.

30. Dean, *Aliens in America,* pp. 8, 201.

3. The New World Order and the Illuminati

1. Bush's statement on March 10, 1991, seemed innocuous to nonmillenarians: "The new world order said that a lot of countries, disparate backgrounds,

with differences, can come together standing for a common principle. And that principle is: You don't take over another country by force." A typical conspiracist response was the one contained in Texe Marrs's *Dark Majesty: The Secret Brotherhood and the Magic of a Thousand Points of Light* (Austin, Tex.: Living Truth, 1992), p. 32.

2. Robert Fuller, *Naming the Antichrist: The History of an American Obsession* (New York: Oxford University Press, 1995), pp. 14–19. For a historical overview, see Bernard McGinn, *Antichrist: Two Thousand Years of the Human Fascination with Evil* (San Francisco: HarperSanFrancisco, 1994).

3. Fuller, *Naming the Antichrist*. Christopher Hill, *Antichrist in Seventeenth-Century England* (London: Oxford University Press, 1971).

4. John F. Walvoord, *Armageddon, Oil, and the Middle East Crisis,* rev. ed. (Grand Rapids, Mich.: Zondervan, 1999). Paul Boyer, *When Time Shall Be No More: Prophecy Belief in Modern American Culture* (Cambridge, Mass.: Harvard University Press, 1992), p. 183.

5. Fuller, *Naming the Antichrist,* p. 161.

6. Boyer, *When Time Shall Be No More,* pp. 108–109. Fuller, *Naming the Antichrist,* p. 161.

7. Leo P. Ribuffo, *The Old Christian Right: The Protestant Far Right from the Great Depression to the Cold War* (Philadelphia: Temple University Press, 1983), pp. 100, 106–108. Gerald B. Winrod, "Antichrist and the Tribe of Dan" (pamphlet; Wichita: Defender, 1936).

8. Winrod, "Antichrist and the Tribe of Dan," pp. 19, 24.

9. Jerry Falwell, "Press Statement: Falwell Clarifies Belief That Biblical Antichrist Will Be Jewish," http://www.falwell.com/jf2/state1.html (February 7, 1999).

10. McGinn, *Antichrist,* p. 79.

11. Boyer, *When Time Shall Be No More,* p. 283; emphasis in original. "Witchcraft and the Illuminati" (pamphlet; Zarephath-Horeb, Mo.: Covenant, Sword and Arm of the Lord, 1981), p. 31 (365 computers). Peter Lalonde and Paul Lalonde, *The Mark of the Beast* (Eugene, Ore.: Harvest House, 1994), p. 197; the famously obscure "mark of the beast" passage is as follows: "And he causeth all, the small and the great, and the rich and the poor, and the free and the bond, that there be given them a mark on their right hand, or upon their forehead; and that no man should be able to buy or to sell, save he that hath the mark, even the name of the beast or the number of his name" (Rev. 13:16–17; King James Version).

12. Grant R. Jeffrey, *Final Warning: Economic Collapse and the Coming World Government* (Toronto: Frontier Research, 1995), p. 218.

13. Richard Hofstadter, *The Paranoid Style in American Politics and Other Essays* (New York: Knopf, 1965), pp. 10–12. David H. Bennett, *The Party of Fear: The American Far Right from Nativism to the Militia Movement,* rev. ed. (New York: Vintage, 1995), pp. 23–26.

14. American Opinion Book Service, 1996 winter catalog (not paginated). John Robison, *Proofs of a Conspiracy,* repr. (Boston: Western Islands, 1967), p. xiv.

15. The account of the Illuminati here is based on James H. Billington, *Fire in the Minds of Men: Origins of the Revolutionary Faith* (New York: Basic Books, 1980), pp. 93–99.

16. Nicholas Goodrick-Clarke, *Black Sun: Aryan Cults, Esoteric Nazism, and the Politics of Identity* (New York: New York University Press, 2002), p. 283.

17. E. J. Hobsbawm, *Primitive Rebels: Studies in Archaic Forms of Social Movements in the Nineteenth and Twentieth Centuries* (New York: W. W. Norton, 1965), chap. 9. The Carbonari, a primarily Italian secret society active during the early nineteenth century, opposed monarchical absolutism. *Carbonari*—literally, "charcoal burners"—were taken as the symbol of freedom for these middle-class intellectuals because the charcoal burners' life in the forest took them out of the reach of human institutions and into the freedom of nature.

18. Nesta H. Webster, *Secret Societies and Subversive Movements,* repr. (Los Angeles: Christian Book Club of America, n.d.), p. 404.

19. Lady Queenborough (a.k.a. Edith Starr Miller), *Occult Theocrasy* [*sic*], repr. (Los Angeles: Christian Book Club of America, n.d.), pp. 662, 184.

20. Gerald B. Winrod, "Adam Weishaupt, a Human Devil" (pamphlet lacking publisher, place of publication, or date), pp. 45, 47. Ribuffo, however, shows the original edition as having been issued in Wichita, Kansas, by Defender Publishers in 1935: *The Old Christian Right,* p. 308. Stephen Eric Bronner, *A Rumor about the Jews: Reflections on Antisemitism and The Protocols of the Elders of Zion* (New York: St. Martin's Press, 2000), pp. 81–88.

21. *The Protocols of the Meetings of the Learned Elders of Zion with Preface and Explanatory Notes,* ed. and trans. Victor E. Marsden (1934). The exposure of *The Protocols* is described in Bronner, *A Rumor about the Jews,* p. 78.

22. Bennett, *The Party of Fear,* p. 317.

23. William H. McIlhany, "Two Centuries of Intrigue," *New American* 12 (September 16, 1996): 37.

24. Larry Abraham, *Call It Conspiracy,* repr. (Gig Harbor, Wash.: Double A, 1985 [orig. 1971]), pp. 134 (emphasis in original), 91.

25. Abraham, *Call It Conspiracy,* pp. 46–47.

26. Eustace Mullins, *The World Order: Our Secret Rulers,* 2d ed. (Staunton, Va.: Ezra Pound Institute of Civilization, 1992), pp. 3–4.

27. William T. Still, *New World Order: The Ancient Plan of Secret Societies* (Lafayette, La.: Huntington House, 1990), pp. 81, 82, 192.

28. Marrs, *Dark Majesty,* p. 18 ("all of these groups"); emphasis in original. Idem, *Project L.U.C.I.D.: The Beast 666 Universal Human Control System* (Austin, Tex.: Living Truth, 1996), p. 185 ("the unseen men" and "will fulfill Bible prophecy").

29. Pat Robertson, *The New World Order* (Dallas: Word, 1991).

30. Michael Lind, "Rev. Robertson's Grand International Conspiracy Theory," *The New York Review of Books,* February 2, 1995, 21–25. Michael Lind and Jacob Heilbrun, "On Pat Robertson," *The New York Review of Books,* April 20, 1995, 71–76. For Robertson's disavowal of anti-Semitism, see "Pat Robertson

Says He Intended No Anti-Semitism in Book He Wrote Four Years Ago," *The New York Times*, March 4, 1995, 10; and *The Forward* (English-language edition), March 31, 1995.

31. Des Griffin, *Fourth Reich of the Rich* (South Pasadena, Calif.: Emissary, 1976).

32. Ibid., pp. 19–21, 25–26, 36. Alexander Hislop, *The Two Babylons; or, The Papal Worship Proved to Be the Worship of Nimrod and His Wife*, repr. (New York: Loizeaux Brothers, 1943). Michael Barkun, *Religion and the Racist Right: The Origins of the Christian Identity Movement*, rev. ed. (Chapel Hill: University of North Carolina Press, 1997), p. 168.

33. Griffin, *Fourth Reich of the Rich*, p. 57.

34. Webster, *Secret Societies and Subversive Movements*, pp. 408–414.

35. Griffin, *Fourth Reich of the Rich*, p. 195.

36. John Todd apparently wrote nothing for publication. A detailed, though hostile, narrative of his life and preaching appears in a work by two evangelists, Darryl E. Hicks and David A. Lewis, *The Todd Phenomenon: Ex-Grand Druid vs. the Illuminati, Fact or Fantasy?* (Harrison, Ark.: New Leaf Press, 1979), pp. 41–42. See also Bill Ellis, *Raising the Devil: Satanism, New Religions, and the Media* (Lexington: University Press of Kentucky, 2000), pp. 192–201.

37. This account of Todd's career draws on Gareth J. Medway's *Lure of the Sinister: The Unnatural History of Satanism* (New York: New York University Press, 2001), pp. 170–172.

38. Todd's diagrams of the conspiracy are reproduced in Hicks and Lewis, *The Todd Phenomenon*, pp. 12, 34, 95.

39. Hicks and Lewis, *The Todd Phenomenon*, pp. 43–44.

40. Ibid., p. 94. "Witchcraft and the Illuminati." See also Barkun, *Religion and the Racist Right*, pp. 216–217.

41. Michael York, "New Age and the Late Twentieth Century," *Journal of Contemporary Religion* 12 (1997): 401–420.

42. *Alternative 3* (videotape; Beverly Hills, Calif.: Underground Video, 1996); originally broadcast on *Science Report*, Anglia Television (U.K.), April 1, 1977. Jim Keith, *Casebook on Alternative 3: UFOs, Secret Societies and World Control* (Lilburn, Ga.: IllumiNet, 1994). Leslie Watkins, *Alternative 3* (London: Sphere, 1978).

43. Stan Deyo, *The Cosmic Conspiracy*, rev. ed. (Kempton, Ill.: Adventures Unlimited, 1994), pp. 61–66.

44. Ibid., pp. 67, 79, 94–96. The official interpretation of the seal appears in Department of State, "The Great Seal of the United States" (pamphlet; Washington, D.C.: Government Printing Office, 1996).

45. Deyo, *The Cosmic Conspiracy*, pp. 102, 103. André Maurois, *The Next Chapter: The War against the Moon* (New York: E. P. Dutton, 1923). Deyo was apparently unaware of Maurois's story.

46. Deyo, *The Cosmic Conspiracy*, pp. 70, 83.

47. Although Pat Robertson continues to claim a premillennialist position, his increasing emphasis on Christians taking control of societal institutions gives

his operational theology a decidedly postmillennial twist. Deyo, *The Cosmic Conspiracy,* pp. 129, 139.

48. Daniel Wojcik, *The End of the World as We Know It: Faith, Fatalism, and Apocalypse in America* (New York: New York University Press, 1997), p. 200. Cooper, *Behold a Pale Horse.* Cooper claimed to operate "the Intelligence Service of the Second Continental Army of the Republic (Militia)," http://in-search-of.com/frames/wwwBoard/messages/1050.html, topic no. 14, posted May 19, 1997 (November 11, 1997). Commander X (pseud.), ed., *William Cooper: Death of a Conspiracy Salesman* (New Brunswick, N.J.: Global Communications, 2002), p. 12. Don Ecker, "Dead Man Talking," *Fortean Times* 155 (March 2002): 38.

49. Cooper, *Behold a Pale Horse,* pp. 75–76.

50. Ibid., pp. 93–94. Stephen Gill, *American Hegemony and the Trilateral Commission* (Cambridge, U.K.: Cambridge University Press, 1990), pp. 129–130, 137. Cooper, *Behold a Pale Horse,* pp. 80, 113–114, 178.

51. Cooper, *Behold a Pale Horse,* pp. 27, 91. A similar story, without the Bilderberg connection, appeared earlier in Watkins, *Alternative 3,* p. 23.

52. Cooper, *Behold a Pale Horse,* pp. 165, 176.

53. Ibid., pp. 200, 202, 208, 221.

54. Ibid., p. 232.

55. Hal Lindsey, *The Late Great Planet Earth* (New York: Bantam, 1973). Boyer, *When Time Shall Be No More.*

56. Boyer, *When Time Shall Be No More,* chap. 10.

4. A World of Black Helicopters

1. http://www.cfr.org/Public/about/mission.html (April 1, 2002).

2. Stephen Gill, *American Hegemony and the Trilateral Commission* (Cambridge, U.K.: Cambridge University Press, 1990), pp. 129–132, 137–141.

3. John F. McManus, *The Insiders* (Appleton, Wisc.: John Birch Society, 1996), pp. 111–140. Larry Abraham, *Call It Conspiracy,* repr. (Gig Harbor, Wash.: Double A, 1985 [orig. 1971]), pp. 295–312.

4. Abraham, *Call It Conspiracy,* p. 98. For leftist attacks on the Trilateral Commission, see Holly Sklar, ed., *Trilateralism: The Trilateral Commission and Elite Planning for World Management* (Boston: South End, 1980). Abraham, *Call It Conspiracy:* the Stewart chart follows p. 313. The chart has been reprinted in many other places, e.g., as an endpaper in Milton William Cooper's *Behold a Pale Horse* (Sedona, Ariz.: Light Technology, 1991); and in Valdamar Valerian's *Matrix III: The Psycho-Social, Chemical, Biological and Electromagnetic Manipulation of Human Consciousness* (Yelm, Wash.: Leading Edge Research Group, 1992), vol. 1, pp. 638–639.

5. John Coleman, *Conspirators' Hierarchy: The Story of the Committee of 300* (Bozeman, Mont.: America West, 1992), p. 265. Texe Marrs, *Circle of Intrigue: The Hidden Inner Circle of the Global Illuminati Conspiracy* (Austin, Tex.: Living Truth, 1995), pp. 275–276.

6. David Icke, . . . *And the Truth Shall Set You Free* (Isle of Wight: Bridge of Love, 1995), p. 208. "Witchcraft and the Illuminati" (pamphlet; Zarephath-Horeb, Mo.: Covenant, Sword and Arm of the Lord, 1981) reproduces a number of the Todd conspiracy diagrams. Valerian, *Matrix III,* vol. 1, pp. 632–637.

7. Milton William Cooper, "Trojan Horse Lt. Col. James 'Bo' Gritz," http://harvest-trust.org/trojan.htm (March 19, 1998).

8. Jim Keith, *Black Helicopters over America: Strikeforce for the New World Order* (Lilburn, Ga.: IllumiNet, 1994). Idem, *Black Helicopters II: The End Game Strategy* (Lilburn, Ga.: IllumiNet, 1997). *Enemies Foreign & Domestic,* part 1: *The United Nations & the New World Order,* Militia of Montana videotape (n.d.). Keith, *Black Helicopters over America,* pp. 18, 35.

9. Mark Koernke, *America in Peril* (videotape; n.d.). Keith, *Black Helicopters over America,* p. 148. Idem, *Black Helicopters II,* chap. 14.

10. Keith, *Black Helicopters over America,* chap. 3.

11. Linda Thompson, "Black Helicopters: Response to Yet Another Media Whore Doing Yet Another Propaganda Piece," posted March 27, 1997, http://www.mindspring.com/~jcargill/articles/b-h-faq2.htm (January 27, 1999).

12. "Black Helicopter Hyperlist," http://weber.ucsd.edu/~dmckiern/blakchop.htm (January 27, 1999); "Black Helicopters," http://www.wkac.ac.uk/research/ccc/Black%20Helicopters.html (January 27, 1999).

13. James Thornton, "Neutralizing Good Americans," *New American* 12 (September 16, 1996): 68.

14. "Garden Plot & SWAT: U.S. Police as New Action Army," *CounterSpy* 2 (Winter 1976): 16–25.

15. Frank J. Donner, *The Age of Surveillance: The Aims and Methods of America's Political Intelligence System* (New York: Vintage, 1981), pp. 163, 166. "Garden Plot & SWAT." I am grateful to Chip Berlet for bringing this material to my attention.

16. William R. Pabst, "Concentration Camp Plans for U.S. Citizens," updated pamphlet, purportedly the transcript of a "taped message." This document has also been posted on the Web, e.g., http://www.geocities.com/CapeCanaveral/2012/camps.txt (January 25, 1999).

17. Pabst, "Concentration Camp Plans," pp. 4, 7, 17.

18. Pabst, "Concentration Camp Plans," p. 5.

19. James Harrer, "Reagan Orders Concentration Camps," *The Spotlight,* April 23, 1984, pp. 1, 3.

20. Fred Blahut, "Emergency Plan Implementation Responsibility of 'Low Key' FEMA," *The Spotlight,* April 23, 1984, 3. "The OMEGA File: The Federal Emergency Management Agency," http://www.omega.tm/file/omega34.thm (October 4, 1998).

21. "Private Institutions Used in C.I.A. Effort to Control Behavior," *The New York Times,* August 2, 1977, section A, 1, 16. Joseph E. Persico, *Casey: From the OSS to the CIA* (New York: Viking, 1990), p. 408. "Subjects of CIA Mind Control View Settlement as a Victory," *The Washington Post,* October 6, 1988.

22. Jonathan D. Moreno, *Undue Risk: Secret State Experiments on Humans* (New York: W. H. Freeman, 2000), pp. 190–200. Michael Ignatieff, "What Did

the C.I.A. Do to His Father?" *The New York Times Magazine*, April 1, 2001, 56–61. Jonathan Vankin, *Conspiracies, Cover-ups, and Crimes: Political Manipulation and Mind Control in America* (New York: Paragon House, 1991), p. 168. "Trance Formation of America's Update on LABOR DAY MARCH on Washington, D.C.," *The American's Bulletin* 15 (September 1996): 1, 3.

23. The fullest account appears in John Marks, *The Search for the "Manchurian Candidate"* (New York: W. W. Norton, 1991).

24. Jim Keith, *Mind Control, World Control* (Kempton, Ill.: Adventures Unlimited, 1997), pp. 293–294. Mark Phillips, "Forward," in Cathy O'Brien with Mark Phillips, *Trance Formation of America* (Nashville: Global Trance Formation Info, 1995), at http://tau.lpl.arizona.edu/~corleyj/wwolf/truth/text/monarch.txt (May 28, 1997).

25. Fritz Springmeier, "Project Monarch: How the U.S. Creates Slaves of Satan," in *Cult Rapture*, ed. Adam Parfrey (Portland, Ore.: Feral House, 1995), p. 241. Keith, *Mind Control, World Control*, p. 296. Phillips, "Forward." Martin Cannon, "Project Monarch: The Tangled Web," http://www.visitations.com/mindcontrol/monarch.html (April 1, 2002).

26. "Mind Control Forum," wysiwyg://31/http://www.mk.net/~mcf/ (January 22, 1999). Jeffrey S. Victor, *Satanic Panic: The Creation of a Contemporary Legend* (Chicago: Open Court, 1993), pp. 24–25. Bill Ellis, *Raising the Devil: Satanism, New Religions, and the Media* (Lexington: University Press of Kentucky, 2000), p. 292. Gareth J. Medway, *Lure of the Sinister: The Unnatural History of Satanism* (New York: New York University Press, 2001), pp. 312–313. David H. Bennett, *The Party of Fear: The American Far Right from Nativism to the Militia Movement*, rev. ed. (New York: Vintage, 1995), pp. 41–47.

27. Relfe cited in Paul Boyer, *When Time Shall Be No More: Prophecy Belief in Modern American Culture* (Cambridge, Mass.: Harvard University Press, 1992), pp. 287–288. Texe Marrs, *Project L.U.C.I.D.: The Beast 666 Universal Human Control System* (Austin, Tex.: Living Truth, 1996), pp. 98–99.

5. UFO Conspiracy Theories, 1975–1990

1. Andrew Macdonald (pseudonym of William L. Pierce), *The Turner Diaries*, 2d ed. (Washington, D.C.: National Alliance, 1980). Typical of the news coverage is Mark Potok and Katy Kelly, "Militia Movement's Draw: A Shared Anger, Fear," *USA Today*, May 16, 1995, 6D.

2. Pat Robertson, *The New World Order* (Dallas: Word, 1991), p. 185. "Buchanan Promises 'Millennial Struggle' against World Government," CNN, January 6, 2000; http://www.cnn.com (January 7, 2000).

3. Phil Patton, "Indeed They Have Landed. Look Around," *The New York Times*, June 15, 1997, section H, 38. Jodi Dean, *Aliens in America: Conspiracy Cultures from Outerspace to Cyberspace* (Ithaca, N.Y.: Cornell University Press, 1998), p. 36. Amy Harmon, "For U.F.O. Buffs, 50 Years of Hazy History," *The New York Times*, June 14, 1997, section A, 1. "Gallup UFO Poll: Some Want to

Believe, Some Don't," http://www.parascope.com/articles/0597/gallup.htm (July 2, 1997).

4. Cynthia Fox, "The Search for Extraterrestrial Life," *Life* (March 2000): 56.

5. Dean, *Aliens in America,* pp. 30, 52.

6. Brenda Denzler, *The Lure of the Edge: Scientific Passions, Religious Beliefs, and the Pursuit of UFOs* (Berkeley: University of California Press, 2001), pp. 164–167.

7. "Gallup UFO Poll." Fox, "The Search for Extraterrestrial Life," p. 56.

8. "Men in Black," in *The UFO Encyclopedia,* ed. John Spencer (New York: Avon, 1993), pp. 210–211. Jerome Clark, *The UFO Files* (Lincolnwood, Ill.: Publications International, 1996), pp. 127–129. Peter Rojcewicz, "The 'Men in Black' Experience and Tradition: Analogues with the Traditional Devil Hypothesis," *Journal of American Folklore* 100 (April–June 1987): 148–160. The first book on the subject, which initially appeared in 1956, was by Gray Barker: *They Knew Too Much about Flying Saucers,* repr. (Lilburn, Ga.: IllumiNet, 1997).

9. The literature on each is very large; but the nature of the material can be gleaned from the following. On Area 51: David Darlington, *Area 51: The Dreamland Chronicles* (New York: Henry Holt, 1997); and Phil Patton, *Travels in Dreamland: The Secret History of Area 51* (London: Millennium, 1997). On Dulce: Branton, *The Dulce Wars: Underground Alien Bases & the Battle for Planet Earth* (New Brunswick, N.J.: Inner Light/Global Communications, 1999); and Commander X, *Underground Alien Bases* (n.p.: Abelard Productions, 1990).

10. "Abduction Phenomenon," in *The UFO Encyclopedia,* ed. Jerome Clark, vol. 1 (Detroit: Apogee, 1990), p. 4. Thomas E. Bullard, *UFO Abductions: The Measure of a Mystery* (n.p.: Fund for UFO Research, 1987), vol. 1, pp. 87–88.

11. "Hollow Earth and UFOs," in *The UFO Encyclopedia,* ed. Jerome Clark, vol. 2 (Detroit: Omnigraphics, 1992), p. 204. Commander X, "Legions of Doom," *UFO Universe, Conspiracies & Cover-ups,* Special Issue 1 (1998): 64–65. The Nazi-UFO stories have been most fully reconstructed by Nicholas Goodrick-Clarke in *Black Sun: Aryan Cults, Esoteric Nazism, and the Politics of Identity* (New York: New York University Press, 2002), chap. 8.

12. "Animal Mutilations and UFOs," in *The UFO Encyclopedia,* ed. Jerome Clark, vol. 3 (Detroit: Omnigraphics, 1996), pp. 18–25. George E. Onet, "Animal Mutilations: What We Know," National Institute for Discovery Science, http://www.nidsci.org/articles/animal1.html (September 13, 2000). Idem, "Animal Mutilations: What We Don't Know," National Institute for Discovery Science, http://www.nidsci.org/articles/animal2.html (September 13, 2000).

13. "Animal Mutilations and UFOs," pp. 18, 23.

14. "Linda Moulton Howe: The 'Alien Harvest' and Beyond," transcript of a conversation in *UFOs and the Alien Presence: Six Viewpoints,* ed. Michael Lindemann (Newberg, Ore.: Wild Flower, 1991), pp. 61–64. Linda Moulton Howe, *An Alien Harvest: Further Evidence Linking Animal Mutilations and Human Abductions to Alien Life Forms* (Huntingdon Valley, Penn.: Linda

Moulton Howe Productions, 1989), p. 224. On Howe, see *Idaho Statesman* (Boise), June 5, 1998, id. Bullard, *UFO Abductions,* pp. 50, 86–87, 91.

15. *Alternative 3* (videotape; Beverly Hills, Calif.: Underground Video, 1996); originally broadcast on *Science Report,* Anglia Television (U.K.), April 1, 1977.

16. *Alternative 3.* Leslie Watkins, *Alternative 3* (London: Sphere, 1978). Jim Keith, *Casebook on Alternative 3: UFOs, Secret Societies and World Control* (Lilburn, Ga.: IllumiNet, 1994). Idem, *Mind Control and UFOs: Casebook on Alternative 3* (Lilburn, Ga.: IllumiNet, 1999). Bob Rickard, "Hoax: Alternative," *Fortean Times* 64 (August–September 1992): 47–49.

17. George C. Andrews, *Extra-Terrestrials among Us,* repr. (St. Paul, Minn.: Llewellyn, 1993 [orig. 1986]), pp. 166, 174–175, 229, 270. William R. Pabst, "Concentration Camp Plans for U.S. Citizens," see, e.g., http://www.geocities.com/CapeCanaveral/2012/camps.txt (January 25, 1999).

18. Patton, *Travels in Dreamland,* p. 236. Stanton T. Friedman, *Top Secret/Majic* (New York: Marlowe, 1997), pp. 20–21, 56. Howe, *An Alien Harvest,* p. 157. The texts appear in Timothy Good, *Above Top Secret: The Worldwide U.F.O. Cover-up* (New York: William Morrow, 1988), pp. 544–551. The MJ-12 documents also appear in Friedman, *Top Secret/Majic,* pp. 222–229, and Howe, *An Alien Harvest,* pp. 165–172. Robert Alan Goldberg provides another description of the affair in *Enemies Within: The Culture of Conspiracy in Modern America* (New Haven, Conn.: Yale University Press, 2001), pp. 205–208.

19. Jacques Vallee, *Revelations: Alien Contact and Human Deception* (New York: Ballantine, 1991), pp. 38–41. "Skeptics Attack," http://www.parascope.com/ds/0996/maj2.htm (July 1, 1997).

20. For example, "Declassified Documents Confirm Recovery of Alien Craft and Bodies!" *Nexus* 6 (February–March 1999): 55–60.

21. "Statement Released By: John Lear, December 29, 1987," William F. Hamilton III, *Alien Magic* (Glendale, Calif.: Uforces, 1989).

22. Ibid.

23. Ibid.

24. Ibid.

25. A brief biographical statement precedes the text of Lear's statement.

26. Donna Kossy, *Kooks* (Portland, Ore.: Feral House, 1994), pp. 191–192. "William Cooper: A Short Biography," http://williamcooper.com/william.htm (August 29, 2000). Milton William Cooper, *Behold a Pale Horse* (Sedona, Ariz.: Light Technology, 1991).

27. Don Ecker, "Dead Man Talking," *Fortean Times* 155 (March 2002): 38.

28. The December 18 statement is reproduced in Howe, *An Alien Harvest,* pp. 177–196.

29. Howe, *An Alien Harvest,* pp. 183, 184–185. Andrews, *Extra-Terrestrials among Us,* p. 184.

30. Howe, *An Alien Harvest,* pp. 185, 190–191. Milton William Cooper, "The Cooper Document: The Absolute True Information Regarding the Alien Presence on Earth" (1989), posted October 29, 1997, http://server.wizards.net/mac/handy/incoming/cooperdoc.html (November 6, 1997); capitalization in original.

31. Howe, *An Alien Harvest*, pp. 187–188.

32. There are some discrepancies in dates for Cooper material between Hamilton, *Alien Magic*, and Howe, *An Alien Harvest*, pp. 290–291.

33. Howe, *An Alien Harvest*, pp. 292–294.

34. Cooper, "The Cooper Document."

35. Howe, *An Alien Harvest*, pp. 297–298.

36. Cooper, *Behold a Pale Horse*, p. 198.

37. Letter from Milton William Cooper, published in Hamilton, *Alien Magic*, unpaginated section.

38. "Petition to Indict," published in Hamilton, *Alien Magic*, unpaginated section.

39. Ibid.

40. Ibid.

41. For a detailed, though partisan, treatment of Gale, see Cheri Seymour, *Committee of the States: Inside the Radical Right* (Mariposa, Calif.: Camden Place Communications, 1991). Michael Barkun, *Religion and the Racist Right: The Origins of the Christian Identity Movement*, rev. ed. (Chapel Hill: University of North Carolina Press, 1997), p. 208.

42. Milton William Cooper, "The Plot Thickens," http://harvest-trust .org/plot.htm (June 30, 1998). Idem, "In Search of . . . Mail Digest, May 11, 1997," http://in-search-of.com/frames/WWWBoard/messages/1050.html (November 11, 1997).

43. For Cooper's quotation, see "Cooper Family Targeted by Feds," http:// www.williamcooper.com/targeted.htm (August 29, 2000). "USMS Major Fugitive Cases," http://www.usdoj.gov/marshals/wanted/major-cases/cases .html#A (August 30, 2000).

44. "Unofficial Link Page for John Grace," http://www.ufomind.com/ people/g/grace/ (September 16, 1998). "Animal Mutilations and UFOs," p. 34. Valdamar Valerian, *Matrix II: The Abduction and Manipulation of Humans Using Advanced Technology*, 3d ed. (Yelm, Wash.: Leading Edge Research Group, 1990–1991). Idem, *Matrix III: The Psycho-Social, Chemical, Biological and Electromagnetic Manipulation of Human Consciousness* (Yelm, Wash.: Leading Edge Research Group, 1992).

45. Valerian, *Matrix III*, vol. 1, pp. 632–637.

46. Valerian, *Matrix II*, p. v.

47. J. Gordon Melton, *Finding Enlightenment: Ramtha's School of Ancient Wisdom* (Hillsboro, Ore.: Beyond Words, 1998), pp. 70–71. Idem, "Ramtha's School of Enlightenment," in *The Encyclopedia of Cults, Sects, and New Religions*, ed. James R. Lewis, 2d ed. (Amherst, N.Y.: Prometheus, 2002), pp. 596–600. "Ramtha's School of Enlightenment," http://cti.itc.virginia.edu/ ~jkh8x/soc257/nrms/Ramtha.html (January 21, 1999). Steven Lee Weinberg, Carol Wright, and John Clancy, eds., *Ramtha Intensive: Change, the Days to Come* (Eastsound, Wash.: Sovereignty, 1987). Valerian, *Matrix II*, p. i. Idem, *Matrix III*, vol. 1, pp. 475–476. Melton, *Finding Enlightenment*, p. 131. "Conspiracies," http://www.ramtha.com/cgi-bin/private/c...&nav_mode = search &frames = &refer = homepage (September 21, 2000). "Cathy O'Brien," *The*

Golden Thread Newspaper (November 1999), http://ramtha.com/golden/11–1999.html (September 21, 2000).

48. "Animal Mutilations and UFOs," p. 33.

6. UFOs Meet the New World Order

1. Nicholas Goodrick-Clarke, *Black Sun: Aryan Cults, Esoteric Nazism, and the Politics of Identity* (New York: New York University Press, 2002), p. 299.

2. "Kenn Thomas email to Conspiracy Journal" and Anjeanette Damon, "Rumors Abound in Death of Conspiracy Theorist," http://users.intercomm.com/gpickard/jimkeith/news.html#anchor148414 (February 4, 2000); Damon's article was reprinted from the *Reno Gazette-Journal,* September 28, 1999. Jim Keith, "Revising Reality," in *Cyberculture Counterconspiracy: A Steamshovel Web Reader,* ed. Kenn Thomas (Escondido, Calif.: The Book Tree, 1999), vol. 1, p. 172.

3. Kenn Thomas, ed., *Popular Alienation: A Steamshovel Press Reader* (Lilburn, Ga.: IllumiNet, 1995), pp. 13–15 and passim.

4. In order of publication date, Keith's books are as follows: *The Gemstone File* (edited; Atlanta, Ga.: IllumiNet, 1992); *Secret and Suppressed: Banned Ideas and Hidden History* (edited; Portland, Ore.: Feral House, 1993); *Black Helicopters over America: Strikeforce for the New World Order* (Lilburn, Ga.: IllumiNet, 1994); *Casebook on Alternative 3: UFOs, Secret Societies and World Control* (Lilburn, Ga.: IllumiNet, 1994); *OKBomb! Conspiracy and Cover-Up* (Lilburn, Ga.: IllumiNet, 1996); *The Octopus: Secret Government and the Death of Danny Casolaro* (with Kenn Thomas; Portland, Ore.: Feral House, 1997); *Black Helicopters II: The End Game Strategy* (Lilburn, Ga.: IllumiNet, 1997); *Casebook on the Men in Black* (Lilburn, Ga.: IllumiNet, 1997); *Mind Control, World Control* (Kempton, Ill.: Adventures Unlimited, 1997); *Mind Control and UFOs: Casebook on Alternative 3* (Lilburn, Ga.: IllumiNet, 1999); *Mass Control: Engineering Human Consciousness* (Lilburn, Ga.: IllumiNet, 1999); and *Saucers of the Illuminati* (Lilburn, Ga.: IllumiNet, 1999; IllumiNet published a photocopied edition of two hundred copies of an earlier version in 1993).

5. "Author Jim Keith Dies under Mysterious Circumstances," "Kenn Thomas email to Conspiracy Journal," and Robert Sterling, "Was Jim Keith Commander X?: Jim Keith's Big Secret," all at http://jsers.intercomm.com/gpickard/jimkeith/news.html#anchor148414 (February 4, 2000). "Jim Keith's Big Secret," http://www.ufomind.com/misc/1999/sep/d29–001.html (February 3, 2000). "Unofficial Link Page Jim Keith," http://www.ufomind.com/people/k/keith/ (February 4, 2000).

6. Keith, *Black Helicopters over America,* pp. 95, 129, 148. Idem, *Casebook on Alternative 3,* p. 155. Idem, *Black Helicopters II,* p. 185.

7. Keith, *Saucers of the Illuminati,* pp. 57–59, 101. Michael Baigent, Richard Leigh, and Henry Lincoln, *The Holy Blood and the Holy Grail* (New York: Delacorte, 1982).

8. Keith, *Black Helicopters over America,* chap. 3, especially p. 94; map after p. 100. Idem, *Black Helicopters II,* pp. 55, 57.

9. Keith, *Black Helicopters II,* chap. 12.

10. Pabst is used in Keith, *Black Helicopters over America,* p. 83; Koernke in Keith, *Black Helicopters over America,* pp. 143–144; Webster in Keith, *Casebook on Alternative 3,* p. 157; *The Spotlight* in Keith, *Black Helicopters over America,* p. 109, and idem, *Black Helicopters II,* pp. 149–151; and Mullins in Keith, *Black Helicopters II,* p. 16.

11. Jim Keith, "Whose Saucers Are They?" in *Popular Alienation,* ed. Thomas, pp. 75–76.

12. Keith, *Black Helicopters over America,* p. 58. Idem, *Mind Control, World Control,* pp. 271, 288, 292. Idem, *Mind Control and UFOs,* p. 88.

13. Keith, *Casebook on Alternative 3,* pp. 120, 155.

14. Keith, *Saucers of the Illuminati,* pp. 14–15, 117, 125. Idem, *Casebook on the Men in Black,* pp. 207–208, 218–220. Idem, "Revising Reality," pp. 171–174.

15. Sam Taylor, "So I Was in This Bar with the Son of God . . . ," *The* [London] *Observer Review,* April 20, 1997, 1, 4.

16. Ibid.

17. David Icke, *The Robots' Rebellion: The Story of the Spiritual Renaissance* (Bath, U.K.: Gateway, 1994), pp. xv, 12, 139, 155, 199, 224.

18. Ibid., p. 212.

19. David Icke, *. . . And the Truth Shall Set You Free* (Isle of Wight: Bridge of Love, 1995), p. 185.

20. Ibid., pp. 37, 9.

21. Ibid., pp. 290–295.

22. David Icke, *The Biggest Secret* (Scottsdale, Ariz.: Bridge of Love, 1999), pp. 1, 24–27, 259–260.

23. David Icke, *Children of the Matrix: How an Interdimensional Race Has Controlled the World for Thousands of Years—and Still Does* (Wildwood, Mo.: Bridge of Love, 2001), pp. 30–31.

24. Rick Martin, "Are 'Their' Aliens among Us? *The Biggest Secret,* an Interview with David Icke 7/30/99 Rick Martin," from *The Spectrum* (August 3, 1999), http://www.spectrumnews10.com/html/writings/Icke-Interview .html (December 21, 2000). Icke, *Children of the Matrix.*

25. "David Coming 2001 World Tour Schedule," http://www.davidicke .com/icke/schedule.html (December 22, 2000). "David Icke The Nation of Texas Tour," http://www.immunotex.com/davidicke/icke/intro.html (December 22, 2000). June Wisniewski, "Sheriff Richard Mack Speaks Out at Reno Conference," *The American's Bulletin* 15.9 (September 1996): 8.

26. "Author David Icke in Tehachapi: A Series," *Contact: The Phoenix Project* 16 (May 6, 1997): 9; 16 (May 13, 1997): 21; 17 (May 20, 1997): 6; 17 (May 27, 1997): 6. Martin, "Are 'Their' Aliens among Us?" "Genetics, Perception, Dimensionality and Individual Action: Excerpts from the David Icke Lecture, Yelm, Washington, March 1997," http://www.trufax.org/menu/ickemar97 .html (November 1, 1997).

27. "The Dark Side of David Icke," *Evening Standard* [London], May 26, 1995.

28. Martin, "Are 'Their' Aliens among Us?" Icke, *The Biggest Secret*, p. 182. Idem, *. . . And the Truth Shall Set You Free*, p. 421.

29. Icke, *The Biggest Secret*, p. 490. Martin, "Are 'Their' Aliens among Us?"

30. "The Dark Side of David Icke."

7. Armageddon Below

1. "Extraterrestrial Biological Entities," in *The UFO Encyclopedia*, ed. Jerome Clark, vol. 1 (Detroit: Apogee, 1990), p. 89; "Animal Mutilations and UFOs," *The UFO Encyclopedia*, ed. Jerome Clark, vol. 3 (Detroit: Omnigraphics, 1996), p. 32.

2. "Animal Mutilations and UFOs," p. 25. Andrew Stiny, "Group Hopes Web Site Helps Solve Mutilations," *The Santa Fe New Mexican*, May 27, 1997, http://web.lexis-nexis.com/universe/doc. . .1&_md5 = 7db08741ff3f57a4fc5e 4fb7e7828918 (September 13, 2000). Christopher O'Brien, *Enter the Valley* (New York: St. Martin's Press, 1999), discusses mutilations and related matters in the Colorado–New Mexico border area, albeit in a highly credulous manner.

3. "Animal Mutilations and UFOs," pp. 32–33. Anne Strieber, "How Disinformation Experts Spread Fear about UFOs," *The Communion Letter* 1 (Autumn 1989): 1–3, 13; http://www.ufo.net/ufodocs/text.documents/d/ dinfufo.txt (February 21, 2000). "Dulce!" wysiwyg://29/http://ufos.about .com/science/ufos/library/weekly/aa112597.htm (February 22, 2001). William F. Hamilton III, *Cosmic Top Secret: America's Secret UFO Program* (New Brunswick, N.J.: Inner Light, 1991), p. 104. Jason Bishop III, "Recollections and Impressions of Visit to Dulce, New Mexico—October 23, 24, 1988," http:// www.rcbbs.com/docs/dulce-x.txt (February 22, 2001). Paul Bennewitz, "Project Beta," http://www.totse.com/en/fringe/flying_saucers_from _andromeda/probetaa.html and. . ./probetab.html (February 22, 2001). "Statement Released by: John Lear December 29, 1987," in William F. Hamilton III, *Alien Magic* (Glendale, Calif.: Uforces, 1989). "A Press Briefing Given by John Lear May 14, 1990 Las Vegas," http://www.shoah.free-online.co.uk/ 801/Lear/Learupd.html (February 22, 2001).

4. Richard Sauder, *Underground Bases and Tunnels: What Is the Government Trying to Hide?* (Kempton, Ill.: Adventures Unlimited, 1995). Jason Bishop III, "The Dulce Base," in Hamilton, *Alien Magic*. Hamilton, *Cosmic Top Secret*, chap. 9.

5. Walter Kafton-Minkel, *Subterranean Worlds: 100,000 Years of Dragons, Dwarfs, the Dead, Lost Races & UFOs from Inside the Earth* (Port Townsend, Wash.: Loompanics Unlimited, 1989), chap. 3 and passim. Daisie Radner and Michael Radner, *Science and Unreason* (Belmont, Calif.: Wadsworth, 1982), pp. 48–50.

6. Henry H. Bauer, *Science or Pseudoscience: Magnetic Healing, Psychic Phenomena, and Other Heterodoxies* (Urbana, Ill.: University of Illinois Press, 2001), p. 188. Brenda Denzler, *The Lure of the Edge: Scientific Passions, Religious Beliefs, and the Pursuit of UFOs* (Berkeley: University of California Press, 2001), p. 91.

7. I reserve the term *hollow earth* for materials that conceive the interior of the planet to be essentially hollow, and *inner earth* for those that view it as solid but honeycombed with interconnected spaces.

8. Stephen Williams, *Fantastic Archaeology: The Wild Side of North American Prehistory* (Philadelphia: University of Pennsylvania Press, 1991), chap. 7. Donna Kossy, *Strange Creations: Aberrant Ideas of Human Origins from Ancient Astronauts to Aquatic Apes* (Los Angeles: Feral House, 2001), pp. 4–7.

9. H. P. Blavatsky, *Isis Unveiled* (Theosophical University Press Online Edition, 1999), vol. 1, p. 595; http://www.theosociety.org/pasadena/isis/iu15.htm (December 28, 1999).

10. Williams, *Fantastic Archaeology,* pp. 14–52.

11. "I AM Religious Activity," in *The Encyclopedia of American Religions,* ed. J. Gordon Melton, 3d ed. (Tarrytown, N.Y.: Triumph, 1991), vol. 3, pp. 90–91. Arthur Francis Eichorn, Sr., "The 'I AM' Story," in *Mount Shasta: Home of the Ancients,* ed. Bruce Walton (Pomeroy, Wash.: Health Research, 1985), pp. 61–66. G. B. Bryan, *The 'I AM' Experiences of Mr. G. W. Ballard* (Los Angeles: self-published, 1936). Bradley Whitsel, "Escape to the Mountains: A Case Study of the Church Universal and Triumphant" (Ph.D. diss., Syracuse University, 1998).

12. Walton, ed., *Mount Shasta,* pp. i, ix. Emilie A. Frank, *Mt. Shasta: California's Mystic Mountain* (Hilt, Calif.: Photografix Publishing, 1998).

13. Pasquale Maranzino, "Denver Mystic Is Constructing Atomic Armageddon Refuge," *Rocky Mountain News* (Denver), August 30, 1946, 22. "Atom Attack Forecast 'This Year,'" *Denver Post,* February 15, 1953, 1. Donna Kossy, *Kooks* (Portland, Ore.: Feral House, 1994), pp. 124–127.

14. "Shaver and Palmer Part I," http://www.thehollowearthinsider.com/news/wmview.php?ArtID = 20 (January 24, 2002). "Shaver Mystery," in *The UFO Encyclopedia,* ed. Jerome Clark, vol. 2 (Detroit: Omnigraphics, 1992), pp. 304–305. Martin Gardner, *The New Age: Notes of a Fringe Watcher* (Buffalo, N.Y.: Prometheus, 1991), p. 220. Raymond Palmer, "The Observatory, by the Editor," *Amazing Stories* 21 (June 1947): 9.

15. Richard S. Shaver, "I Remember Lemuria!" *Amazing Stories* 19.1 (March 1945). Raymond Palmer, "The Shaver Mystery," in *The Shaver Mystery and the Inner Earth,* ed. Timothy Green Beckley (Clarksburg, W. Va.: Saucerian Publications, 1967), pp. 115–118. "Shaver Mystery," p. 304. Raymond Palmer to "Long John," radio station WOR, February 4, 1957, Gray Barker Collection, Clarksburg-Harrison (W. Va.) Public Library; I am indebted to Brad Whitsel for bringing this correspondence to my attention. David Hatcher Childress, "Introduction," in David Hatcher Childress and Richard S. Shaver, *Lost Continents & the Hollow Earth* (Kempton, Ill.: Adventures Unlimited, 1999), pp. i–vii. For a bibliography of Shaver's writings, see Bruce A. Walton, *A Guide to the Inner Earth* (Pomeroy, Wash.: Health Research, 1985), pp. 77–78.

16. Gardner, *The New Age,* p. 212. Editors, "The Shaver Mystery," *Amazing Stories* 20 (August 1946): 160–161. Letter from Dr. M. Doreal, *Amazing Stories* 20 (September 1946): 177–178.

17. "Shaver Mystery," p. 306. Childress and Shaver, *Lost Continents & the Hollow Earth,* p. vi. Richard Toronto, "The Shaver Mystery," http://www .parascope.com/nb/articles/shaverMystery.htm (October 13, 1999). Gardner, *The New Age,* p. 214.

18. "Discussions," *Amazing Stories* 21 (October 1947): 172. Letter from W. C. Hefferlin, *Amazing Stories* 22 (January 1948): 162. The most complete scholarly treatment of the place occupied by polar regions in esoteric literature is in Joscelyn Godwin, *Arktos: The Polar Myth in Science, Symbolism and Nazi Survival* (Kempton, Ill.: Adventures Unlimited, 1996), pp. 137 and passim. Michael X (pseudonym of Michael Barton), *Rainbow City and the Inner Earth People,* repr. (Clarksburg, W. Va.: Saucerian Books, 1969 [orig. 1960]).

19. Godwin, *Arktos,* pp. 79–81. Nicholas Goodrick-Clarke, *The Occult Roots of Nazism: Secret Aryan Cults and Their Influence on Nazi Ideology, the Ario-sophists of Austria and Germany, 1890–1935,* repr. (New York: New York University Press, 1992), p. 218. Kafton-Minkel, *Subterranean Worlds,* pp. 168–175. Shambhala is sometimes seen as a center of evil, but for an example of it as a seat of virtue and wisdom, see James Redfield, *The Secret of Shambhala: In Search of the Eleventh Insight* (New York: Warner Books, 1999). As with Agharti (some-times rendered "Agarti" or "Agharta"), Shambhala is subject to many variant spellings.

20. Godwin, *Arktos,* pp. 86–87. Goodrick-Clarke, *The Occult Roots of Na-zism,* p. 218. Ferdinand Ossendowski, *Beasts, Men and Gods* (New York: E. P. Dutton, 1922).

21. Ossendowski, *Beasts, Men and Gods,* pp. 312, 314.

22. Kafton-Minkel, *Subterranean Worlds,* p. 178.

23. Raymond Palmer, "The King of the World?" *Amazing Stories* 20 (May 1946): inside back cover. Heinrich Hauser, "Agharti," *Amazing Stories* 20 (June 1946): 8–9.

24. For Costello, see Branton, *The Dulce Wars: Underground Alien Bases & the Battle for Planet Earth* (New Brunswick, N.J.: Inner Light/Global Com-munications, 1999), chap. 11. Hamilton, *Cosmic Top Secret,* p. 36; emphasis in original. Bishop, "The Dulce Base."

25. Maurice Doreal, "Mysteries of the Gobi" (pamphlet; Sedalia, Colo.: Brotherhood of the White Temple, n.d.), pp. 6, 10. Idem, "Flying Saucers: An Occult Viewpoint," repr. (pamphlet; Sedalia, Colo.: Brotherhood of the White Temple, 1992), pp. 29, 47–50.

26. Doreal [*sic*], *The Emerald Tablets of Thoth the Atlantean: A Literal Trans-lation and Interpretation of One of the Most Ancient and Secret of the Great Works of the Ancient Wisdom* (Nashville: Source Books, n.d.), pp. i, ii, 44–45. David Icke, *Children of the Matrix: How an Interdimensional Race Has Con-trolled the World for Thousands of Years—and Still Does* (Wildwood, Mo.: Bridge of Love, 2001), pp. 133, 140, 143, 144.

27. Kafton-Minkel, *Subterranean Worlds,* p. 154.

28. Robert E. Howard, "The Shadow Kingdom," *Weird Tales* (August 1929). Idem, *Kull,* repr. (New York: Baen, 1995), pp. 33–34, 37.

29. L. Sprague de Camp, *Lovecraft: A Biography* (Garden City, N.Y.: Doubleday, 1975), p. 397. Most of the mythology originated with Lovecraft. For a summary, see Timothy K. Beal, *Religion and Its Monsters* (New York: Routledge, 2002), pp. 179–188.

30. Robert Ernst Dickhoff, *Agharta,* repr. (New York: Fieldcrest, 1965 [orig. 1951]). Kafton-Minkel, *Subterranean Worlds,* p. 184. Dickhoff, *Agharta,* pp. 32, 76.

31. "For the Record—Info? On 'Branton,'" http://www.ufomind.com/ ufo.updates/1998/nov/m16–004.shmtl (December 6, 2000). "Re: Who Is 'Branton'?" http://www.ufomind.com/ufo/updates/1997/apr/m18–002 .shmtl (December 3, 2000). "Branton," http://www.ufomind.com/people/ b/branton/ (December 3, 2000). As indicated previously, Branton now has three conventional hard-copy books available: *The Dulce Wars* (1999; see n. 24 above), *The Secrets of the Mojave* (Abilene, Tex.: Creative Arts & Science Enterprises, 1999), and *The Omega Files: Secret Nazi UFO Bases Revealed!* (New Brunswick, N.J.: Global Communications, 2000), not paginated. Bruce A. Walton has published *A Guide to the Inner Earth* (see n. 15 above) and *Mount Shasta* (see n. 11 above), both in 1985; he lists additional items by himself, most of them articles, in *A Guide to the Inner Earth,* p. 86. Branton cites Walton in *The Secrets of the Mojave,* pp. 34, 163, and 179.

32. Branton, "The Alien/LDS Connection," http://www.srv.net/bhw/ favorite.htm (September 27, 2000). "For the Record—Info? On 'Branton.'" Michael Corbin, "Dulce, New Mexico & the Ashtar Connection," http:// www.eagle-net.org/dulce/R-ASHTAR.html (December 2, 1997). B. Alan Walton, "Reptilian Encounters in Utah, Time to Kick Ass," *World of the Strange* (July 30, 2001), http://www.orion-web-maintenance.com/iuf. . .e_zines_ august_01_01_03_world_of_the.htm (February 5, 2002).

33. "For the Record—Info? On 'Branton.'" Branton, "Dreamland in the Rockies—part 1 of 2," http://www.geocities.com/Area51/Shadowlands/ 6583/et18/html (April 28, 1999); capitalization in original.

34. Icke, *Children of the Matrix,* pp. 140, 263, 383. Idem, "The Reptilian Connection," http://www.davidicke.com/icke/temp/reptconnectionmenu .html (August 30, 2000). John Rhodes, "Reptoids.com," http://www .reptoids.com/ (February 11, 2001).

35. David Icke, *The Biggest Secret* (Scottsdale, Ariz.: Bridge of Love, 1999), p. 21. Branton, *The Secrets of the Mojave,* p. 55. Idem, *The Dulce Wars,* p. 93. John Rhodes, "Probing Deeper into the Dulce Enigma," http://www.eagle-net .org/dulce/W-RHODES.html (October 23, 1997); capitalization in original.

36. Michael Barkun, *Religion and the Racist Right: The Origins of the Christian Identity Movement,* rev. ed. (Chapel Hill: University of North Carolina Press, 1997), chaps. 8–9.

37. "The Cosmic Grand Deception," http://athena.gmu.edu/~cleo/ crim002.txt (June 4, 1997). TAL (a.k.a. Jason Bishop III), quoted in Branton, *The Secrets of the Mojave,* p. 127. Reptilians are sometimes referred to as draco-

nians or Draco in the belief that they originated in star systems in the constellation Draco, which has the symbolic advantage of being a constellation said to resemble a dragon.

38. Commander X, *The Controllers: The Hidden Rulers of Earth Identified* (n.p.: Abelard Productions, 1994), p. 9.

8. Anti-Catholicism and Anti-Masonry

1. John Higham, *Strangers in the Land: Patterns of American Nativism, 1860–1925,* repr. (New Brunswick, N.J.: Rutgers University Press, 1998), p. 4. David H. Bennett, *The Party of Fear: The American Far Right from Nativism to the Militia Movement,* rev. ed. (New York: Vintage, 1995), p. xii.

2. Higham, *Strangers in the Land,* pp. 5–11.

3. Richard Hofstadter, *The Paranoid Style in American Politics and Other Essays* (New York: Knopf, 1965), pp. 21–22.

4. Higham, *Strangers in the Land,* p. 29. Bennett, *The Party of Fear,* p. 172.

5. Hofstadter, *The Paranoid Style in American Politics,* pp. 14–18. Seymour Martin Lipset and Earl Raab, *The Politics of Unreason: Right-Wing Extremism in America, 1790–1977,* 2d ed. (Chicago: University of Chicago Press, 1978), p. 43. Bennett, *The Party of Fear,* p. 50.

6. This account of Masonic history follows that of Margaret C. Jacob in *The Radical Enlightenment: Pantheists, Freemasons and Republicans* (London: George Allen & Unwin, 1981), chap. 4 passim.

7. Hofstadter, *The Paranoid Style in American Politics,* p. 18.

8. Lipset and Raab, *The Politics of Unreason,* p. 92. Bennett, *The Party of Fear,* p. 169.

9. Bennett, *The Party of Fear,* p. 408.

10. Commander X, *The Controllers: The Hidden Rulers of Earth Identified* (n.p.: Abelard Productions, 1994), p. 50. David Icke, *The Biggest Secret* (Scottsdale, Ariz.: Bridge of Love, 1999), pp. 52–53. Branton, *The Secrets of the Mojave* (Abilene, Tex.: Creative Arts & Science Enterprises, 1999), p. 36.

11. Michael Barkun, *Religion and the Racist Right: The Origins of the Christian Identity Movement,* rev. ed. (Chapel Hill: University of North Carolina Press, 1997), p. 168. Alexander Hislop, *The Two Babylons; or, The Papal Worship Proved to Be the Worship of Nimrod and His Wife,* repr. (New York: Loizeau Brothers, 1943); a brief first edition was published in Edinburgh in 1853, and a much-expanded second edition in 1858.

12. Milton William Cooper, *Behold a Pale Horse* (Sedona, Ariz.: Light Technology), pp. 100–102.

13. Branton, *The Secrets of the Mojave,* pp. 31–32. Commander X, ed., *Cosmic Patriot Files* (n.p.: Abelard Productions, n.d.), vol. 1, p. 12. Branton, *The Secrets of the Mojave,* pp. 31–32.

14. "Phil Schneider vs. the New World Order," http://www.eagle-net.org/dulce/Y92SNIDR.html (December 3, 1997); this purports to be a lecture delivered by Schneider in May 1995, and is annotated by Branton. UFO conspir-

acists believe Schneider to have been an engineer involved in construction of the Dulce base who discovered the alien presence and was subsequently murdered: Branton, *The Dulce Wars: Underground Alien Bases & the Battle for Planet Earth* (New Brunswick, N.J.: Inner Light/Global Communications, 1999), chap. 13.

15. Bennett, *The Party of Fear,* pp. 41–47. Mark Phillips, "Forward," in Cathy O'Brien with Mark Phillips, *Trance Formation of America* (Nashville: Global Trance Formation Info, 1995), at http://tau.lpl.arizona.edu/~corleyj/wwolf/truth/text/monarch.txt (May 28, 1997). Icke, *The Biggest Secret,* pp. 324–325.

16. O'Brien with Phillips, *Trance Formation of America.* Icke, *The Biggest Secret,* chap. 16.

17. Icke, *The Biggest Secret,* p. 324.

18. Branton, "The Alien/LDS Connection," http://www.srv.net/~bhw/favorite.htm (September 27, 2000). Idem, *The Secrets of the Mojave,* p. 227.

19. Michael W. Cuneo, *The Smoke of Satan: Conservative and Traditionalist Dissent in Contemporary American Catholicism* (New York: Oxford University Press, 1997), pp. 134–144. Congregation for the Doctrine of the Faith, "The Message of Fatima," http://www.cesnur.org/testi/fatima/en.htm (June 26, 2000).

20. Cooper, *Behold a Pale Horse,* pp. 212–213. Cooper's discussion of Fatima, with Branton's commentary, appears in Branton, *The Secrets of the Mojave,* pp. 77–78. Milton William Cooper, "Satanism in Vatican?" http://harvesttrust.org/satanism.htm (February 27, 1998).

21. George C. Andrews, *Extra-Terrestrials among Us,* repr. (St. Paul, Minn.: Llewellyn, 1993 [orig. 1986]), pp. 18–19. Commander X, ed., *Cosmic Patriot Files,* vol. 1, p. 12. "Darkest Secrets of Our Time: A Letter to My Darling Daughter Josephine, Part II," *Contact: The Phoenix Project* 18 (September 9, 1997): 8.

22. Darryl E. Hicks and David A. Lewis, *The Todd Phenomenon: Ex-Grand Druid vs. the Illuminati, Fact or Fantasy?* (Harrison, Ark.: New Leaf, 1979), pp. 25–26, 95. Des Griffin, *Descent into Slavery?* (South Pasadena, Calif.: Emissary, 1980), p. 38.

23. Cooper, *Behold a Pale Horse,* pp. 78–79. Icke, *The Biggest Secret,* p. 167.

24. Nesta H. Webster, *Secret Societies and Subversive Movements,* repr. (Los Angeles: Christian Book Club of America, n.d.), p. 293. Lady Queenborough (a.k.a. Edith Starr Miller), *Occult Theocrasy [sic],* repr. (Los Angeles: Christian Book Club of America, n.d.), p. 32; emphasis in original.

25. David Icke, *. . . And the Truth Shall Set You Free* (Isle of Wight: Bridge of Love, 1995), p. 188. Branton, *The Omega Files: Secret Nazi UFO Bases Revealed!* (New Brunswick, N.J.: Global Communications, 2000), not paginated.

26. John Coleman, *Conspirators' Hierarchy: The Story of the Committee of 300* (Bozeman, Mont.: America West, 1992), p. 39. "The Cult of the Serpent," http://www.balaams-ass.com/journal/prophecy/srpntcit.htm (June 3, 1997).

27. Griffin, *Descent into Slavery?* pp. 38–39.

28. Branton, *The Omega Files.* Ray Bilger, "The Untold History of America, Part XVI," *Contact: The Phoenix Project* 17 (June 24, 1997): 8. Milton William Cooper claims that John F. Kennedy was assassinated to keep him from reveal-

ing relationships between the government and the aliens: *Behold a Pale Horse,* p. 215.

29. Daniel (pseud.), *Signs and Symbols in the Seat of Government* (self-published, n.d.), p. 3. Much of this anti-Masonic conspiracism appears to derive from material issued by evangelist Ralph Woodrow: http://www.ralphwoodrow.org/ (February 15, 2000). For nonconspiracist speculation about the Washington, D.C., street plan, see David Ovason, *The Secret Architecture of Our Nation's Capital: The Masons and the Building of Washington, D.C.* (New York: HarperCollins, 2000).

30. Branton, *The Omega Files.*

31. Commander X, ed., *Cosmic Patriot Files,* vol. 1, pp. 6–7; capitalization in original.

32. Icke, *The Biggest Secret,* pp. 356–360.

33. "What on Earth Is Going on at Denver International Airport?" http://www.geocities.com/Baja/5692/ (March 18, 1998).

34. "The KSEO 4/26/96 Interview with Alex Christopher," *The Leading Edge* 92 (n.d.): 3. Jon King, "Deep Underground: Part I," *UFO Reality* 4 (1996): 44. Branton, *The Dulce Wars,* pp. 100–101.

35. Branton, *The Dulce Wars,* p. 100.

9. Anti-Semitism among the Aliens

1. "Ernst Zundel & Flying Saucers: A Source," http://www.ca.nizkor.org/hweb/people/z/zundel-ernst/flying-saucers.html (February 15, 1999). Joscelyn Godwin, *Arktos: The Polar Myth in Science, Symbolism and Nazi Survival* (Kempton, Ill.: Adventures Unlimited, 1996), p. 73. Alan Baker, *Invisible Eagle: The History of Nazi Occultism* (London: Virgin, 2000), pp. 268–273.

2. Branton, *The Dulce Wars: Underground Alien Bases & the Battle for Planet Earth* (New Brunswick, N.J.: Inner Light/Global Communications, 1999), p. 44; capitalization in original. Branton, *The Omega Files: Secret Nazi UFO Bases Revealed!* (New Brunswick, N.J.: Global Communications, 2000), not paginated.

3. Branton, *The Omega Files.*

4. Stan Deyo, *The Cosmic Conspiracy,* rev. ed. (Kempton, Ill.: Adventures Unlimited, 1994), p. 133. Idem, *The Vindicator Scrolls* (Perth: West Australian Texas Trading, 1989), pp. 229–232.

5. Jacques Vallee, *Revelations: Alien Contact and Human Deception* (New York: Ballantine, 1991), p. 66. George C. Andrews, *Extra-Terrestrial Friends and Foes* (Lilburn, Ga.: IllumiNet, 1993), pp. 142–144. Branton, *The Dulce Wars,* p. 79.

6. Milton William Cooper, *Behold a Pale Horse* (Sedona, Ariz.: Light Technology, 1991), p. 96. Valdamar Valerian, *Matrix III: The Psycho-Social, Chemical, Biological and Electromagnetic Manipulation of Human Consciousness* (Yelm, Wash.: Leading Edge Research Group, 1992), vol. 1, pp. 632–637.

7. Icke, . . . *And the Truth Shall Set You Free* (Isle of Wight: Bridge of Love, 1995), p. 76. Idem, *The Biggest Secret* (Scottsdale, Ariz.: Bridge of Love, 1999), p. 87. Idem, *Children of the Matrix: How an Interdimensional Race Has Controlled the World for Thousands of Years—and Still Does* (Wildwood, Mo.: Bridge of Love, 2001), pp. 408, 431–432, 436, 438, 440.

8. Icke, . . . *And the Truth Shall Set You Free*, pp. 106, 123.

9. Stephen Eric Bronner, *A Rumor about the Jews: Reflections on Antisemitism and the Protocols of the Elders of Zion* (New York: St. Martin's Press, 2000), pp. 81–88. Norman Cohn, *Warrant for Genocide: The Myth of the Jewish World-Conspiracy and the Protocols of the Elders of Zion* (London: Eyre and Spottiswoode, 1967).

10. *The International Jew*, a compilation of articles from the *Dearborn Independent*, was issued in four volumes by the Dearborn Publishing Company, in Dearborn, Michigan: vol. 1, *The World's Foremost Problem* (1920); vol. 2, *Jewish Activities in the United States* (1921); vol. 3, *Jewish Influences in American Life* (1921); and vol. 4, *Aspects of Jewish Power in the United States* (1922). Michael Barkun, *Religion and the Racist Right: The Origins of the Christian Identity Movement*, rev. ed. (Chapel Hill: University of North Carolina Press, 1997), pp. 33–39.

11. Deyo, *The Cosmic Conspiracy*, p. 66.

12. Cooper, *Behold a Pale Horse*, p. 267 (both quotes). Commander X, ed., *Cosmic Patriot Files* (n.p.: Abelard Productions, n.d.), vol. 1, p. 42. The term *Sion* in the quotation from Cooper apparently refers to the Priory of Sion, an organization alleged by occultists and conspiracists to have provided the foundation for the medieval Templars and, with them, to have been the custodians of secret knowledge and power.

13. Icke, . . . *And the Truth Shall Set You Free*, pp. 54–55. Idem, *The Biggest Secret*, p. 212. Barkun, *Religion and the Racist Right*, pp. 136–142.

14. Barkun, *Religion and the Racist Right*, pp. 136–142.

15. Jim Marrs, *Rule by Secrecy: The Hidden History That Connects the Trilateral Commission, the Freemasons, and the Great Pyramids* (New York: HarperCollins, 2000), p. 152.

16. Des Griffin, *The Fourth Reich of the Rich* (South Pasadena, Calif.: Emissary, 1976), p. 195. Nesta H. Webster, *Secret Societies and Subversive Movements*, repr. (Los Angeles: Christian Book Club of America, n.d.), p. 413.

17. Patrick H. Bellringer (probable pseudonym), "People of the Lie: What Is the Truth—or The 'New' Contact Newspaper," http://www.fourwinds10.com/phb/what_is.htm (November 16, 2000).

18. "Background Information—about CONTACT: The Phoenix Project," wysiwyg://6http://www.rapidnet.com/contact/background.html (June 10, 1998). "Hatonn Appears on Radio Talk-Show," *The Phoenix Liberator* 17 (January 14, 1992): 15–20; this is a transcript of a broadcast of the Jay Lawrence show on KTAR (Phoenix), January 5, 1992.

19. J. Gordon Melton, "Ancient Wisdom Family," in *The Encyclopedia of American Religions*, 3d ed., repr. (Tarrytown, N.Y.: Triumph, 1991), vol. 3, pp. 1–4.

20. "Background Information—about CONTACT: The Phoenix Project."

21. J. Gordon Melton and George M. Eberhart, "The Flying Saucer Contactee Movement, 1950–1994: A Bibliography," in *The Gods Have Landed: New Religions from Other Worlds*, ed. James R. Lewis (Albany: State University of New York Press, 1995), pp. 251–332. J. Gordon Melton, *Finding Enlightenment: Ramtha's School of Ancient Wisdom* (Hillsboro, Ore.: Beyond Words, 1998), pp. 53–55 ("a source other than"). Brenda Denzler, *The Lure of the Edge: Scientific Passions, Religious Beliefs, and the Pursuit of UFOs* (Berkeley: University of California Press, 2001), p. 46. Wayne Spencer, "To Absent Friends: Classical Spiritual Mediumship and New Age Channeling Compared and Contrasted," *Journal of Contemporary Religion* 16 (2001): 350.

22. Thomas E. Bullard, *UFO Abductions: The Measure of a Mystery* (n.p.: Fund for UFO Research, 1987), vol. 1, pp. 5–20. Melton and Eberhart, "The Flying Saucer Contactee Movement." James W. Moseley and Karl T. Pflock, *Shockingly Close to the Truth! Confessions of a Grave-Robbing Ufologist* (Amherst, N.Y.: Prometheus, 2002), pp. 60, 136–137. Denzler, *The Lure of the Edge*, pp. 41–42. Donna Kossy, *Strange Creations: Aberrant Ideas of Human Origins from Ancient Astronauts to Aquatic Apes* (Los Angeles: Feral House, 2001), pp. 11–12. Colin Bennett, *Looking for Orthon: The Story of George Adamski, the First Flying Saucer Contactee, and How He Changed the World* (New York: Paraview, 2001), pp. 33–36; the latter is a colorful, if credulous, account. For a systematic debunking of Adamski's claims, see Moseley and Pflock, *Shockingly Close to the Truth!* pp. 333–352.

23. George Hunt Williamson, *Other Tongues, Other Flesh* (Amherst, Wis.: Amherst Press, 1953), pp. 95, 381, 378, 386. Idem, *The Saucers Speak: A Documentary Report of Interstellar Communication by Radiotelegraphy* (London: Neville Spearman, 1963), pp. 75–76.

24. Richard T. Miller, *Star Wards III* (Folsom, Calif.: Advent, 2000), pp. 26–35, 37, 61. Moseley and Pflock, *Shockingly Close to the Truth!* p. 137. Michael Corbin, "Review of the 'Phoenix Project' by ParaNet," approximate posting date August 16, 1992, http://www.ufobbs.com/txt3/2495.ufo (October 22, 1997). Richard T. Miller, "Rebuttal of Paranet's Review of the 'Phoenix Project,'" posted August 12, 1992; http://www.ufobbs.com/txt3/2496.ufo (October 12, 1997); notwithstanding the fact that the rebuttal bears a date prior to the review being rebutted, Miller is clearly responding to Corbin.

25. James R. Lewis, *The Encyclopedia of Cults, Sects, and New Religions*, 2d ed. (Amherst, N.Y.: Prometheus, 2002): "Ashtar Command," p. 78, and "Ministry of Universal Wisdom," p. 493. Kenn Thomas, "The Giant Rock Conventions," wysi://105/http://www.virtuallystrange.net/ufo/updates/1998/dec/m17-013.shtml (January 16, 2002); republished from *Fortean Times*. Tuella (a.k.a. Thelma B. Terrell), "Compiled through Tuella by the Ashtar Command," in *Project World Evacuation*, ed. Timothy Green Beckley (New Brunswick, N.J.: Inner Light, 1993), p. 81.

26. "George Green Clarifies Role in Meier Case," dated January 1, 1999, http://www.ufomind.com/misc/1999/jan/d02-001.shtml (March 17, 2000).

Undated letter from George Green to potential customers on the letterhead of America West Publishers.

, 27. Miller, *Star Wards III*. "The Ultimate Secret: An Intelligence Evaluation and Overview" (pamphlet; Carson City, Nev.: Advent, May 5, 1992). "The K-2 Report: The Discovery of a Secret Alien Base in Northern California" (pamphlet; Carson City, Nev.: Advent, May 27, 1992). "The Dulce Report: A Field Investigation and Evaluation" (pamphlet; Carson City, Nev.: Advent, May 27, 1992). *Insights,* a monthly newsletter, began publication in February 1995.

28. John Coleman, *Conspirators' Hierarchy: The Story of the Committee of 300* (Bozeman, Mont.: America West, 1992), pp. 160, 243. "George Green Clarifies Role in Meier Case." *Victoria* [British Columbia] *Times-Colonist,* January 22, 1992. Arthur Koestler, *The Thirteenth Tribe: The Khazar Empire and Its Heritage* (New York: Random House, 1976).

29. "Like a *Bad* Dream . . . More on George Green," *Contact: The Phoenix Project* 1 (June 22, 1993): 40–43. "Another Fabulous Fable from 'Honest' George Green," *Contact: The Phoenix Project* 1 (June 1, 1993): 21–24. "CON-TACT Staff Locked-out under Cloak of Darkness," *Contact: The Phoenix Educator* 24 (March 26, 1999): 1–2. "What Has Happened since the CONTACT Lock-out?" *The Spectrum* 1 (June 1, 1999): 26. "Objective Investigation into the Situation between the Old and New CONTACT Staff," http://www .fourwinds10.com/corner/watchers-staff.html (November 28, 2000); capitalization in original.

30. "A Few Important Historical Definitions," *Phoenix Liberator* 19 (May 5, 1992): 8; emphasis in original. "*Rise of Antichrist,* Vols. 1–4," *Contact: The Phoenix Educator* 23 (December 1, 1998): 18. Rick Martin, "Are 'Their' Aliens among Us? *The Biggest Secret,* an Interview with David Icke 7/30/99 Rick Martin," *The Spectrum* (August 3, 1999), http://www.spectrumnews10.com/html/ writings/Icke-Interview.html (December 1, 2000).

31. John M. Werly, "Premillennialism and the Paranoid Style," *American Studies* 18 (1977): 39–55. Leo P. Ribuffo, *The Old Christian Right: The Protestant Far Right from the Great Depression to the Cold War* (Philadelphia: Temple University Press, 1983), pp. 49–59.

32. Ribuffo, *The Old Christian Right,* p. 229.

33. Alec Hidel, "George Hunt Williamson & the Genesis of the Contactees," http://www.ufomind.com/misc/1997/mar/d21–002.shtml (April 18, 2000). Jacques Vallee, *Messengers of Deception: UFO Contacts and Cults* (Berkeley, Calif.: And/Or Press, 1979), pp. 192–193.

34. For information on Pelley's UFO writings, I am indebted to Vance Pollock. William Dudley Pelley, *Star Guests: Design for Mortality* (Noblesville, Ind.: Soulcraft Chapels, 1950).

35. Gen. 6:1–4. Pelley, *Star Guests,* pp. 75, 100–101, 167.

36. Pelley, *Star Guests,* pp. 99, 165–166, 240, 242.

37. Moseley and Pflock, *Shockingly Close to the Truth!* p. 74. Williamson, *Other Tongues, Other Flesh,* book 3, chap. 1, pp. 287–288.

38. George Hunt Williamson and John McCoy, *UFOs Confidential! Behind the Most Closely Guarded Secret of All Time* (Corpus Christi, Tex.: Essene Press, 1958), pp. 42–44, 53; emphasis in original. Glen Jeansonne, *Gerald L. K. Smith: Minister of Hate* (New Haven, Conn.: Yale University Press, 1988), p. 122.

39. J. Gordon Melton, "Brotherhood of the Seven Rays," in *The Encyclopedia of American Religions,* 3d ed., repr. (Tarrytown, N.Y.: Triumph, 1991), vol. 2, p. 296. Brother Philip (pseudonym of George Hunt Williamson), *Secret of the Andes,* repr. (Novato, Calif.: Leaves of Grass, 1976 [orig. 1961]), pp. 118, 138.

40. Leon Festinger, Henry W. Riecken, and Stanley Schachter, *When Prophecy Fails: A Social and Psychological Study of a Modern Group That Predicted the Destruction of the World,* repr. (New York: Harper, 1964 [orig. 1956]).

41. Ibid., p. 193.

42. Ibid., pp. 34, 41. For an influential attack on the Ballards emphasizing links to Pelley, see Gerald B. Bryan, *Psychic Dictatorship in America,* repr. (Livingston, Mont.: Paolini International, 2000 [orig., 1940]), chap. 3. Melton, "Brotherhood of the Seven Rays," pp. 295–296. "The Teachings of Sananda," http://home.iae.nl/users/lightnet/celestial/jesus.htm (October 30, 2000).

10. September 11: The Aftermath

1. For a summary of September 11 urban legends, see About Urban Legends and Folklore, "Current Netlore: Terrorist Attacks on the U.S.: Internet Hoaxes, Small Rumors and Urban Legends," wysiwyg://144/http://urbanlegends.about.com/library/bixterror.html (October 18, 2001).

2. John Hagee, *Attack on America: New York, Jerusalem, and the Role of Terrorism in the Last Days* (Nashville, Tenn.: Thomas Nelson, 2001), pp. 4–5. Arno Froese, *Terror over America: Understanding the Tragedy* (West Columbia, S.C.: Midnight Call Ministries, 2001), p. 123.

3. Grant R. Jeffrey, *War on Terror: Unfolding Bible Prophecy* (Toronto: Frontier Research Publications, 2002), pp. 181–182.

4. *End-Time Informer* (December 2001), e-journal for subscribers (November 30, 2001); *End-Time Informer* (November 2001), e-journal for subscribers (November 2, 2001); issued by Armageddon Books, http://www.armageddonbooks.com.

5. "Year-End Google Zeitgeist: Search Patterns, Trends, and Surprises," http://www.google.com/press/zeitgeist.html (January 7, 2002).

6. "CSICOP Tracks Misinformation and Hoaxes in Wake of the Terrorist Attacks," http://www.csicop.org/hoaxwatch (October 23, 2001). Joe McNally, "Spinning Nostradamus," *Fortean Times* 152 (December 2001): 17.

7. Richard Hoagland, "The Twin Towers and the Great Masonic Experiments: Has the 'End of Days' Begun?" *Paranoia* 20 (Spring 2002): 52–58. On Khalifa's numerology, see "Dr. Rashad Khalifa, the Man, the Issues, and the Truth," http://www.submission.org/khalifa.html (November 18, 1998).

8. Editors, "11.09.2001," *Fortean* Times 152 (December 2001): 9. Kenn Thomas, "Nine Eleven," http://www.steamshovelpress.com/fromeditor.htm (October 9, 2001). Among the sites showing segments of the video was http://www.globalchanges.com/news/091701.htm (October 23, 2001). Sister Tynetta Muhammad, "In Search of the Messiah: U.F.O.s Appear at the Time of Horrific Explosions of Twin Towers at the Trade Center," *The Final Call Online* (October 15, 2001), http://finalcall.com/columns/num19/num19%5F10%2D16%2D2001.html (October 26, 2001).

9. Duncan M. Roads, "Editorial," *Nexus* 9 (January–February 2002): 2. Texe Marrs, "The Mysterious Riddle of Chandra Levy," http://www.texemarrs.com/112001/mysterious_riddle_chandra.htm (January 29, 2002). Clayton R. Douglas, "Publisher's Corner," *Free American* (January 2002): 5.

10. Editors, "The Day the Earth Stood Still," *The Spectrum* 3 (October 2001), http://www.spectrumnews10.com/images/sb/2001/sb3-100901.gif (December 11, 2001). Leonard G. Horowitz, "The CIA's Role in the Anthrax Mailings," *The Spectrum* 3 (January 2002), http://www.spectrumnews10.com/images/sb/2002/01JAN-1-Large.gif (February 13, 2002). Leonard G. Horowitz, "Could the Anthrax Mailings Be Military-Industrial Sabotage?" *Paranoia* 29 (Spring 2002): 8.

11. "Public Disclaimer," http://www.fourwinds10.com/index.html (December 12, 2001). Patrick H. Bellringer (probable pseudonym), "Update: September 18, 2001," http://www.fourwinds10.com/index.html (December 12, 2001).

12. "Branton Update Mon. April 8, 2002," http://www.alienjoes.com/branton/update.html (April 23, 2002). TCA, "The Truth about the September 11th Terrorist Attack to [*sic*] USA," http://www.angelfire.com/ab/libertas/terrorism.html (March 22, 2002).

13. David Icke, "Alice in Wonderland & the WTC Disaster," *Conspiracy Planet* (January 28, 2002), http://www.conspiracyplanet.com/channel.cfm (January 28, 2002), republished from *The Spectrum* (October 9, 2001).

14. David Icke, "An Other-Dimensional View of the American Catastrophe from a Source They Cannot Silence: How Bush and Blair 'Knew'; the China Scenario; and the Manipulation to Come by Mind-Controlled 'Celebrities,'" http://www.davidicke.com/articles3/bushblairknew.html (March 8, 2002).

15. Ibid.

16. Milton William Cooper, "Who Benefits? The Question No One Dares to Ask!" wysiwyg://64/http://www.williamcooper.com/vnexclusivesarchives.html (September 28, 2001).

17. Mark Shaffer, "Officers Kill Militia Voice; Deputy Shot," *The Arizona Republic* (November 7, 2001), http://www.azcentral.com/news/articles/breaking/1107cooper07.html (November 7, 2001).

18. Ibid.

19. Ibid. (Moore quote). Norio Hayakawa, "My Thoughts on the Late Bill Cooper," in Commander X, ed., *William Cooper: Death of a Conspiracy Salesman* (New Brunswick, N.J.: Global Communications, 2002), pp. 51, 53, 91.

20. "Shot Dead! WBCQ Short-Wave Radio Talk Show Host William 'Bill' Cooper," http://www.halturnershow.com/BillCooper.htm (November 7, 2001). Clay Douglas, "The Death of William Cooper," *Free American* 9 (January 2002): 5–6.

21. Kenn Thomas, "Bullets before Brains," *Fortean Times* 155 (March 2002): 39. Commander X, ed., *William Cooper*, pp. 90, 95.

22. James Moseley, "Rebel without a Pause: The Life & Death of Former Ufologist William Milton [*sic*] Cooper," *Saucer Smear* 48 (December 1, 2001), http://www.martiansgohome.com/smear/v48/ss001201.htm (January 15, 2002). Hamilton is in Commander X, ed., *William Cooper*, p. 16. Don Ecker, "Dead Man Talking," *Fortean Times* 155 (March 2002): 41.

23. Nicholas Goodrick-Clarke, *Black Sun: Aryan Cults, Esoteric Nazism, and the Politics of Identity* (New York: New York University Press, 2002), p. 123.

24. "Osama in Shambhala?" *UFO Roundup* 7 (January 1, 2002), http://www.100megsfree4.com/farshores/ufor071.htm (March 14, 2002).

25. David Hatcher Childress, "The Ancient Heart of Central Asia: Was Afghanistan Once Home to the Garden of Eden?" *Atlantis Rising* 31 (January–February 2002): 24.

26. Michael Barkun, *Religion and the Racist Right: The Origins of the Christian Identity Movement*, rev. ed. (Chapel Hill: University of North Carolina Press, 1997), part 1 passim.

27. Ibid., p. 183.

28. Michael Barkun, "Defending against the Apocalypse: The Limits of Homeland Security," in *Governance and Public Security* (Syracuse, N.Y.: Campbell Public Affairs Institute, Maxwell School, Syracuse University, 2002), pp. 17–28.

11. Conclusion

1. Philip Lamy, "UFOs, Extraterrestrials, and the Apocalypse—the Making of a Subculture," in *Millennial Visions*, ed. Martha Lee (Westport, Conn.: Praeger, 2000), pp. 115–134. Vicki Ecker, "A Clone of Their Own," *UFO Magazine* 16 (February–March 2001): 44–51.

2. Milton William Cooper, *Behold a Pale Horse* (Sedona, Ariz.: Light Technology, 1991), pp. 3, 177, 21; capitalization in original.

3. Commander X, *The Controllers: The Hidden Rulers of Earth Identified* (Wilmington, Del.: Abelard Productions, 1994), pp. 55–56. Idem, "Legions of Doom," *UFO Universe, Conspiracies & Cover-ups*, Special Issue 1 (1998): 63. Branton, *The Omega Files: Secret Nazi UFO Bases Revealed!* (New Brunswick, N.J.: Global Communications, 2000), "Scriptural References."

4. Timothy Green Beckley, *Psychic & UFO Revelations in the Last Days* (New Brunswick, N.J.: Inner Light, 1989), pp. 55–56. *Phoenix Operator-Owner Manual Including Flight Instruction* (Tehachapi, Calif.: America West, 1991), p. 9.

5. "Sannada [*sic*] on Earth Changes," http://www.fourwinds10.com/v-of-r/032195g-sananda.html (November 28, 2000); emphasis in original; first published in *Contact: The Phoenix Project* (March 21, 1995): 33.

6. "Channeling Movement," in *The Encyclopedia of Cults, Sects, and New Religions,* ed. James R. Lewis, 2d ed. (Amherst, N.Y.: Prometheus, 2002), pp. 157–158. Gordon-Michael Scallion, *Notes from the Cosmos: A Futurist's Insights into the World of Dream Prophecy and Intuition* (West Chesterfield, N.H.: Matrix Institute, 1997), pp. 17–18. Steven Lee Weinberg, Carol Wright, and John Clancy, eds., *Ramtha Intensive: Change, the Days to Come* (Eastsound, Wash.: Sovereignty, 1987), p. 130.

7. David Icke, *The Biggest Secret* (Scottsdale, Ariz.: Bridge of Love, 1999), p. 474.

8. José Arguelles, *The Mayan Factor: Path beyond Technology* (Santa Fe, N.M.: Bear, 1987), p. 218.

9. Arguelles, *The Mayan Factor,* pp. 190, 219–220.

10. Icke, *The Biggest Secret,* p. 472.

11. Ibid., pp. 472–473.

12. Valdamar Valerian, *Matrix II: The Abduction and Manipulation of Humans Using Advanced Technology,* 3d ed. (Yelm, Wash.: Leading Edge Research Group, 1990–1991), pp. 10, 15, 28.

13. Valdamar Valerian, *Matrix III: The Psycho-Social, Chemical, Biological and Electromagnetic Manipulation of Human Consciousness* (Yelm, Wash.: Leading Edge Research Group, 1992), vol. 1, pp. 691–697.

14. Chip Berlet, "Apocalypse," in *Encyclopedia of Millennialism and Millennial Movements,* ed. Richard Landes (Great Barrington, Mass.: Berkshire Reference Works, 2000), p. 25. Catherine Wessinger, ed., *Millennialism, Persecution, and Violence* (Syracuse, N.Y.: Syracuse University Press, 2000). Her "catastrophic millennialism" has many of the characteristics of the more traditional term *premillennialism.*

15. Wessinger's "progressive millennialism" has many of the characteristics of the more traditional term *postmillennialism.* On the historical relationship of millennialism and progress, see Ernest Tuveson, *Millennium and Utopia: A Study in the Background of the Idea of Progress* (New York: Harper Torchbooks, 1964).

16. Richard Hofstadter, "The Paranoid Style in American Politics," in *The Paranoid Style in American Politics and Other Essays* (New York: Knopf, 1965), p. 30.

17. W. Warren Wagar, *Terminal Visions: The Literature of Last Things* (Bloomington: Indiana University Press, 1982), pp. 185–186, 194–195, 204.

18. Michael Barkun, *Religion and the Racist Right: The Origins of the Christian Identity Movement,* rev. ed. (Chapel Hill: University of North Carolina Press, 1997), pp. 247–249.

19. "Statement of Purpose," *Nexus: New Times Magazine* 9 (March–April 2001): 2. Although its headquarters is in Australia, the magazine maintains offices in the United States, Great Britain, and the Netherlands.

20. My use of *bridging mechanisms* here differs from my use of it in an earlier book, where I employed it in a sense that conflated it with what is here called *mainstreaming;* cf. Barkun, *Religion and the Racist Right,* pp. 287–290.

21. David Cook, "America the Second 'Ad: Prophecies about the Downfall of the United States,'" http://www.mille.org/scholarship/papers/ADAM .html (March 8, 2002).

22. Jodi Dean, *Aliens in America: Conspiracy Cultures from Outerspace to Cyberspace* (Ithaca, N.Y.: Cornell University Press, 1998), pp. 8–9.

23. On Aum Shinrikyo, see for example Robert Jay Lifton, *Destroying the World to Save It: Aum Shinrikyo, Apocalyptic Violence, and the New Global Terrorism* (New York: Henry Holt, 1999).

Bibliography

Books, Articles, Pamphlets, and Videotapes

Abraham, Larry. 1985 [orig. 1971]. *Call It Conspiracy*. Reprint. Gig Harbor, Wash.: Double A.

Alternative 3. 1996. Videotape. Beverly Hills, Calif.: Underground Video. Originally aired on Anglia Television [U.K.], April 1, 1977.

American Opinion Book Service. 1996. Winter catalog.

Andrews, George C. 1993. *Extra-Terrestrial Friends and Foes*. Lilburn, Ga.: IllumiNet.

———. 1993 [orig. 1986]. *Extra-Terrestrials among Us*. Reprint. St. Paul, Minn.: Llewellyn.

"Another Fabulous Fable from 'Honest' George Green." 1993. *Contact: The Phoenix Project* 1 (June 1).

Arguelles, Jose. 1987. *The Mayan Factor: Path beyond Technology*. Santa Fe, N.M.: Bear.

"Atom Attack Forecast 'This Year.'" 1953. *Denver Post*, February 15, 1.

"Author David Icke in Tehachapi: A Series." 1997. *Contact: The Phoenix Project* 16 (May 6), 16 (May 13), 17 (May 20), and 17 (May 27).

Baigent, Michael, Richard Leigh, and Henry Lincoln. 1982. *The Holy Blood and the Holy Grail*. New York: Delacorte.

Baker, Alan. 2000. *Invisible Eagle: The History of Nazi Occultism*. London: Virgin.

Barker, Gray. 1997. *They Knew Too Much about Flying Saucers*. Reprint. Lilburn, Ga.: IllumiNet.

Barkun, Michael. 1997. *Religion and the Racist Right: The Origins of the Christian Identity Movement*. Rev. ed. Chapel Hill: University of North Carolina Press.

———. 1998. "Conspiracy Theories as Stigmatized Knowledge: The Basis for a New Age Racism?" In *Nation and Race: The Developing Euro-American*

Racist Subculture, edited by Jeffrey Kaplan and Tore Bjorgo. Boston: Northeastern University Press.

———. 1998. "Politics and Apocalypticism." In *The Encyclopedia of Apocalypticism,* edited by Stephen J. Stein. New York: Continuum.

———. 2002. "Defending against the Apocalypse: The Limits of Homeland Security." In *Governance and Public Security.* Syracuse, N.Y.: Campbell Public Affairs Institute, Maxwell School, Syracuse University.

Barton, Michael. *See* Michael X.

Bauer, Henry H. 2001. *Science or Pseudoscience: Magnetic Healing, Psychic Phenomena, and Other Heterodoxies.* Urbana: University of Illinois Press.

Beal, Timothy K. 2002. *Religion and Its Monsters.* New York: Routledge.

Beckley, Timothy Green. 1967. *The Shaver Mystery and the Inner Earth.* Clarksburg, W. Va.: Saucerian Publications.

———. 1989. *Psychic & UFO Revelations in the Last Days.* New Brunswick, N.J.: Inner Light.

Bell, Daniel. 1961. *The End of Ideology: On the Exhaustion of Political Ideas in the Fifties.* Rev. ed. New York: Collins.

Bennett, Colin. 2001. *Looking for Orthon: The Story of George Adamski, the First Flying Saucer Contactee, and How He Changed the World.* New York: Paraview.

Bennett, David H. 1995. *The Party of Fear: The American Far Right from Nativism to the Militia Movement.* Rev. ed. New York: Vintage.

Bilger, Ray. 1997. "The Untold History of America, Part XVI." *Contact: The Phoenix Project* 17 (June 24).

Billington, James H. 1980. *Fire in the Minds of Men: Origins of the Revolutionary Faith.* New York: Basic Books.

Blahut, Fred. 1984. "Emergency Plan Implementation Responsibility of 'Low Key' FEMA." *The Spotlight* (April 23).

Boyer, Paul. 1992. *When Time Shall Be No More: Prophecy Belief in Modern American Culture.* Cambridge, Mass.: Harvard University Press.

Branton [pseudonym]. 1999. *The Dulce Wars: Underground Alien Bases & the Battle for Planet Earth.* New Brunswick, N.J.: Inner Light/Global Communications.

———. 1999. *The Secrets of the Mojave.* Abilene, Tex.: Creative Arts & Science Enterprises.

———. 2000. *The Omega Files: Secret Nazi UFO Bases Revealed!* New Brunswick, N.J.: Global Communications.

Bronner, Stephen Eric. 2000. *A Rumor about the Jews: Reflections on Antisemitism and the Protocols of the Elders of Zion.* New York: St. Martin's Press.

Brother Philip. *See* Williamson, George Hunt.

Brunvand, Jan Harold. 1981. *The Vanishing Hitchhiker: American Urban Legends and Their Meanings.* New York: W. W. Norton.

———. 1989. *Curses! Boiled Again! The Hottest Urban Legends Going.* New York: W. W. Norton.

Bryan, G. B. 1936. *The "I AM" Experiences of Mr. G. W. Ballard*. Los Angeles: self-published.

———. 2000 [orig. 1940]. *Psychic Dictatorship in America*. Reprint. Livingston, Mont.: Paolini International.

Bullard, Thomas E. 1987. *UFO Abductions: The Measure of a Mystery*. N.p.: Fund for UFO Research.

Bulwer-Lytton, Edward. 1871. *The Coming Race*. Edinburgh: W. Blackwood.

Campbell, Colin. 1972. "The Cult, the Cultic Milieu and Secularization." *Sociological Yearbook of Religion in Britain* 5: 119–136. London: SCM Press.

Childress, David Hatcher. 1999. "Introduction." In David Hatcher Childress and Richard S. Shaver, *Lost Continents & the Hollow Earth*. Kempton, Ill.: Adventures Unlimited.

———. 2002. "The Ancient Heart of Central Asia: Was Afghanistan Once Home to the Garden of Eden?" *Atlantis Rising* 31 (January–February): 24.

Clark, Jerome. 1990. "Abduction Phenomenon." In *The UFO Encyclopedia*, edited by Jerome Clark. Vol. 1. Detroit: Apogee.

———. 1992. "Hollow Earth and UFOs." In *The UFO Encyclopedia*, edited by Jerome Clark. Vol. 2. Detroit: Omnigraphics.

———. 1996. "Animal Mutilations and UFOs." In *The UFO Encyclopedia*, edited by Jerome Clark. Vol. 3. Detroit: Omnigraphics.

———. 1996. *The UFO Files*. Lincolnwood, Ill.: Publications International.

Cohn, Norman. 1967. *Warrant for Genocide: The Myth of the Jewish World-Conspiracy and the Protocols of the Elders of Zion*. London: Eyre and Spottiswoode.

Coleman, John. 1992. *Conspirators' Hierarchy: The Story of the Committee of 300*. Bozeman, Mont.: America West.

Commander X [pseudonym]. 1990. *Underground Alien Bases*. Wilmington, Del.: Abelard Productions.

———. 1994. *The Controllers: The Hidden Rulers of Earth Identified*. Wilmington, Del.: Abelard Productions.

———. 1998. "Legions of Doom." *UFO Universe, Conspiracies & Coverups* Special Issue 1.

———, ed. 2002. *William Cooper: Death of a Conspiracy Salesman*. New Brunswick, N.J.: Global Communications.

———, ed. n.d. *Cosmic Patriot Files*. Wilmington, Del.: Abelard Productions.

"CONTACT Staff Locked-out under Cloak of Darkness." 1999. *Contact: The Phoenix Educator* 24 (March 26).

Cooper, Milton William. 1991. *Behold a Pale Horse*. Sedona, Ariz.: Light Technology.

Cuneo, Michael W. 1997. *The Smoke of Satan: Conservative and Traditionalist Dissent in Contemporary American Catholicism*. New York: Oxford University Press.

Daniel [pseudonym]. n.d. *Signs and Symbols in the Seat of Government*. Self-published.

"Darkest Secrets of Our Time: A Letter to My Darling Daughter Josephine, Part II." 1997. *Contact: The Phoenix Project* 18 (September 9).

"The Dark Side of David Icke." 1995. *Evening Standard* [London], May 26.

Darlington, David. 1997. *Area 51: The Dreamland Chronicles.* New York: Henry Holt.

Dean, Jodi. 1998. *Aliens in America: Conspiracy Cultures from Outerspace to Cyberspace.* Ithaca, N.Y.: Cornell University Press.

De Camp, L. Sprague. 1975. *Lovecraft: A Biography.* Garden City, N.Y.: Doubleday.

"Declassified Documents Confirm Recovery of Alien Craft and Bodies!" 1999. *Nexus* 6 (February–March).

Denzler, Brenda. 2001. *The Lure of the Edge: Scientific Passions, Religious Beliefs, and the Pursuit of UFOs.* Berkeley: University of California Press.

Department of State. 1996. "The Great Seal of the United States." Pamphlet. Washington, D.C.: Government Printing Office.

De Walton, Bruce Alan. *See* Branton.

Deyo, Stan. 1989. *The Vindicator Scrolls.* Perth: West Australia Texas Trading.

———. 1994. *The Cosmic Conspiracy.* Rev. ed. Kempton, Ill.: Adventures Unlimited.

Dickhoff, Robert Ernst. 1965 [orig. 1951]. *Agharta.* New York: Fieldcrest.

"Discussions." 1947. *Amazing Stories* 21 (October).

Doan, Ruth Alden. 1987. *The Miller Heresy, Millennialism, and American Culture.* Philadelphia: Temple University Press.

Donner, Frank J. 1981. *The Age of Surveillance: The Aims and Methods of America's Political Intelligence System.* New York: Vintage.

Doreal, Maurice [pseudonym]. 1946. Letter. *Amazing Stories* 20 (August): 177–178.

———. 1992. "Flying Saucers: An Occult Viewpoint." Pamphlet. Reprint. Sedalia, Colo.: Brotherhood of the White Temple.

———. n.d. *The Emerald Tablets of Thoth the Atlantean: A Literal Translation and Interpretation of One of the Most Ancient and Secret of the Great Works of the Ancient Wisdom.* Nashville: Source Books.

———. n.d. "Mysteries of the Gobi." Pamphlet. Sedalia, Colo.: Brotherhood of the White Temple.

Douglas, Clayton R. 2002. "The Death of William Cooper." *Free American* 9 (January).

———. 2002. "Publisher's Corner." *Free American* 9 (January).

The Dulce Report: A Field Investigation and Evaluation. 1992. Carson City, Nev.: Advent.

Ecker, Don. 2002. "Dead Man Talking." *Fortean Times* 155 (March).

Ecker, Vicki. 2001. "A Clone of Their Own." *UFO Magazine* 16 (February–March).

Eichorn, Arthur Francis, Sr. 1985. "The 'I AM' Story." In *Mount Shasta: Home of the Ancients,* edited by Bruce Walton. Pomeroy, Wash.: Health Research.

"11.09.2001." 2001. *Fortean Times* 152 (December).

Ellis, Bill. 2000. *Raising the Devil: Satanism, New Religions, and the Media*. Lexington: University Press of Kentucky.

Elwood, Robert S. 1995. "Theosophy." In *America's Alternative Religions*, edited by Timothy Miller. Albany: State University of New York Press.

Enemies Foreign & Domestic, part 1: *The United Nations & the New World Order*. n.d. Videotape. Militia of Montana.

Festinger, Leon, Henry W. Riecken, and Stanley Schachter. 1964 [orig. 1956]. *When Prophecy Fails: A Social and Psychological Study of a Modern Group That Predicted the Destruction of the World*. Reprint. New York: Harper.

"A Few Important Historical Definitions." 1992. *Phoenix Liberator* 19 (May 5).

Fox, Cynthia. 2000. "The Search for Extraterrestrial Life." *Life* (March).

Frank, Emilie A. 1998. *Mt. Shasta: California's Mystic Mountain*. Hilt, Calif.: Photografix Publishing.

Friedman, Stanton T. 1997. *Top Secret/Majic*. New York: Marlowe.

Froese, Arno. 2001. *Terror over America: Understanding the Tragedy*. West Columbia, S.C.: Midnight Call Ministries.

Fukuyama, Francis. 1992. *The End of History and the Last Man*. New York: Avon.

Fuller, Robert. 1995. *Naming the Antichrist: The History of an American Obsession*. New York: Oxford University Press.

Galbreath, Robert. 1986. "Explaining Modern Occultism." In *The Occult in America: New Historical Perspectives*, edited by Howard Kerr and Charles L. Crow. Urbana: University of Illinois Press.

"Garden Plot & SWAT: U.S. Police as New Action Army." 1976. *CounterSpy* 2 (Winter).

Gardner, Martin. 1991. *The New Age: Notes of a Fringe Watcher*. Buffalo, N.Y.: Prometheus.

"George Green Clarifies Role in Meier Case." 1992. *Victoria* [British Columbia] *Times-Colonist*, July 22.

Gill, Stephen. 1990. *American Hegemony and the Trilateral Commission*. Cambridge, U.K.: Cambridge University Press.

Godwin, Joscelyn. 1996. *Arktos: The Polar Myth in Science, Symbolism and Nazi Survival*. Kempton, Ill.: Adventures Unlimited.

Goldberg, Robert Alan. 2001. *Enemies Within: The Culture of Conspiracy in Modern America*. New Haven, Conn.: Yale University Press.

Good, Timothy. 1988. *Above Top Secret: The Worldwide U.F.O. Cover-up*. New York: William Morrow.

Goodrick-Clarke, Nicholas. 1992. *The Occult Roots of Nazism: Secret Aryan Cults and Their Influence on Nazi Ideology, the Ariosophists of Austria and Germany, 1890–1935*. Reprint. New York: New York University Press.

———. 2002. *Black Sun: Aryan Cults, Esoteric Nazism, and the Politics of Identity*. New York: New York University Press.

Grace, John. *See* Valerian, Valdamar.

Griffin, Des. 1976. *Fourth Reich of the Rich*. South Pasadena, Calif.: Emissary.

———. 1980. *Descent into Slavery?* South Pasadena, Calif.: Emissary.

Hagee, John. 2001. *Attack on America: New York, Jerusalem, and the Role of Terrorism in the Last Days.* Nashville, Tenn.: Thomas Nelson.

Hamilton, William F., III. 1989. *Alien Magic.* Glendale, Calif.: Uforces.

———. 1991. *Cosmic Top Secret: America's Secret UFO Program.* New Brunswick, N.J.: Inner Light.

Harmon, Amy. 1997. "For U.F.O. Buffs, 50 Years of Hazy History." *The New York Times,* June 14, section A, 1.

"Hatonn Appears on Radio Talk Show." 1992. *The Phoenix Liberator* 17 (January 24).

Hauser, Heinrich. 1946. "Agharti." *Amazing Stories* 20 (June).

Hayward, Chris. n.d. "Trick or Treat?" *Sightings* [no issue number]: 37–38.

Hefferlin, W. C. 1948. Letter. *Amazing Stories* 22 (January): 162.

Hicks, Darryl E., and David A. Lewis. 1979. *The Todd Phenomenon: Ex-Grand Druid vs. the Illuminati, Fact or Fantasy?* Harrison, Ark.: New Leaf.

Higham, John. 1998. *Strangers in the Land: Patterns of American Nativism, 1860–1925.* Reprint. New Brunswick, N.J.: Rutgers University Press.

Hill, Christopher. 1971. *Antichrist in Seventeenth-Century England.* London: Oxford University Press.

Hislop, Alexander. 1943 [orig. 1858]. *The Two Babylons; or, The Papal Worship Proved to Be the Worship of Nimrod and His Wife.* Reprint. New York: Loizeaux Brothers.

Hoagland, Richard. 2002. "The Twin Towers and the Great Masonic Experiments: Has the 'End of Days' Begun?" *Paranoia* (Spring).

Hobsbawm, E. J. 1965. *Primitive Rebels: Studies in Archaic Forms of Social Movements in the Nineteenth and Twentieth Centuries.* New York: W. W. Norton.

Hofstadter, Richard. 1965. *The Paranoid Style in American Politics and Other Essays.* New York: Knopf.

Horowitz, Leonard G. 2002. "Could the Anthrax Mailings Be Military Industrial Sabotage?" *Paranoia* 29 (Spring).

Howard, Robert E. 1929. "The Shadow Kingdom." *Weird Tales* (August).

———. 1995. *Kull.* Repr. New York: Baen.

Howe, Linda Moulton. 1989. *An Alien Harvest: Further Evidence Linking Animal Mutilations and Human Abductions to Alien Life Forms.* Huntingdon Valley, Penn.: Linda Moulton Howe Productions.

Huntington, Samuel P. 1996. *The Clash of Civilizations and the Remaking of World Order.* New York: Simon and Schuster.

Icke, David. 1994. *The Robots' Rebellion: The Story of the Spiritual Renaissance.* Bath, U.K.: Gateway.

———. 1995. *. . . And the Truth Shall Set You Free.* Isle of Wight: Bridge of Love.

———. 1999. *The Biggest Secret.* Scottsdale, Ariz.: Bridge of Love.

———. 2001. *The Children of the Matrix: How an Interdimensional Race Has Controlled the World for Thousands of Years—and Still Does.* Wildwood, Mo.: Bridge of Love.

Ignatieff, Michael. 2001. "What Did the C.I.A. Do to His Father?" *The New York Times Magazine,* April 1, 56–61.

The International Jew. 1920–1922. 4 vols. Dearborn, Mich.: Dearborn Publishing Co.

Jacob, Margaret C. 1981. *The Radical Enlightenment: Pantheists, Freemasons and Republicans.* London: George Allen & Unwin.

Jeansonne, Glen. 1988. *Gerald L. K. Smith: Minister of Hate.* New Haven, Conn.: Yale University Press.

Jeffrey, Grant R. 1995. *Final Warning: Economic Collapse and the Coming World Government.* Toronto: Frontier Research.

———. 2002. *War on Terror: Unfolding Bible Prophecy.* Toronto: Frontier Research.

Kafton-Minkel, Walter. 1989. *Subterranean Worlds: 100,000 Years of Dragons, Dwarfs, the Dead, Lost Races & UFOs from Inside the Earth.* Port Townsend, Wash.: Loompanics Unlimited.

Keith, Jim. 1994. *Black Helicopters over America: Strikeforce for the New World Order.* Lilburn, Ga.: IllumiNet.

———. 1994. *Casebook on Alternative 3: UFOs, Secret Societies and World Control.* Lilburn, Ga.: IllumiNet.

———. 1996. *OKBomb! Conspiracy and Cover-Up.* Lilburn, Ga.: IllumiNet.

———. 1997. *Black Helicopters II: The End Game Strategy.* Lilburn, Ga.: IllumiNet.

———. 1997. *Mind Control, World Control.* Kempton, Ill.: Adventures Unlimited.

———. 1999. *Mass Control and UFOs: Engineering Human Consciousness.* Lilburn, Ga.: IllumiNet.

———. 1999. *Mind Control and UFOs: Casebook on Alternative 3.* Lilburn, Ga.: IllumiNet.

———. 1999. "Revising Reality." In *Cyberculture Counterconspiracy: A Steamshovel Web Reader,* edited by Kenn Thomas. Escondido, Calif.: The Book Tree.

———. 1999. *Saucers of the Illuminati.* Lilburn, Ga.: IllumiNet.

———, ed. 1992. *The Gemstone File.* Atlanta, Ga.: IllumiNet.

———, ed. 1993. *Secret and Suppressed: Banned Ideas and Hidden History.* Portland, Ore.: Feral House.

Keith, Jim, with Kenn Thomas. 1997. *The Octopus: Secret Government and the Death of Danny Casolaro.* Portland, Ore.: Feral House.

King, Jon. 1996. "Deep Underground: Part I." *UFO Reality* 4.

Koernke, Mark. n.d. *America in Peril.* Videotape.

Koestler, Arthur. 1976. *The Thirteenth Tribe: The Khazar Empire and Its Heritage.* New York: Random House.

Kossy, Donna. 1994. *Kooks.* Portland, Ore.: Feral House.

———. 2001. *Strange Creations: Aberrant Ideas of Human Origins from Ancient Astronauts to Aquatic Apes.* Los Angeles: Feral House.

"The KSEO 4/26/96 Interview with Alex Christopher." n.d. *The Leading Edge* 92.

The K-2 Report: The Discovery of a Secret Alien Base in Northern California. 1992. Carson City, Nev.: Advent.

Lady Queenborough (a.k.a. Edith Starr Miller). n.d. *Occult Theocrasy.* Reprint. Los Angeles: Christian Book Club of America.

Lalonde, Peter, and Paul Lalonde. 1994. *The Mark of the Beast.* Eugene, Ore.: Harvest House.

Lamy, Philip. 2000. "UFOs, Extraterrestrials, and the Apocalypse—the Making of a Subculture." In *Millennial Visions,* edited by Martha Lee. Westport, Conn.: Praeger.

Landes, Richard, ed. 2000. *The Encyclopedia of Millennialism and Millennial Movements.* Great Barrington, Mass.: Berkshire Reference Works.

Lévi-Strauss, Claude. 1966. *The Savage Mind.* Chicago: University of Chicago Press.

Lewis, James R. 2002. *The Encyclopedia of Cults, Sects, and New Religions.* 2d ed. Amherst, N.Y.: Prometheus.

Lifton, Robert Jay. 1999. *Destroying the World to Save It: Aum Shinrikyo, Apocalyptic Violence, and the New Global Terrorism.* New York: Henry Holt.

Lind, Michael. 1995. "Rev. Robertson's Grand International Conspiracy Theory." *The New York Review of Books,* February 2, 21–25.

Lind, Michael, and Jacob Heilbrun. 1995. "On Pat Robertson." *The New York Review of Books,* April 20, 71–76.

"Linda Moulton Howe: The 'Alien Harvest' and Beyond." 1991. In *UFOs and the Alien Presence: Six Viewpoints,* edited by Michael Lindemann. Newberg, Ore.: Wild Flower.

Lindsey, Hal, with C. C. Carlson. 1973. *The Late Great Planet Earth.* New York: Bantam.

Lipset, Seymour Martin, and Earl Raab. 1978. *The Politics of Unreason: Right-Wing Extremism in America, 1790 –1977.* 2d ed. Chicago: University of Chicago Press.

Macdonald, Andrew [pseudonym of William L. Pierce]. 1980. *The Turner Diaries.* 2d ed. Washington, D.C.: National Alliance.

Maclellan, Alec. 1996. *The Lost World of Agharti: The Mystery of Vril Power.* London: Souvenir.

Mannion, Michael. 1998. *Project Mindshift: The Re-education of the American Public Concerning Extraterrestrial Life 1947–Present.* New York: M. Evans.

Maranzino, Pasquale. 1946. "Denver Mystic Is Constructing Atomic Armageddon Refuge." *Rocky Mountain News* [Denver], August 30, 22.

Marks, John. 1991. *The Search for the "Manchurian Candidate."* New York: W. W. Norton.

Marrs, Jim. 2000. *Rule by Secrecy: The Hidden History That Connects the Trilateral Commission, the Freemasons, and the Great Pyramids.* New York: HarperCollins.

Marrs, Texe. 1992. *Dark Majesty: The Secret Brotherhood and the Magic of a Thousand Points of Light.* Austin, Tex.: Living Truth.

———. 1995. *Circle of Intrigue: The Hidden Inner Circle of the Global Illuminati.* Austin, Tex.: Living Truth.

———. 1996. *Project L.U.C.I.D.: The Beast 666 Universal Human Control System.* Austin, Tex.: Living Truth.

Marty, Martin E., and R. Scott Appleby, eds. 1995. *Fundamentalisms Comprehended.* Chicago: University of Chicago Press.

Maurois, André. 1923. *The Next Chapter: The War against the Moon.* New York: E. P. Dutton.

McGinn, Bernard. 1994. *Antichrist: Two Thousand Years of the Human Fascination with Evil.* San Francisco: HarperSanFrancisco.

McIlhany, William H. 1996. "Two Centuries of Intrigue." *New American* 12 (September 16).

McLoughlin, William G. 1978. *Revivals, Awakenings, and Reform: An Essay on Religion and Social Change in America, 1607–1977.* Chicago: University of Chicago Press.

McManus, John F. 1996. *The Insiders.* Appleton, Wis.: John Birch Society.

Medway, Gareth J. 2001. *Lure of the Sinister: The Unnatural History of Satanism.* New York: New York University Press.

Melton, J. Gordon. 1992. *Encyclopedic Handbook of Cults in America.* Rev. ed. New York: Garland.

———. 1998. *Finding Enlightenment: Ramtha's School of Ancient Wisdom.* Hillsboro, Ore.: Beyond Words.

———, ed. 1991. *The Encyclopedia of American Religions.* Reprint of 3d ed. Tarrytown, N.Y.: Triumph.

Melton, J. Gordon, and George M. Eberhart. 1995. "The Flying Saucer Contactee Movement, 1950–1994: A Bibliography." In *The Gods Have Landed: New Religions from Other Worlds,* edited by James R. Lewis. Albany: State University of New York Press.

Michael X [pseudonym of Michael Barton]. 1969 [orig. 1960]. *Rainbow City and the Inner Earth People.* Reprint. Clarksburg, W. Va.: Saucerian Books.

Michel, Lou, and Dan Herbeck. 2001. *American Terrorist: Timothy McVeigh and the Oklahoma City Bombing.* New York: Regan Books.

Miller, Richard T. 2000. *Star Wards III.* Folsom, Calif.: Advent.

Moreno, Jonathan D. 2000. *Undue Risk: Secret State Experiments on Humans.* New York: W. H. Freeman.

Moseley, James W., and Karl T. Pflock. 2002. *Shockingly Close to the Truth! Confessions of a Grave-Robbing Ufologist.* Amherst, N.Y.: Prometheus.

Mullins, Eustace. 1992. *The World Order: Our Secret Rulers.* 2d ed. Staunton, Va.: Ezra Pound Institute of Civilization.

Nash, Alanna. 1998. "Confused or Not, X-Philes Keep Coming." *The New York Times,* January 11, 41.

Noble, Kerry. 1998. *Tabernacle of Hate: Why They Bombed Oklahoma City.* Prescott, Ont.: Voyageur.

O'Brien, Christopher. 1999. *Enter the Valley.* New York: St. Martin's Press.

O'Leary, Stephen D. 1994. *Arguing the Apocalypse: A Theory of Millennial Rhetoric.* New York: Oxford University Press.

Ossendowski, Ferdinand. 1922. *Beasts, Men and Gods.* New York: E. P. Dutton.

Ovason, David. 2000. *The Secret Architecture of Our Nation's Capital: The Masons and the Building of Washington, D.C.* New York: HarperCollins.

Pabst, William R. n.d. "Concentration Camp Plans for U.S. Citizens." Pamphlet. N.p.

Palmer, Raymond. 1946. "The King of the World?" *Amazing Stories* 20 (May): inside back cover.

———. 1947. "The Observatory, by the Editor." *Amazing Stories* 21 (June).

———. 1957. Letter to "Long John," radio station WOR. February 4. In the Gray Barker Collection, Clarksburg-Harrison [W. Va.] Public Library.

———. 1967. "The Shaver Mystery." In *The Shaver Mystery and the Inner Earth*, edited by Timothy Green Beckley. Clarksburg, W. Va.: Saucerian Books.

Patton, Phil. 1997. "Indeed They Have Landed. Look Around." *The New York Times*, June 15, section H.

———. 1997. *Travels in Dreamland: The Secret History of Area 51*. London: Millennium.

Pelley, William Dudley. 1950. *Star Guests: Design for Mortality*. Noblesville, Ind.: Soulcraft Chapels.

Persico, Joseph E. 1990. *Casey: From the OSS to the CIA*. New York: Viking.

Pierce, William L. *See* Macdonald, Andrew.

The Protocols of the Meetings of the Learned Elders of Zion, with Preface and Explanatory Notes. 1934. Edited and translated by Victor E. Marsden. N.p.

Radner, Daisie, and Michael Radner. 1982. *Science and Unreason*. Belmont, Calif.: Wadsworth.

Redfield, James. 1999. *The Secret of Shambhala: In Search of the Eleventh Insight*. New York: Warner Books.

Ribuffo, Leo P. 1983. *The Old Christian Right: The Protestant Far Right from the Great Depression to the Cold War*. Philadelphia: Temple University Press.

Rickard, Bob. 1992. "Hoax: Alternative." *Fortean Times* 64 (August–September).

"Rise of Antichrist, Vols. 1–4." 1998. *Contact: The Phoenix Educator* 23 (December 1).

Roads, Duncan M. 2002. "Editorial." *Nexus* 9 (January–February): 2.

Robertson, Pat. 1991. *The New World Order*. Dallas: Word.

Robins, Robert S., and Jerrold M. Post. 1997. *Political Paranoia: The Psychopolitics of Hatred*. New Haven, Conn.: Yale University Press.

Robison, John. 1967. *Proofs of a Conspiracy*. Repr. Boston: Western Islands.

Rojcewicz, Peter. 1987. "The 'Men in Black' Experience and Tradition: Analogues with the Traditional Devil Hypothesis." *Journal of American Folklore* 100 (April–June).

Rux, Bruce. 1997. *Hollywood vs. the Aliens: The Motion Picture Industry's Participation in UFO Disinformation*. Berkeley: Frog.

Sauder, Richard. 1995. *Underground Bases and Tunnels: What Is the Government Trying to Hide?* Kempton, Ill.: Adventures Unlimited.

Scallion, Gordon-Michael. 1997. *Notes from the Cosmos: A Futurist's Insights into the World of Dream Prophecy and Intuition*. West Chesterfield, N.H.: Matrix Institute.

Seymour, Cheri. 1991. *Committee of the States: Inside the Radical Right*. Mariposa, Calif.: Camden Place Communications.

"The Shaver Mystery." 1946. *Amazing Stories* 20 (September).

Sklar, Holly, ed. 1980. *Trilateralism: The Trilateral Commission and Elite Planning for World Management*. Boston: South End.

Spencer, John, ed. 1993. *The UFO Encyclopedia*. New York: Avon.

Spencer, Wayne. 2001. "To Absent Friends: Classical Spiritual Mediumship and New Age Channeling Compared and Contrasted." *Journal of Contemporary Religion* 16.

Springmeier, Fritz. 1995. "Project Monarch: How the U.S. Creates Slaves of Satan." In *Cult Rapture*, edited by Adam Parfrey. Portland, Ore.: Feral House.

"Statement of Purpose." 2001. *Nexus: New Times Magazine* 9 (March–April).

Steinberg, Gene. 1998. "Ray Palmer's Son: Remembrances of a UFO Pioneer." *UFO Universe* 5, "Richard Shaver's Last Interview."

Still, William T. 1990. *New World Order: The Ancient Plan of Secret Societies*. Lafayette, La.: Huntington House.

Taylor, Sam. 1997. "So I Was in This Bar with the Son of God . . ." *The* [London] *Observer Review* (April 20): 1, 4.

Terrell, Thelma B. *See* Tuella.

Thomas, Kenn. 2002. "Bullets before Brains." *Fortean Times* 155 (March).

———, ed. 1995. *Popular Alienation: A Steamshovel Press Reader*. Lilburn, Ga.: IllumiNet.

Thornton, James. 1996. "Neutralizing Good Americans." *New American* 12 (September 16).

"Trance Formation in America's Update on LABOR DAY MARCH on Washington, D.C." 1996. *The American's Bulletin* 15 (September).

Tuella [pseudonym of Thelma B. Terrell]. 1993. "Compiled through Tuella by the Ashtar Command." In *Project World Evacuation*, edited by Timothy Green Beckley. New Brunswick, N.J.: Inner Light.

Turner, Patricia A. 1993. *I Heard It through the Grapevine: Rumor in African-American Culture*. Berkeley: University of California Press.

Tuveson, Ernest. 1964. *Millennium and Utopia: A Study in the Background of the Idea of Progress*. New York: Harper Torchbooks.

The Ultimate Secret: An Intelligence Evaluation and Overview. 1992. Carson City, Nev.: Advent.

Valerian, Valdamar [pseudonym of John Grace]. 1990–1991. *Matrix II: The Abduction and Manipulation of Humans Using Advanced Technology*. 3d ed. Yelm, Wash.: Leading Edge Research Group.

———. 1992. *Matrix III: The Psycho-Social, Chemical, Biological and Electromagnetic Manipulation of Human Consciousness*. Vol. 1. Yelm, Wash.: Leading Edge Research Group.

Vallee, Jacques. 1979. *Messengers of Deception: UFO Contacts and Cults*. Berkeley, Calif.: And/Or Press.

———. 1991. *Revelations: Alien Contact and Human Deception*. New York: Ballantine.

Vankin, Jonathan. 1991. *Conspiracies, Cover-ups, and Crimes: Political Manipulation and Mind Control in America*. New York: Paragon House.

Victor, Jeffrey S. 1993. *Satanic Panic: The Creation of a Contemporary Legend*. Chicago: Open Court.

Wagar, W. Warren. 1982. *Terminal Visions: The Literature of Last Things*. Bloomington: Indiana University Press.

Walton, Bruce A. 1985. *A Guide to the Inner Earth*. Pomeroy, Wash.: Health Research.

———. *See also* Branton.

Walvoord, John F. 1999. *Armageddon, Oil, and the Middle East Crisis*. Rev. ed. Grand Rapids, Mich.: Zondervan.

Watkins, Leslie. 1978. *Alternative 3*. London: Sphere.

Webb, James. 1974. *The Occult Underground*. LaSalle, Ill.: Open Court.

———. 1976. *The Occult Establishment*. LaSalle, Ill.: Open Court.

Webster, Nesta H. n.d. [orig. 1924]. *Secret Societies and Subversive Movements*. Reprint. Los Angeles: Christian Book Club of America.

Weinberg, Steven Lee, Carol Wright, and John Clancy, eds. 1987. *Ramtha Intensive: Change, the Days to Come*. Eastsound, Wash.: Sovereignty.

Werly, John M. 1977. "Premillennialism and the Paranoid Style." *American Studies* 18.

Wessinger, Catherine, ed. 2000. *Millennialism, Persecution, and Violence*. Syracuse, N.Y.: Syracuse University Press.

"What Has Happened since the CONTACT Lock-out?" 1999. *The Spectrum* 1 (June 1).

Whitsel, Bradley. 1998. "Escape to the Mountains: A Case Study of the Church Universal and Triumphant." Ph.D. dissertation, Syracuse University.

Williams, Stephen. 1991. *Fantastic Archaeology: The Wild Side of North American Prehistory*. Philadelphia: University of Pennsylvania Press.

Williamson, George Hunt. 1953. *Other Tongues, Other Flesh*. Amherst, Wis.: Amherst Press.

———. 1963. *The Saucers Speak: A Documentary Report of Interstellar Communication by Radiotelegraphy*. London: Neville Spearman.

——— [using pseudonym Brother Philip]. 1976 [orig. 1961]. *Secret of the Andes*. Reprint. Novato, Calif.: Leaves of Grass.

Williamson, George Hunt, and John McCoy. 1958. *UFOs Confidential! Behind the Most Closely Guarded Secret of All Time*. Corpus Christi, Tex.: Essene Press.

Winrod, Gerald B. 1936. "Antichrist and the Tribe of Dan." Pamphlet. Wichita, Kan.: Defender.

———. n.d. "Adam Weishaupt, a Human Devil." Pamphlet. N.p.

Wisniewski, June. 1996. "Sheriff Richard Mack Speaks Out at Reno Conference." *The American's Bulletin* 15 (September).

"Witchcraft and the Illuminati." 1981. Pamphlet. Zarephath-Horeb, Mo.: Covenant, Sword and Arm of the Lord.

Wojcik, Daniel. 1997. *The End of the World as We Know It: Faith, Fatalism, and Apocalypse in America*. New York: New York University Press.

York, Michael. 2001. "New Age Commodification and Appropriation of Spirituality." *Journal of Contemporary Religion* 16.

Internet Sites

The date on which the site was accessed appears following the URL.

"Author Jim Keith Dies under Mysterious Circumstances." http://jsers.intercomm.com/gpickard/jimkeith/news.html#anchor148414. February 4, 2000.

"Background Information—about CONTACT: The Phoenix Project." wysiwyg://6http://www.rapidnet.com/contact/background.html. June 10, 1998.

Bell, Art. http://www.artbell.com.

Bellringer, Patrick H. [probable pseudonym]. "People of the Lie: What Is the Truth—or The 'New' Contact Newspaper." http://www.fourwinds10.com/phb/what_is.htm. November 16, 2000.

———. "Update: September 18, 2001." http://www.fourwinds10.com/index.html. December 12, 2001.

Bennewitz, Paul. "Project Beta." http://www.totse.com/en/fringe/flying_saucers_from_andromeda/probetaa.html and. . ./probetab.html. February 22, 2001.

Bishop, Jason, III. "Recollections and Impressions of Visit to Dulce, New Mexico—October 23, 24, 1988." http://www.rcbbs.com/docs/dulce-x.txt. February 22, 2001.

"Black Helicopters." http://www.wkac.ac.uk/research/ccc/Black%20 Helicopters.html. January 27, 1999.

"Black Helicopters Hyperlist." http://weber.ucsd.edu/~dmckiern/blakchop.htm. January 27, 1999.

Blavatsky, H. P. *Isis Unveiled.* Theosophical University Press Online Edition, 1999. http://www.theosociety.org/Pasadena/isis/iu1.5.htm. December 28, 1999.

Branton [pseudonym]. "The Alien/LDS Connection." http://www.srv.net/~bhw/favorite.htm. September 27, 2000.

———. "Dreamland in the Rockies—part 1 of 2." http://www.geocities.com/Area51/Shadowlands/6583/et18/html. April 28, 1999.

"Branton." http://www.ufomind.com/people/b/branton. December 3, 2000.

"Branton Update Mon. April 8, 2002." http://www.alienjoes.com/branton/update.html. April 23, 2002.

Cannon, Martin. "Project Monarch: The Tangled Web." http://www.visitations.com/mindcontrol/monarch.html. April 1, 2002.

"Cathy O'Brien." *The Golden Thread Newspaper* (November 1999). http://www.ramtha.com/golden/11–1999.html. September 21, 2000.

Congregation for the Doctrine of the Faith. "The Message of Fatima." http:// www.cesnur.org/testi/fatima/en.htm. June 26, 2000.

"Conspiracies." http://www.ramtha.com/cgi-bin.private/c. . .&nav_mode =search&frames=&refer=homepage. September 21, 2000.

Cook, David. "America the Second 'Ad: Prophecies about the Downfall of the United States.'" http://www.mille.org/scholarship/papers/ADAM.html. March 8, 2002.

Cooper, [Milton] William. "The Cooper Document: The Absolute True Information Regarding the Alien Presence on Earth." Dated 1989; posted October 29, 1997. http://server.wizards.net/mac/handy/incoming/ cooperdoc.html. November 6, 1997.

———. "Cooper Family Targeted by Feds." http://www.williamcooper.com/ targeted.htm. August 29, 2000.

———. "Majestytwelve." http://harvest-trust.org/majestyt.htm. February 27, 1998. Cooper's Internet site subsequently changed to http://www .williamcooper.com.

———. "The Plot Thickens." http://harvest-trust.org/plot.htm. June 30, 1998.

———. "Trojan Horse Lt. Col. James 'Bo' Gritz." http://harvest-trust .org/trojan.htm. March 19, 1998.

———. "Who Benefits? The Question No One Dares to Ask!" wysiwyg://64/ http://www.williamcooper.com/vnexclusivesarchives.html. September 28, 2001.

Corbin, Michael. "Dulce New Mexico & the Ashtar Connection." http:// www.eagle-net.org/dulce/R-ASHTAR.html. December 2, 1997.

———. "Review of the 'Phoenix Project' by ParaNet." Approximate posting date August 16, 1992. http://www.ufobbs.com/txt3/2495.ufo. October 22, 1997.

"The Cosmic Grand Deception." http://athena.gmu.edu/~cleo/crim002.txt. June 4, 1997.

"CSICOP Tracks Misinformation and Hoaxes in Wake of the Terrorist Attacks." http://www.csicop.org/hoaxwatch. October 23, 2001.

"The Cult of the Serpent." http://www.balaams-ass.com/journal/prophecy/ srpntcit.htm. June 3, 1997.

"Current Netlore: Terrorist Attacks on the U.S.: Internet Hoaxes, Small Rumors and Urban Legends." wysiwyg://144/http://urbanlegends.about .com/library/bixterror.html. October 18, 2001.

Damon, Anjeanette. "Rumors Abound in Death of Conspiracy Theorist." http://users.intercomm.com/gpickard/jimkeith/news.html# anchor148414. February 4, 2000.

"David Coming 2001 World Tour Schedule." http://www.davidicke.com/ icke/schedule.html. December 22, 2000.

"David Icke The Nation of Texas Tour." http://www.immunotex.com/ davidicke/icke/intro.html. December 22, 2000.

"The Day the Earth Stood Still." *The Spectrum* 3 (October 2001). http://

www.spectrumnews10.com/images/sb/2001/sb3–100901.gif.   December 11, 2001.

"Dr. Rashid Khalifa, the Man, the Issues, and the Truth." http://www .submission.org/khalifa.html. November 18, 1998.

"Dulce!" wysiwyg://29/http://ufos.about.com/science/ufos/library/ weekly/aa112597.htm. February 22, 2001.

End-Time Informer. E-journal of Armageddon Books. http://www .armageddonbooks.com. November 2, 2001.

"Ernst Zundel and Flying Saucers: A Source." http://www.ca.nizkor.org/ hweb/people/z/zundel-ernst/flying-saucers.html. February 15, 1999.

Falwell, Jerry. "Press Statement: Falwell Clarifies Belief That Biblical Antichrist Will Be Jewish." http://www.falwell.com/jf2/state1.html. February 7, 1999.

"For the Record—Info? On 'Branton.'" http://www.ufomind.com/ufo .updates/1998/nov/m16–004.shmtl. December 9, 2000.

"Gallup UFO Poll: Some Want to Believe, Some Don't." http://www .parascope.com/articles/0597/gallup.htm. July 2, 1997.

"George Green Clarifies Role in Meier Case." Dated January 1, 1999. http:// www.ufomind.com/misc/1999/jan/d02–001.shmtl. March 17, 2000.

Hidel, Alec. "George Hunt Williamson and the Genesis of the Contactees." http://www.ufomind.com/misc/1997/mar/d21–002.shmtl. April 18, 2000.

Hoffman, Michael A., II. "His Pursuers Are Not Theoretical." http://www .hoffman-info.com/occult.html. December 8, 1998.

Horowitz, Leonard G. "The CIA's Role in the Anthrax Mailings." *The Spectrum* 3 (January 2002). http://www.spectrumnews10.com/images/sb/2002/ 01JAN-1-Large.gif. February 13, 2002.

Icke, David. "Alice in Wonderland & the WTC Disaster." *Conspiracy Planet* (January 28, 2002). http://www.conspiracyplanet.com/channel.cfm. January 28, 2002.

———. "An Other-Dimensional View of the American Catastrophe from a Source They Cannot Silence: How Bush and Blair 'Knew'; the China Scenario; and the Manipulation to Come by Mind-Controlled 'Celebrities.'" http://www.davidicke.com/articles3/bushblairknew.html. March 8, 2002.

———. "The Reptilian Connection." http://www.davidicke.com/icke/ tempo/reptconnectionmenu.html. August 30, 2000.

"Intelligence Service of the Second Continental Army of the Republic (Militia)." http://in-search-of.com/frames/wwwBoard/messages/1050.html. November 11, 1997.

"Jim Keith's Big Secret." http://www.ufomind.com/misc/1999/sep/d29 -001.html. February 3, 2000.

Jones, Alex. http://www.infoware.com.

"Kenn Thomas email to Conspiracy Journal." http://users.intercomm.com/ gpickard/jimkeith/news.html#anchor 148414. February 4, 2000.

Left Behind series. http://www.leftbehind.com. March 27, 2002.

Marrs, Texe. "The Mysterious Riddle of Chandra Levy." http://www.texemarrs.com/112001/mysterious_riddle_chandra.htm. January 29, 2002.

Martin, Rick. "Are 'Their' Aliens among Us? *The Biggest Secret,* an Interview with David Icke 7/30/99 Rick Martin." *The Spectrum* (August 3, 1999). http://www.spectrumnews10.com/html/writings/Icke-Interview.html. December 21, 2000.

Miller, Richard T. "Rebuttal of Paranet's Review of the 'Phoenix Project.'" Posted August 12, 1992. http://www.ufobbs.com/tx3/2496.ufo. October 12, 1997.

"Mind Control Forum." wysiwyg://31/http://www.mk.net/~mcf/. January 22, 1999.

Moseley, James. "Rebel without a Pause: The Life & Death of Former Ufologist William Milton [*sic*] Cooper," *Saucer Smear* 48 (December 1, 2001). http://www.martiansgohome.com/smear/v48/see001201.htm. January 15, 2002.

"Objective Investigation into the Situation between the Old and the New CONTACT Staff." http://www.fourwinds10.com/corner/watchers-staff.html. November 28, 2000.

"The OMEGA File: The Federal Emergency Management Agency." http://www.omega.tm/file/omega34/thm. October 4, 1998.

Onet, George E. "Animal Mutilations: What We Don't Know." National Institute for Discovery Science. http://www.nidsci.org/articles/animal2.html. September 13, 2000.

———. "Animal Mutilations: What We Know." National Institute for Discovery Science. http://www.nidsci.org/articles/animal1.html. September 13, 2000.

"Osama in Shambhala?" *UFO Roundup* 7 (January 1, 2002). http://www.100megsfreed.com/farshores/ufor071.htm. March 14, 2002.

Pabst, William R. "Concentration Camp Plans for U.S. Citizens." http://www.geocities.com/CapeCanaveral/2012/camps.txt. January 23, 1999.

"Phil Schneider vs. the New World Order." http://www.eagle-net.org/dulce/Y92SNIDR.html. December 3, 1997.

Phillips, Mark. "Forward." In Cathy O'Brien with Mark Phillips, *Trance Formation of America* (Nashville: Global Trance Formation Info, 1995). http://tau.ipl.arizona.edu/~corleyj/wwolf/truth/text/monarch.txt. May 28, 1997.

"A Press Briefing Given by John Lear May 14, 1990 Las Vegas." http://www.shoah.free-online.co.uk/801/Lear/Learupd.html. February 22, 2001.

"Public Disclaimer." http://www.fourwinds10.com/index.html. Decemer 12, 2001.

"Ramtha's School of Enlightenment." http://cti.itc.virginia.edu/~jkh8x/soc257/nrms/Ramtha.html. January 21, 1999.

"Re: Who Is 'Branton'?" http://ufomind.com/ufo/updates/1997/apr/m18-002.shmtl. December 3, 2000.

Rhodes, John. "Probing Deeper into the Dulce Enigma." http://www.eagle -net.org/dulce/W-RHODES.html. October 23, 1997.

———. "Reptoids.com." http://www.reptoids.com/. February 11, 2001.

Rossman, Randi, and Lori A. Carter. "Bohemian Grove Intruder Says He Feared Human Sacrifices." *Sonoma Press Democrat,* January 22, 2002. http://www.rense.com/general19/bo.htm. April 15, 2002.

"Sannada [*sic*] on Earth Changes." http://www.fourwinds10.com/v-of-r/ 032195g-sananda.html. November 28, 2000.

"Satanism in Vatican?" http://harvest-trust.org/satanism.htm. February 27, 1998.

"Shaver and Palmer Part I." http://www.thehollowearthinsider.com/news/ wmview.php?ArtID=20. January 24, 2002.

"Shot Dead! WBCQ Short-Wave Radio Talk Show Host William 'Bill' Cooper." http://www.halturnershow.com/BillCooper.htm. November 7, 2001.

"Skeptics Attack." http://www.parascope.com/ds/0996/maj2.htm. July 1, 1997.

Sterling, Robert. "Was Jim Keith Commander X?: Jim Keith's Big Secret." http://jsers.intercomm.com/gpickard/jimkeith/news.html# anchor148414. February 4, 2000.

Stiny, Andrew. "Group Hopes Web Site Helps Solve Mutilations." *The Santa Fe New Mexican,* May 27, 1997. http://web.lexis-nexis.com/universe/doc . . .1&_md5=7db08741ff5f57a4fc5e4fb7e7828918. September 13, 2000.

Strieber, Anne. "How Disinformation Experts Spread Fears about UFOs." *The Communion Letter* 1 (Autumn 1989): 1–3, 13. http://www.ufo.net/ ufodocs/text.documents/d/dinfufo.txt. February 21, 2000.

TCA. "The Truth about the September 11th Terrorist Attack to [*sic*] USA." http://www.angelfire.com/ab/libertas/terrorism.html. March 22, 2002.

"The Teachings of Sananda." http://home.iac.nl/users/lightnet/celestial/ jesus.htm. October 30, 2000.

Thomas, Kenn. "The Giant Rock Conventions." wysiwyg://105/http://www .virtuallystrange.net/ufo/updates/1998/dec/m17–013.shtml, January 16, 2002.

———. "Nine Eleven." http://www.steamshovelpress.com/fromeditor.htm. October 9, 2001.

Thompson, Linda. "Black Helicopters: Response to Yet Another Media Whore Doing Yet Another Propaganda Piece." Posted March 27, 1997. http:// www.mindspring.com/~jcargill/articles/b-h-faq2.htm. January 27, 1999.

Toronto, Richard. "The Shaver Mystery." http://www.parascope.com/ub/ articles/shaverMystery.htm. October 13, 1999.

"Unofficial Link Page Jim Keith." http://www.ufomind.com/people/ k/keith/. February 4, 2000.

"Unofficial Link Page for John Grace." http://www.ufomind.com/people/ g/grace/. September 16, 1998.

"USMS Major Fugitive Cases." http://www.usdoj.gov/marshals/wanted/ major-cases.html#A. August 30, 2000.

Walton, B. Alan. "Reptilian Encounters in Utah: Time to Kick Ass." *World of the Strange* (July 30, 2001). http://www.orion-web-maintenance.com/iuf. . .e_zines_august_01_01_03_world_of_the.htm. February 5, 2002.

———. *See also* Branton.

"William Cooper: A Short Biography." http://www.williamcooper.com/william.htm. August 29, 2000.

"William Cooper Exhibit." http://www.teleport.com/ndkossy/cooper.html. December 4, 1997.

Woodrow, Ralph. http://www.ralphwoodrow.org/. February 15, 2000.

"Year-End Google Zeitgeist: Search Patterns, Trends, and Surprises." http://www.google.com/press/zeitgeist.html. January 7, 2002.

Index

Compositor: G&S Typesetters, Inc.
Text: 10/13 Galliard
Display: Galliard
Printer and Binder: Edwards Brothers, Inc.

JOHNSON STATE COLLEGE
337 College Hill
Johnson, VT 05605

DATE DUE